Economic Citizenship

Economic Citizenship
Neoliberal Paradoxes of Empowerment

Amalia Sa'ar

berghahn
NEW YORK · OXFORD
www.berghahnbooks.com

Published in 2016 by
Berghahn Books
www.berghahnbooks.com

© 2016, 2018 Amalia Sa'ar
First paperback edition published in 2018

All rights reserved. Except for the quotation of short passages for the purposes of criticism and review, no part of this book may be reproduced in any form or by any means, electronic or mechanical, including photocopying, recording, or any information storage and retrieval system now known or to be invented, without written permission of the publisher.

Library of Congress Cataloging-in-Publication Data

Names: Sa'ar, Amalia, author.
Title: Economic citizenship : neoliberal paradoxes of empowerment / Amalia Sa'ar.
Description: New York : Berghahn Books, 2016. | Includes bibliographical references and index.
Identifiers: LCCN 2015047970| ISBN 9781785331794 (hardback : alk. paper) | ISBN 9781785331800 (ebook)
Subjects: LCSH: Women—Israel—Social conditions. | Women—Israel—Economic conditions. | Women—Employment—Israel. | Poor women—Israel—Social conditions. | Discrimination—Israel. | Inequality—Israel. | Citizenship—Israel.
Classification: LCC HQ1728.5 .S23 2016 | DDC 305.4095694—dc23
LC record available at hkp://lccn.loc.gov/2015047970

British Library Cataloguing in Publication Data

A catalogue record for this book is available from the British Library

ISBN 978-1-78533-179-4 hardback
ISBN 978-1-78533-830-4 paperback
ISBN 978-1-78533-180-0 ebook

In memory of my sister
Avi Dror-Sircovich.

Contents

List of Tables	viii
List of Abbreviations and Research Projects	ix
Acknowledgments	x
Introduction	1

Part I. Paradoxes of the Pursuit of Solidarity amid Polarizing Social Inequalities

Chapter 1. Social Economy: The Quest for Social Justice under Neoliberalism	27

Part II. Women Making Sense of the Demand to Make Money

Chapter 2. Vulnerability	71
Chapter 3. Empowerment	109
Chapter 4. Entitlement	154

Part III. Economic Citizenship—Between the Right to Work and the Obligation to Be Productive

Chapter 5. Discussion—The Emergence of a Hybrid Local Discourse on Inclusion, Productivity, and Care	193
Conclusion	219
References	225
Index	241

List of Tables

1.1 Selected data on social inequalities in Israel — 34

1.2 Incidence of poverty among families by population groups (percentages) — 37

1.3 Wage gaps in Israel, by ethnonationality and gender, 2012 (in Israeli New Shekel) — 37

2.1 Arabs aged 15 and over, by labor force characteristics, sex, and selected characteristics, 2013 — 88

2.2 Single mothers—selected data — 104

List of Abbreviations and Research Projects

Abbreviations

BONPO business-organized nonprofit organization
CED community economic development
EEW Economic Empowerment for Women (name of organization)
GONGO government-organized nongovernmental organization
Histadrut General Union of Hebrew Workers in the Land of Israel
JDC Joint Distribution Committee
MITL Ministry of Industry, Trade, and Labor
MATI (merkaz tipuah yazamut) State-sponsored centers for fostering entrepreneurship
NGO nongovernmental organization
NII National Insurance Agency (central state agency responsible for all social benefits)
NPO nonprofit organization
OECD Organization for Economic Co-operation and Development

Research Projects

al-Tufula (Arabic, "childhood") Center
Atida project
Bedouin Village Study (focused on the Sawa Empowerment Project)
Mahut Center
Microentrepreneurship Study
Van Leer Research Group Survey

Acknowledgments

It is with great pleasure that I acknowledge the many people and institutions who have supported me and contributed to the research and writing of this book.

During several periods of fieldwork, spanning more than a decade, I met and became friends with many incredible women, and some men, Palestinian and Jewish, whose struggles to live full, dignified lives filled me with awe and inspiration, and whose kindness and generosity in letting me into their lives continue to imbue me with gratitude and humility. These women are not mentioned here by name because I am committed to protect their privacy. I hope that those of them who read the book will feel that I have communicated their perspectives with fairness and respect, although, of course, the presentation and interpretations are solely my responsibility.

I was blessed with numerous talented assistants who took part in various stages of the research. Most of them were my graduate students; some even wrote their MA theses on specific topics within the larger frame of the research. I thank Chava Nishri, Chava Rubin, Tamar Kaneh-Shalit, Ya'ara Buksbaum, Itay Alter, Guy Bruker, Nisreen Mazzawi, Adi Romano, Yevgenia Gorbachevich, Ma'ayan Agmon, Yael Shostak-Pascal, Noor Falah, Kifah Daghash, and Samiyya Sharkawi for conducting sensitive interviews, collecting archival and public materials, coding and analyzing, and helping me think through the many paradoxes that emerged with the unfolding of the research.

A wonderful reward of working on this book was the opportunity to forge intellectual partnerships with other feminist colleagues who, like me, have been fascinated by the effects of the neoliberal turn on Israeli civil society, and by the penetration of the ideology of self-governmentality into feminist and human rights circles. I am grateful to Nitza Berkovitch, Adriana Kemp, and Mimi Ajzenstadt for inviting me to the Van Leer research group on the NGOization of civil spaces and for the opportunity to converse in a common theoretical language. Additional critical sustenance came from friends and colleagues in the field itself, who were a constant source of ideological and intellectual innovation. I thank Ruti Gur, Khawla Reihani, Michal Dagan, Nabila Espanioly, and Johayna Hussain for allowing me a close look at the wonderful work they have been doing, and my many friends at Isha-L-Isha, the Haifa Feminist Center, which has been my political home for so many years and which has served as a springboard for important feminist empowerment initiatives. I thank and acknowledge, with love, Ayelet Ilany for her wisdom and insights, for teaching me so much that I did not know, and for inspiring me with her capacity to imagine and fight for a better society, while keeping her heart open to human injustices and human beauty.

I wrote the book in Boston, during my sabbatical year at the Department of Anthropology at Boston University. I thank Rob Weller for offering me the affiliation and for his kind and warm hospitality. My gratitude to Chuck Lindholm, also from Boston University, dates long before this book, whose progress he accompanied with careful reading and thoughtful comments. As my former dissertation adviser, Chuck has been a true teacher, setting a very high intellectual standard combined with an open mind and a good sense of humor. Diana Wylie read and commented on the entire manuscript and contributed to making my year in Boston a nourishing writing period by engaging me in stimulating intellectual conversation along with wonderful social and cultural recreation. I thank Val Moghadam, whose rich feminist scholarship on women in the Middle East and North Africa has been a major analytical reference point for me, for her warm, generous friendship during my stay in Boston and for her attentive reading of some of the chapters of this book. Other colleagues who enriched and supported me during the writing period away from home were Michal Frenkel, Alanna Cooper, Joyce Dalsheim, Pnina Lahav, Shahla Haeri, and Paula Rayman, and of course my beloved aunt and cousins Lea (Loly), Tammy, Marc, and Daniel Kamionkowski.

In Israel, I thank my colleagues at the University of Haifa Department of Anthropology and surrounding departments, Tamar Katriel, Carol Kidron, Nurit Bird-David, Yuval Yonay, Debbie Bernstain, Dalit Simchai, Alisa Lewin, Tally Katz-Gerro, Asaf Darr, Rebeca Raijman, and Regev Nathanson, for providing a sound intellectual environment for debate and discussion. Particular thanks go to Tsipy Ivry, whose feminist anthropological outlook converges so perfectly with mine and who therefore has been among the most immediate partners for sharing ideas, dilemmas, frustrations, and revelations.

I have been fortunate to receive generous financial support for several of the projects that comprise this research. I thank the Israel National Insurance Institute, whose three-year research grant to evaluate an empowerment project effectively jump-started my decade-long immersion in the field. This grant was followed by a three-year grant from the Israel Science Foundation, which allowed me to reorient my research to broader theoretical questions and to conduct time-consuming ethnographic fieldwork. The Van Leer Institute in Jerusalem, where I enjoyed a share of a two-year group research grant, allowed me to add an in-depth exploration of the structural contours of Israeli social economy. Lastly, I thank a philanthropic foundation, which preferred to remain anonymous, for a one-year grant to document and explore a back-to-work project for Palestinian women in Nazareth.

I am grateful to Berghahn Books for believing in this manuscript and for the smooth production process of the book, and I thank the anonymous readers for their excellent comments.

Lastly, at home, Murray Rosovsky was a pillar of strength and reassurance throughout. I thank him for his careful language editing of the entire book, and much more—for taking care of our daughter when I was out doing fieldwork and during the long hours of writing. I thank him for believing in me, and for his unconditional love. I thank my family—Oscar and Olga Sircovich-Sa'ar, Yashi Sa'ar, and Dafi Hochman-Sa'ar—for their love and support, and Lyla for being the light of my life.

Introduction

April 2008, graduation party of a business-entrepreneurship course in Haifa. After some speeches and handing out the certificates, while women were enjoying the refreshments, each graduate was asked to say a few words about her business. Rachel Rosen, who had asked to be the last one, used the opportunity to perform a short standup piece that she had written for the occasion. Rachel was a certified medical masseur and self-employed for more than fifteen years. Although like many of the others she had to supplement her income through work as a shop assistant because her business was not economically sustainable, her profile was somewhat atypical in that she had more cultural and social capital than most other participants. A never-married mother of one in her late forties, she had a university education, her father was a white-collar professional, and her social circle included many friends with higher education. "My name is Rachel and I'm a love-and-energy entrepreneur," she opened, talking in a very soft voice. "I sell capsules that will make you fill out with love and help you give love. You should try one of them, because love is really necessary for your economic success...." She continued like that for a few more minutes, then said, "You'd never guess what happened to me last week when I went down to the desert to meditate. I opened one of my love capsules, sat down and did some breathing. All of a sudden I heard a weird sound, like thunder. Before I knew what was going on, a huge sack came down from the sky and landed right in my lap. And guess what, it was full of money! Just like that, all that money came tumbling down on me...." As I was standing in the audience, listening with a big grin to what I thought was a really witty parody, I got a nudge from one of the other graduates. "Why is Rachel talking in this odd voice and using her hands like that?" This woman, it suddenly hit me, didn't get it. "She's doing standup," I said, "It's a joke." "Ah," she said, then turned around and passed the explanation on to the women on her other side. "It's a joke...." I could see the nods from the corner of my eye.[1]

This book tells the story of economic empowerment projects for low-income women in Israel and dwells on the manifold paradoxes that they engender. I portray the institutional context, called "social economy," in which such projects are operated, and describe how the women at the receiving end accommodate the new expectation that they should become economically independent with existing cultural scripts of feminine propriety. As the opening anecdote conveys, the projects are saturated with a New Age lingo of love and money, itself the upshot of emotional capitalism, which collapses together work, care, entitlement, and the very notion of self, in an ever-expanding imaginary shopping mall where "everything," from moral value to utility value to personhood, is marketable.

On a broader level, this is a book about neoliberalism and its localization in a particular cultural context. The Israeli social economy field features collaborations between business tycoons, social services professionals, state functionaries, grassroots activists, and women from disempowered backgrounds, who together create a discourse full of contradictions. On the one hand, economic empowerment projects are replete with talk about individual self-sufficiency and open opportunities; they urge low-income women to abandon the positon of needy, passive recipients of public support and see themselves, instead, as agents of change and the key to their own failure or success. On the other hand, many actors in the field are long-time social-change activists who are deeply committed to feminism and minority rights. Hence, involvement in social economy projects typically entails a complex and somewhat inner contradictory process of gender and ethnic consciousness-raising alongside a depoliticizing approach to economic disadvantage. As noted, this odd-mixture of ideas and perspectives is typically packaged in a hyperemotional language of love, care, and self-fulfillment; it is also inadvertently entrapped in the neoliberal belief that the market is an obvious regulator of morality and identity. All this makes social economy a distinct arena of neoliberal cultural production. In exploring it, I dwell on the fallacies—the fact that most of the women do not become less poor as a result of their enrollment in the projects or that the flow of capital into the field does nothing to mitigate the polarized structure of social inequalities—as well as the unintended consequences—the subtle but meaningful benefits that the women draw from the projects, or the infiltration of a language of universal care and solidarity into the core of a capitalist-patriarchal-nationalist order.

I use two main analytical concepts: economic citizenship and gender contracts. The first connotes the idea that civil entitlement should be somehow conditioned on individual economic productivity. The second represents a generic cultural script regarding the appropriate balance between care and cash work in normative femininity and masculinity. These are two generic cultural schemas that bind together morality, belonging, gender, and economic productivity. Arguably, they are too crude for a satisfactory grounded analysis, as their practical implications differ vastly across and even within cultural settings. At the same time, their analytical value lies precisely in their generality. The ethnography looks at the local adaptations of these general schemas. I explore how they travel globally and how they adapt to specific subsettings within a single political entity: How does the idea of measuring civil entitlement by individual economic productivity make sense in a locale dominated by collective, ethno-national sentiments? And what specific tokens does it assume for Jews and for Palestinians? How does the preoccupation with the economic productivity of women, and minority women at that, fit in with a cultural atmosphere of enduring racist and patriarchal attitudes? And how does the idea that normative women should work for cash and even become economically independent adapt across social classes, national collectivities, and gender regimes?

Thematic Concerns

Community Economic Development

For several decades now, but mainly in the past twenty-odd years, approaches to reduce poverty in postindustrial countries have come strongly to focus on local communities. At the background are several historical processes: social movements, such as the civil rights and the feminist movements that fostered community-based agency already in the 1960s and 1970s; global processes of economic restructuring, which generated substantial pressures to reduce government bureaucracies and privatize welfare; and neoliberal beliefs in the market's capacity to self-regulate and achieve optimal results in all spheres of human activity, including the handling of poverty and social inequalities. The incorporation of these processes into contemporary schemes of community economic development (CED) has meant, among other things, moderating the old socialist conviction that capitalist profit accumulation is the prime generator of class inequalities and social injustice. Gradually, the view that the main engine of economic growth is not labor and direct production but profits made in the business and financial sectors has become common wisdom beyond the circles of hard-core capitalists. Growing numbers of actors in progressive grassroots and academic circles have shifted their efforts from struggles to limit and regulate such profits by supporting strong state interventions and unionized work to becoming partners in programs to channel them directly from corporations "back to the community." Usually the streaming of funds has also entailed inculcation of the *ethos* of profit making, thus opening the door wide to the involvement of corporations in poverty reduction schemes, not just as financial benefactors but as ethical and cultural leaders.

As mentioned, and as will be shown ethnographically in Chapter 1, the cross-sectorial collaborations of businesses, government, and civil society organizations, which occur as part of CED schemes, have complex social effects. They tend to tame and some say coopt radical worldviews, but encounters on the ground yield refreshing interchanges among actors from very different social locations. These encounters facilitate the mainstreaming of critical and feminist outlooks, and legitimize minority claims for inclusion, by reframing arguments for women's and minorities' rights as "diversity" rather than as political radicalism. But at the same time they propagate neoliberal tenets, primarily that individual self-fulfillment is the key to social and economic success, into grassroots milieus that have traditionally focused on structural violence and political oppression.

These general characteristics of community economic development are to be found in the Israeli social economy as well, albeit with specific implications that are discussed at length in Chapter 1. Three themes in particular inform the ideological bridging in Israeli social economy: the national division between the dominant Jewish majority and the subordinate Palestinian minority, the intra-Jewish cleavage between Mizrahim and Ashkenazim, and the contradictory singling out of women as problem subjects and agents of change. Economic empowerment initiatives throughout the country, with their mission of reaching out to groups on the margins, operate precisely where the tensions surrounding ethnicity, nationality, and gender are the greatest: at their intersection with the lower-class and social periphery. These projects bring together, in pragmatic day-to-day operations, lower-class women from any number of subgroups: old-time Mizrahim, more recent Jewish immigrants from the former Soviet Union or Ethiopia, Palestinian-Israelis of various religions and lifestyles, and ultra-Orthodox Jewish women. They likewise assemble social activists from these different groups together with professionals, scholars, state officials, and donors.

In more than one respect, the encounters created in the field are very untraditional, and therefore challenge their participants to address issues that are difficult to talk about. The long-lasting discrimination against Mizrahim, which official discourses tend to downplay by treating it as a thing of the past, or the subordination of the Palestinian citizens, which Jewish Israelis generally prefer to overlook in the name of national security, are made acutely present in the projects. To accommodate these and related tensions, a certain semantic labor attempts to depoliticize them without denying them. Notable expressions here, which I analyze in some detail, are the familiar Israeli trope of "the social," which indicates that a certain topic is not political and therefore presumably less explosive than it may appear; or the English term "diversity," which is used interchangeably with "multiculturalism" to urge tolerance for the claims of Palestinian Israelis. The overwhelming focus on women, lastly, has the oxymoronic effect of bringing feminist jargon to the heart of mainstream debates while reinforcing the stigmatization of women as needy subjects who lack the natural instinct for self-sustainability.

Another important preoccupation of CED projects, besides economic justice and social solidarity, is to reinforce democratic culture. The idea of corporate social responsibility (CSR), now a widespread subindustry in the field worldwide, encourages businesses to integrate social and environmental concerns into their activities by volunteering resources, skills, and workers' time to community projects. As detailed in Chapter 5, this common practice, which is rationalized as a win-win situation—the well-being of businesses is seen as co-dependent on that of society—is increasingly also articulated in terms of good citizenship. Adding an overtly moral tone to the familiar emphasis on economic optimization, CSR discourses preach social involvement, active responsibility, and some restraint on rampant profit making as corporations' contribution to a sustainable democratic culture.

The democratic claims of CED platforms are fraught with contradictions, as is the field throughout. One source of incongruity is the neoliberal embedment of these claims. Under neoliberalism, writes Ahiwa Ong (2006), the elements that we think of as blending to create citizenship—rights, entitlements, territoriality, a nation—become disarticulated and rearticulated. In Israel, where civic privileges are drawn primarily according to ethno-national belonging, the recent neoliberal focus on the perceived economic productivity of individuals (the idea of economic citizenship) entails a significant shift in orientation. Not diminishing the importance of collective affiliation, this idea nevertheless expands and reorients the definition of worthy citizens to include subjects who have been outside the traditional consensus. Chapter 5 is dedicated to the complex implications of this most recent addition to the discourses of Israeli citizenship, with particular attention to their effects on women at the outer edges of a polarizing political economy. Emphatically, the focus on economic citizenship that emerges in the field is pragmatic before it is ideological. It evolves through practice, although eventually it does acquire a moral wrap as well. Accordingly, the discussion of economic citizenship in Chapter 5 draws on the four preceding ethnographic chapters that provide the situated context of its evolution: Chapter 1 on the field of social economy, and chapters 2 through 4 on the women who enroll in the projects. The vulnerabilities and the agency of these women, and of those who seek to empower them, provide a lens to view the pragmatic significance of economic citizenship.

Intersectionality

Throughout this study I am guided by the perspective of intersectionality. By now widely accepted among feminist scholars (e.g., McCall 2005; Yuval-Davis

2006; Davis 2008; Walby, Armstrong, and Strid 2012), this perspective refers to the intersections of gender and other mechanisms of distinction and domination, primarily class, ethnicity, race, and heteronormativity. This theoretical approach to the study of inequalities sees patriarchy as a power structure in dynamic interaction with other power structures, which are historically and culturally contingent. Like many components of feminist scholarship, the contemporary focus on intersections begins in feminist *political practice*, which is grounded in the real-life experiences and the struggles for justice of minority women. As the black lesbian activists of the Combahee River Collective put it in their famous 1979 statement, "The synthesis of these oppressions creates the conditions of our lives" (Combahee River Collective 1983, 272).

Also in the background of intersectionality is a long-standing debate between Marxist and radical feminists on the order of analytical priority between patriarchy and capitalism: is gender akin to class? Do men as a group dominate women as a group? Are wives and husbands distinct classes? Is the domestic mode of production analytically and substantially distinct from the capitalist mode of production? How should we conceptualize the relation of capitalism to patriarchy—are they two autonomous, if interconnected systems? Are they entirely fused? Or are they initially distinct? And what is the role of the state in the perpetuation of women's subjugation? Is the state capitalist *and* patriarchal? Or is it only the former?[2] The introduction of intersectionality, which was suggested in the late 1980s (e.g., Crenshaw 1989) and which became increasingly popular in the following decade or two, marked a development in this discourse. It complicated the gender/class debate by highlighting much more the component of race (later also ethnicity and sexuality), thus pushing it beyond the either/or binary. It also challenged scholars writing about the multiple oppressions of minority women to move beyond a simple additive approach (see Yuval-Davis 2006). To refer to gender, class, ethnicity, race, and sexuality as intersecting means not only that women are oppressed three or four times more harshly if they are also of minority background, lower class, or lesbians: it means also that as social analysts we are challenged to tease out the *effects of the interaction* among various mechanisms of exclusion and domination. While poor Palestinian Israeli women are most likely vulnerable in many more ways than middle-class, educated, Jewish-Ashkenazi Israeli women, the effects of the multiple intersections are ultimately qualitative, not quantitative. Sometimes they may actually imply a complex of disadvantages and prerogatives.

A third inspiration of intersectionailty, which is directly connected to the first mentioned above (the experiences and struggles of minority women), is the politics of identity. The calls from the margins of the feminist movement, which eventually reached the center and changed the way we now look at gender in academia too, were fueled by a quest for inclusion of women who had been active in all the major social-change projects, but felt that their own pressing concerns continued to be overlooked even within these radical settings. In the United States these, among others, were the civil rights, the Black Panther, and the feminist movements; in Israel the struggles for Mizrahi and the Palestinian rights, and again the feminist movement. These women therefore wished to find and articulate their unique voices and make them the central energetic source of their activism. To cite the statement of the Combahee River Collective again, "This focusing upon our own oppression is embodied in the concept of identity politics. We believe that the most profound and potentially most radical politics comes directly out of our own identity, as opposed to working to end somebody else's oppression" (Combahee River Collective 1983, 275). Identity politics has changed and evolved since the 1980s. In some important respects it has come under attack, at least by younger members of the feminist movement who are preoccupied with the right to individual self-expression and resent being "locked in a box" as it were, even in the cause of naming hidden oppressions (Sa'ar and Gooldin 2009). But the focus on the intersections of multiple oppressions still remains highly relevant to feminist analysis.

The heterogeneity of the women who participate in the Israeli social economy projects is a distinct characteristic of this field. Chapter 2 presents an elaborate description of women's vulnerabilities, which shows up their diverse backgrounds. I dedicate specific sections to the situation of Palestinian, ultra-Orthodox, and new immigrant women, and of single mothers. These titles, of course, do not exhaust all the relevant social locations, and in fact more locations—Mizrahi Jews, Bedouins, Christians, non-Jewish new immigrants, or middle-aged women—are introduced through the ethnographic examples and the discussion of welfare and workforce conditions. The interactions of ethnicity, national affiliation, class, or family status evince significant distinctions among these subgroups, in access to state subsidies, in chances of upward mobility, in internalized sense of belonging or disregard, or in fact in whether women who are objectively poor actually feel poor. They also show how the polarizing effects of economic liberalization and the restructuring of the job market are ultimately correlated with majority/minority status, and how female gender works to the disadvantage of the latter.

Before closing the theme of complex inequalities I note two social identities that are not included in this book. One is sexuality. During fieldwork I encountered participants with lesbian, bisexual, or otherwise queer identities, but the topic did not arise as "an issue" in local discourse; after some deliberation I too decided not to pursue it, because of the complexity of the analysis already. The second topic is noncitizen status. As I explain at some length in Chapter 1, the presence of migrant workers, refugees, and commuters from the Palestine Authority is an important catalyst in the progressive polarization of the Israeli workforce, with direct implications for women in peripheral groups. My decision not to include these people in the analysis stems from their not being the regular target groups of local social economy projects, with minor exceptions.

Empowerment as Enchantment

Of the various terms that circulate in the Israeli field of social economy, as in CED more generally, *empowerment* is probably the most emblematic of the type of cultural production that occurs in it—hybrid, and at once co-opting radical ideas and opening spaces for them within the mainstream. As I show ethnographically in Chapter 3, empowerment, which is used concurrently in social economy and in several interfacing fields, operates as a lingua franca that facilitates communication across seemingly incompatible ideological settings. Used simultaneously in radical, liberal, and conservative circles, empowerment seems to mean different or even contradictory things, a quality that makes it liable to strategic interpretations by actors aiming to make the most of their opportunities and resources.

Much has been written about the failure of empowerment schemes to achieve tangible economic results for women in poverty; much has also been written about the irony of channeling development funds to educate women instead of improving infrastructure, or about the cynical upshot of using "empowerment" to attach poor women to multinational financial corporations. The present ethnography lends support to this criticism but also complicates it. Careful analysis of the ways women respond to and appropriate the empowerment language that they encounter in the workshops rules out any one-dimensional conclusion. It shows instead that despite the very partial economic results that the projects yield—often no significant ones at all, women express high levels of satisfaction with their participation. The workshops, it appears, give them some valuable cultural capital and opportunities for self-growth, intellectual engagement, social networking, and leisure activity. In particular, they provide a protected setting in which to experiment with cultural performances of self, which have become hugely popular, but also increasingly pertinent for a variety of workforce environments.

Participants appear very comfortable with the emotional discourse offered in the empowerment workshops. Inspired by the style of the group-discussion moderators, who encourage reflexivity and emotional self-exploration, they incline heavily to a vocabulary of love, care, and giving when talking about their work experiences and aspirations. At the same time, many—particularly among the Jewish participants—tend to avoid talking about the practicalities of earning money or about discordances related to work. In Chapter 4, in attempting to analyze this disproportionate emphasis on the affectionate aspects of work and a certain disregard for its practical and aggressive aspects, I integrate two lines of scholarly literature: feminist writings about the gender contract—the cultural expectation that women should prioritize unpaid care work without withdrawing from the waged workforce altogether, and the anthropology and sociology of emotions. The analysis, not surprisingly perhaps, allows potentially conflicting interpretations. In some important respects the women's discourse sounds self-defeating: the overt goal of the workshops is to help them increase their income; their culture accords general importance to their labor force participation, even as secondary breadwinners; and they themselves are eager to be gainfully employed. So in a sense, their inclination to talk about their work as a form of emotional altruism implicitly above material calculations reinforces the prevalent argument that empowerment schemes deceive women into believing that if only they learned to talk and walk middle class—like wives who are supported and therefore work primarily for fun, not as an economic imperative—they would actually become middle class. However, from a careful reading of the women's discourse during the workshops I also suggest that their enthusiastic immersion in emotional talk has an intrinsic value that cannot be dismissed merely because it is uncritical or nonpractical. The discourse, I argue, gives the workshop participants a ready opportunity to practice a popular cultural style that is symbolically beyond their reach. It also charges them with affective energy and a sense of togetherness, offering some relief from their tiresome and mostly lonely daily struggles.

Numerous scholars to date have addressed the spectacular expansion of the psychotherapeutic domain since the middle of the twentieth century, and its infiltration into practically every aspect of social and cultural life. Philip Rieff (1966), already in the 1960s, linked it to the demise of the tyranny of the primary group. He commented that as people became increasingly crowded together in cities they learned to live more distantly from one another by maintaining strategically varied and numerous contacts. This move away from the cloying warmth of family and a small, face-to-face community meant a gradual reversal of the orientation of the self. Whereas in the former way of life the self was directed outward to communal purposes in which alone it could be realized and satisfied, it now had to redirect inward, yet without becoming lost in anomy. Psychotherapy offered just the right language and institutional setting for this.

Nikolas Rose (1990), in his exploration of the formation of modern governmentality, pointed out the role of the psychological sciences in producing knowledge about human subjectivity and intersubjectivity, and in shaping the self as a private entity, which is perpetually engaged in self-regulation. Similarly, Philip Cushman (1995) in his cultural history of psychotherapy in the United States traced the manifold ways in which the ideology of self-contained individualism or the valuing of inner feelings operate as technologies of self. Despite its explicit claim to objectivity, he argued, psychotherapy was inevitably involved in the exercise of power and in reproducing the existing social order.

Arlie R. Hochschild (1983) looked at the commodification of emotions in the workforce, as job descriptions require employees to exercise emotions in selective and highly controlled ways; she likewise looked at the commercialization of intimate lives, for example, in the self-help book industry, and the recasting of therapeutic language in a spirit of instrumental consumption (Hochschild 2003). Following Hochschild's groundbreaking work, a substantial body of studies now documents the growing demands on employees' emotional labor across a whole range of service professions: preparing and serving food; responding at call centers, rape-crisis and trauma hotlines, or sex lines; working in the global care chain that sends people from poor countries to nurse and serve others in rich countries, and many more.

In many cultures, including in Israel, emotions and economic activity are imagined as separate and even hostile spheres, so their merger assumes a form of symbolic defilement. But in practice, as Viviana Zelizer shows for the United States, this intersection is essential for the maintenance of social relations: "money cohabits regularly with intimacy, and even sustains it" (2005: 28). Along similar lines, but with greater focus on the working of capitalism as a system, Eva Illouz (2007) looks at how the integration of psychotherapeutic narratives into the market creates commodified forms of selfhood. A wide variety of talk shows, self-help books, well-being workshops, meditation and purification retreats, dating websites, co-counseling circles, and related opportunities for self-modification flood the marketplace, drawing people to reinvent themselves through a supply of ever-cheaper and more accessible tools. Intriguingly, this method works by appearing to lift people above material consumption, which is deemed necessary for a truly authentic engagement. This consumption is commonly imagined as antithetic to the more traditional kind, where material goods are flaunted as status symbols. Ostensibly independent of economic means, it draws on emotional competence, namely, the capacity to talk reflexively about the self and about relationships. Yet as Illouz (1997, 2007) shows, it is as entangled as before in the capitalist class system, where taste, style, and cultural competence replace material commodities that have become too common.

Last but not least, the enormous popularity of therapeutic narratives feeds on a deep-seated quest for authenticity dating back to the early phases of modernity and continues unabated through the present late modernity. Charles Lindholm (2008, 2013) traces the yearning for authenticity to the philosophy of Jean-Jacques Rousseau, who believed it was necessary to demand absolute honesty from the world and from himself by indulging his own inner emotional demands regardless of the opinions of others. Attired in different garb according to period and cultural context, the quest for authenticity has propagated into more and more spheres of cultural production. It is found in music, the arts, or culinary fashions; in the evaluation of work and leisure alike by the degree to which they allow connection to the inner self; in the pursuit of self-realization in adventure sports; and of course in romantic relationships. In Israel too, as Tamar Katriel (2004) shows, the quest for authentic dialogue has characterized Hebrew ways of speaking since the early decades of the twentieth century, although it has also undergone significant changes in style and focus over time. Ironically, as Lindholm (2008) notes, the more people intensify their search for authenticity in "the marketplace of the soul" and engage in an intricate dialectics of authenticity and imitation, the more it becomes *commodified* and *standardized*.

Paradoxes, in fact, abound in this mutual entanglement of psychotherapy and consumer capitalism. For example, handing over emotional life from relatives to experts and professionals—psychologists, life-coaches, talk show hosts, authors of advice books—entails an inner-contradictory outcome of emotional flooding and overall cooling (Hochschild 2003). While people are encouraged to talk and dissect their emotions to their minutest components, perhaps to the accompaniment of dramatic effects such as tears, moans, or shouts, the ultimate purpose is to attain better control and purposeful management of these emotions. Another paradox is that emotional discourses that focus on relationships (how to bring them about, manage them, and optimize their benefits) prosper precisely when traditional support institutions, primarily the family, become looser and less important. Third, as already mentioned, splicing authenticity and the culture of mass consumption produces a poignant irony. People are *trained* to be authentic by means of neatly packaged consumer products that inundate them from all directions: as bonuses that come with the job, in courses that prepare them to find a job, or in settings that offer to help them get away from the job. A fourth and last example in this partial list of paradoxes is when service workers who do emotional labor because they are obliged to—because emotions have become a job requirement in itself—use this acquired skill to exercise agency and alter their state of estrangement (Hochschild 2011).

This last point brings us back to the protagonists of the present ethnography, the low-income women in economic empowerment workshops who endorse the idea that work done out of love is the most authentic and therefore also a wise economic strategy. To continue the conflicting interpretations presented earlier of this prevalent attitude among women, and without making light of the problematic of women reinforcing the stigma of their work as falling outside the sphere of economic productivity, I will argue that the tendency of low-income women to talk about work through a terminology of love should *also* be read as a form of enchantment. True, the affective charge that it exerts is not unilaterally positive—in fact it is deeply ambivalent. Nor does it by any means operate as a radicalizing force. Yet it has a clearly charismatic effect of generating commitment, emotional satisfaction, and a sense of inner transformation.

Ethnography of Neoliberalism

According to David Harvey (2005: 2), "Neoliberalism is a theory of political economic practices that proposes that human well-being can best be advanced by liberating individual entrepreneurial freedoms and skills within an institutional framework characterized by strong private property rights, free markets, and free trade." The main role of the state is to facilitate the conditions for profitable capital accumulation by private property owners, businesses, multinational corporations, and financial markets. Neoliberalism was conceived in the US academic elite and gradually consolidated during the 1970s as a new economic orthodoxy in the governments of the United States and Britain. It then spread globally to governments worldwide, which were persuaded or coerced to restructure their economic policies to adapt to the new political-economic hegemony. Concurrently, it has also entered popular imagination as a general ethos of human well-being, that is, calculations of efficacy and optimization are the best core criteria for profit making, but also for ethics and morality more broadly. A market-driven perspective has infiltrated, for example, politics, affecting questions of civic belonging and entitlement; or the home, where it has been increasingly influential in shaping ideas and practices of commitment, attachment, or intimacy.

This book focuses on the latter aspect of neoliberalism and how it translates into real-life practices. I explore the incorporation of the ethos of self-entrepreneurship into Israeli society and how local strategies of making a living and making meaningful lives become dominated by the logic of the market. As many have argued, convincingly to my mind, in its translation into context-bound images and action scenarios, neoliberalism becomes a technology of subjectivity that "grounds the imperatives of modern government upon the self-activating capacities of free human beings, citizens, subjects" (Ong 2006: 13; see also Rose 1990). The entanglement of subjectivity and government occurs through the engulfing of human subjects in myriad suggestions for self-betterment: health regimes, body designs, skills acquisition classes, business entrepreneurial ventures, and other techniques of self-engineering and capital accumulation (Ong 2006; Greenhouse 2010). Almost without exception, these products are wrapped in the scientific dress of expert psychological knowledge.

Techniques of subjectivity travel globally, yet their incorporation into particular locales entails important adaptations (see, e.g., Greenhouse 2010; Comaroff and Comaroff 2001a). In the case of Israel, the neoliberal emphasis on economic efficacy, individual self-sufficiency, and optimizing financial opportunities appears counterintuitive to local discourses of belonging, which are articulated primarily in ethnic, national, and religious terms. Still, the ethnography shows that these ideas do strike a chord and do become absorbed into local renditions of entitlement and inclusion. I analyze concrete encounters in the field for the dialectical effects of this process. The book therefore documents how neoliberal ideas adjust when they travel globally, while local ideas of belonging and entitlement too adapt to the new, catchy focus on individual self-sufficiency, and to the growing prominence of the logic of the market where the dominant logic has been one of blood bonds and essential differences.

The Research—Multiple Sites, Multiple Methodologies, Multiple Positions

The book is based on a series of five studies conducted over ten years, from 2002 to 2012. Three of them were ethnographic. They included participant observations, in-depth interviews, and many informal conversations with people I met repeatedly over extended periods of time. The other two consisted primarily of preset or semistructured interviews. As explained in the outline of each of the projects below, throughout this research my position shifted several times. I initially came upon the topic of studying women's economic empowerment through my direct involvement, as a feminist activist, in the initial stages of Economic Empowerment for Women, the organization that later became the first site of my research. As explained shortly in the description of the different research projects that comprise this book, my involvement was informed by a constant tension between potentially conflicting subject positions: as a grassroots activist I had longstanding friendships and an ideological affinity with some of the key actors in the field. These friends expected me to contribute my time and my skills to document their efforts and to lend academic validation to their discourse, which was quite innovative in the beginning; in late-1990s Israel, talk of a feminist bank or even the very idea of economic empowerment were almost esoteric outside the small circles of radical feminists. As a university professor I was in a convenient position to raise research funds from the same bodies that supported the field projects. These bodies, however, expected from me "objective," pragmatic recommendations, which stood in diametric opposition to the expectations of my friends in the field. To complicate things further, from my own professional perspective, I was actually uncomfortable with both the position of the ideologically committed, action-oriented researcher and that of the detached evaluator. As an anthropologist, my main intellectual motivation was to flesh out the paradoxes of social economy, to explore the mysterious ways in which the neoliberal logic managed to creep into the vision of social change activists, and to understand—without judgment—how the women at the receiving end were making their involvement in the projects meaningful in terms that typically evaded both the activists who wanted to politicize them and the professionals who aimed to discipline them.

Economic Empowerment for Women— Training Women in Microentrepreneurship

Economic Empowerment for Women (EEW) was established in Haifa in 1997 by a group of feminist activists from the Haifa Feminist Center Isha le Isha (Hebrew, "woman to woman"), and was registered as an independent organization in 2000.[3] Its mission is to bring about economic change for women in Israel through a multilevel approach that includes assisting in small business development, broadening public policy, and developing need-specific programs for diverse populations, with a focus on women from the disadvantaged sectors of society. EEW's main program, A Business of One's Own, is a year-long empowerment and entrepreneurial training course. It runs several such courses yearly throughout Israel, in Hebrew and in Arabic. Other projects include a Business Incubator for course graduates, Savings for the Future to foster and promote asset development strategies, Creative Marketing via Technology for Arab women, and lobbying for policy change. During the first decade of its operation EEW also collaborated with the Koret Israel Economic Development Fund in a microcredit loan fund, in which partnership it is no longer active. To date it reports having served over 4,000 women and played an active role in the establishment and growth of over 1,700 small businesses among graduates and loan recipients. As I explain in detail in Chapter 1, EEW, like most civil society organizations in the field, works in close collaboration with a diverse array of agencies, including government and municipal agencies, members of the business community, and civil society groups.

In 2002 I was commissioned by the National Insurance Institute (NII), the major state agency in charge of welfare benefits, to do evaluation research of A Business of One's Own, following NII's entry into this project as a donor and strategic partner. As part of this study I carried out six months of participant observation in an Arabic-speaking economic empowerment course in Haifa, followed by another six months of less intense observations at the escort meetings for the graduates who opened businesses. For the three and a half years of the study, I also participated in periodic meetings of the projects' steering committee, attended events that EEW held for its employees and volunteers, and collected relevant articles published in the local press. Throughout this period, I kept a systematic record of my observations, informal conversations, and reflections.

Besides my direct participant observations, the Microentrepreneurship Study escorted, over the course of three and a half years, fifteen groups, each averaging twenty participants. Fifty-one percent of them were Arabic speakers, the rest predominantly Hebrew speakers. Groups were located in different parts of Israel and covered a wide diversity of linguistic, religious, and ethnic backgrounds. Jewish participants included Mizrahi and Ashkenazi; secular, observant, and ultra-Orthodox women; Hebrew speakers; and recent immigrants. Palestinian participants included women living in cities, villages, and semiurbanized communities. They were mostly Muslims, but there were also Christian women and one group of Bedouins. The members of these groups answered two rounds of structured questionnaires (239 in the first round and 195 in the second), administered to them by research assistants upon their enrollment in the project and again a year later after they completed the course and the business escort period. Fifty-eight of them also gave us open-ended, face-to-face life-history interviews, of which I conducted five (in Arabic) and several research assistants conducted the rest. All the in-depth interviews were recorded and transcribed. Five of them, in Russian, were also translated into Hebrew. Lastly, I conducted four focus groups with participants and graduates of the courses, and fourteen semistructured interviews with EEW staff members and freelancers, and with some of their local partners in the Haifa-based course.

After the official completion of the study and the submission of my report to the NII (Sa'ar 2007c), I decided to expand my research to the field of social economy more generally. I was also eager to break away from the position of evaluator, with which I was very uncomfortable. I now aimed at a more open-ended exploration of the structural dynamics of the field, asking comparative and theoretical questions rather than being bound by issues of "success" and "failure," which I had regarded all along as *discursive* preoccupations integral to the field. Thanks to financial support from the Israel Science Foundation (ISF) I was able to move to this more open-ended phase of the study a year after I completed the first one. In 2007 I returned to EEW to conduct a second round of participant observations in an economic empowerment course. This time it was in Hebrew, and again took place in my home town of Haifa. The funding from the ISF also allowed me to conduct research with two other organizations, al-Tufula and Mahut Center, which are described in the following sections, and to hold more interviews with professionals and functionaries in the field.

Atida—Training Palestinian Women to Be Employees

The al-Tufula (Arabic, "childhood") center was established in Nazareth in 1989 by a group of Palestinian women citizens of Israel.[4] Since its establishment the center has been working in two main fields: early childhood care and development, and women's empowerment. Working toward a vision of society in which all members have equal opportunities to exercise their full capacities, al-Tufula's focus on women and children in early childhood stems from the belief that these two fields are in particular need of nurturing and support. The center runs an early childhood daycare service. It sponsors the translation into Arabic of quality children's books and the publication of original books for and about children and women. It has a library that also sells books. It runs regular programs for early childhood educators and programs for youth. It holds conferences and recreational events for women and for families with small children. It performs advocacy and networking, mostly in collaboration with other grassroots organizations. And it runs community volunteers' projects.

In 2010 I was invited to research two of al-Tufula's projects. One, called Atida, was an economic empowerment project conducted collaboratively by four organizations and a large philanthropic foundation, which also acted as a strategic partner. Here I was invited to be an evaluator by the representative of the donor organization. While the project did not belong to al-Tufula alone, this body managed the actual activity: the classes and workshops, the bulk of the administration, and most of the meetings of the partners. It was also the direct employer of three of the five employees hired to work in the project. By the end of a three-year pilot, the partnership of the four organizations that ran Atida dissolved and the project in its new phase became fully absorbed by al-Tufula. My involvement was during the second year.

Atida[5] aimed to help integrate Palestinian-Israeli women with twelve years of schooling or above into the waged workforce in gainful jobs that matched with their skills and capacities. Its operative targets were to

- introduce a working model for partnership among expert organizations
- introduce a working model for working with women, based on acknowledgment of their capacities, and escort them through the training and job placement to help them keep their jobs and obtain all their rights
- be an address for any Arab woman in search of a job
- change the attitudes of Israeli employers to make them more open to employ Arab women.
- develop and disseminate unique, culturally sensitive knowledge and tools by integrating formal and practical expertise, in order to promote the employment of Arab women.

In practice, Atida compiled a database of women job seekers in the Nazareth area and a parallel database of potential employers. It offered intense two-month courses in skill enhancement (primarily Hebrew language, computer, and Internet skills) and general empowerment, intended to nurture among the participants a sense of entitlement to work for wages. It accompanied its graduates through the job search and during their early stages on the job. A planned component that did not mature during the pilot period was to work directly with both Arab and Jewish employers to encourage them to absorb Arab women into their ranks.

The two main tools used in this research (see Sa'ar 2011) were semistructured interviews with sixteen of the participants and with all twelve professionals employed in the project, as well as observations during selected sessions of the course. Research assistant Noor Falah conducted all the interviews with the participants and most of the observations; occasionally I substituted her. Both of us together held the interviews with the professionals. All the interviews were recorded and transcribed.

Sawa—Community Empowerment of Women in a Bedouin Village in Galilee

Between 2003 and 2011 al-Tufula conducted a community empowerment project with women in several Bedouin villages in Galilee that had been unrecognized for decades and therefore suffered extreme deprivation of the bare basics of infrastructure and social services. Until the mid-1990s these villages had no sewer systems, running water, electricity, or roads; no public transportation, telephone lines, or proper building permits; no schools or medical clinics (Kanaaneh et al. 1995). These extreme conditions started to improve after the villages gained state recognition, although by 2010 they were still highly deficient (Hossein 2012). Al-Tufula started working with women in six villages, at first in collaboration with other grassroots organizations and afterwards on its own, inspiring holistic, community-oriented feminist empowerment. It was determined to break away from the common tendency to focus on the needs of the women, who are on the very edge of the social periphery and indeed face tremendous objective difficulties, and instead engage them from the start as capable and knowledgeable agents.

For nearly a decade al-Tufula representatives paid regular visits to the villages, dedicating the first two years to reaching out and building trust among the women; later, groups of village activists met weekly or biweekly to discuss their vision, share their experiences, create a language of capacities, and define projects that they wanted to promote in their villages. With certain differences in intensity and success, each different group managed to obtain a room to meet in—a striking achievement considering that in the initial stages none of the villages had a public facility that could be used for that purpose. They opened small libraries for children where they ran extracurricular activities, wrote histories of the villages from the perspective of their womenfolk, organized activities for women, and lobbied and petitioned the regional council for improved public services and facilities. In one village the women even managed to seat a regular representative on the village committee, which was unprecedented in this all-men's institution. Over the decade of al-Tufula's involvement, some groups were active more or less continuously, while others operated for a while, then stopped for various reasons. For one thing, many women became employed and therefore had less time to attend group meetings. For another, many were deterred by their relatives' and neighbors' resentment. Although the activities focused by and large on consensual topics such as education and health, they still provoked hostility, as people suspected that the women might become too radical and undermine men's authority. Toward the end of al-Tufula's involvement only one village—Hseiniyye—still had an active group. In the others the groups had ceased to operate although individual members remained socially involved.

In 2010 the director of al-Tufula invited me to document the project in the recently recognized villages in the Galilee, as a form of participatory feminist action research. Nisreen Mazzawi, an anthropology master's student who had been the first coordinator of that project, joined me in conducting a six-month study in Hseiniyye. This consisted of interviews and participant observation at the weekly meetings of the women's project, called Sawa (Arabic, "equal" or "alike"). For the first two months Nisreen and I attended the group meetings together and compiled our field notes into a joint diary. Thereafter Nisreen went to most meetings on her own; from time to time I accompanied her, and I read and commented on her weekly reports. Nisreen also collected the life histories of twelve of the group's core members; I interviewed another member and the four employees from al-Tufula, who had worked in the project over the years. All these interviews were recorded and transcribed. A first publication from this study (Sa'ar 2012) appeared in a book edited by Johayna Hossein, the then coordinator of the project, which detailed the story of the villages and the story of the project.

Mahut Center—Training Jewish Women to Be Employees

Mahut Center was established in Haifa in 2005 as a nonprofit women's organization. It had actually started a year earlier as a project of the Haifa coalition of women's organizations that aimed to help victims of domestic violence become economically independent. After it became an independent organization, Mahut expanded its mission to improving the economic situation of low-income and marginalized women in the Israeli employment market, and to fostering a just and secure employment market, in which women might enjoy their right to a respectable livelihood free of discrimination and harm.[6] Mahut carried out four main activities. First, it offered job-placement services to individual Jewish and Arab women, escorting them over extended periods of time and offering diverse types of support. After an initial in-depth interview so that Mahut's operatives could grasp the complexity of the women's situation, they would teach them how to search and apply for jobs, write a CV, and manage an interview. The operatives would keep in touch with women even after they became employed, since often the job did not last and women had to start all over again (I discuss the discontinuous employment pattern at length in Chapter 2). The support mostly took the form of personal and/or group conversations. When possible, Mahut also referred its clients to other organizations for vocational training, and in at least one case even initiated such a course.

The second activity was knowledge production. Over the years of its operation, Mahut initiated four research projects: Women in a War Economy (documenting the crisis of women in the periphery during the 2006 war with Hizbulla), Women in a Precarious Workforce (on the gendered aspects of nonstandard jobs), Managers in Chains (on low-level store managers), and Women between Age and Employment (on ageism at the workforce). The publication of each final report was accompanied by a conference, to which Mahut invited high-profile policy makers. Each report was the basis for subsequent advocacy work. Besides the research reports Mahut published several position papers on issues pertaining to women's employment.

Mahut's third line was working directly with employers, challenging them to be more active in employing women, alerting them to the concept of abusive employment, and attempting to engage them in changing this norm. And lastly, like many of its sister organizations, Mahut dedicated many of its resources to cross-sectorial networking, another characteristic activity of the social economy field, on which I elaborate in the next chapter.

Mahut is represented in this study through a set of sixteen semistructured interviews with low-income Jewish women who were its clients. The interviews were conducted by Ya'ara Buksbaum, who was an employee of Mahut and the author (in partnership) of at least two of its reports. During her years with Mahut Ya'ara was also a master's student in sociology, and wrote her thesis under my supervision on the employment of low-income Jewish women. I sponsored part of her research with my ISF grant, and in return she shared with me the content of the interviews. I interviewed the founder and director of Mahut, who also participated in a focus group I held in 2009. She was one of several leading actors in the field who became close friends of mine, and subsequently key informants. Mahut Center closed down in December 2013 due to difficulties in securing continuous financial support.

Interviews with Activists and NGO Workers

In 2010–2011 I participated in a research group sponsored by the Van Leer Jerusalem Institute, titled "NGO-ization of Civil Spaces: Transformation of

Welfare and Women's Organizations in Civil Society." As part of this project, Nitza Berkovitch, Adriana Kemp, and I conducted a survey of organizations that work in economic empowerment, with particular focus on microentrepreneurship and microfinance. Senior representatives of thirty organizations participated in the survey. Research assistant Liraz Sapir interviewed them by phone using a structured questionnaire. Thirteen of these organizations worked only with Arab women, eleven worked only with Jewish women, five worked with both, and one targeted African asylum seekers. Sixteen of the organizations did business training, while the remaining fourteen ran general job training, skills enhancement, and job placement, or employed women in nonprofit projects that they started especially for that purpose. The survey, whose primary goal was to explore the institutional structure of the field, focused on cross-sectorial partnerships, funding, organizational structures, and self-measurement of efficiency and success.

Alongside these concentrated and focused interviews, I also used my share of the Van Leer grant to enlarge the sample of face-to-face interviews with actors in the field, at the level of project directors, group moderators, professionals and officials in the civil society, business, philanthropy, and government sectors. Several research assistants held face-to-face semistructured interviews with Arabic- and Hebrew-speaking actors from different parts of the country. All the interviews were recorded and transcribed. These interviews were added to those I had conducted at earlier stages, bringing them to a total of 42 (17 Jews and 25 Palestinians, 7 men and 35 women).

Two Notes on Language Use

Explaining the Referential Value of Some of the Terms Used in the Book

Because I am a non-English speaker writing in English, describing a non-English-speaking setting, I realize that some of the vocabulary that I use in this book carries a specific referential value that may not be self-evident to native English readers. Four expressions in particular—"feminist," "radical activists," "global," and "low-income women"—which recur throughout the book, may merit explanation. "Feminist" appears in a variety of meanings. Besides scholarly or theoretical uses, which are accompanied by references to the relevant literatures, when I use the word "feminist" as part as the ethnography, I refer to grassroots activism against multiple forms of women's oppression and patriarchal injustice. In the context at hand, people involved in such activism—"activists"—are usually also involved in the pro-peace/antioccupation camp, hence they are perceived and see themselves as "radical." This word usually implies an antiestablishment stance, which in Israel commonly means non-Zionist or anti-Zionist, as well as support for an independent Palestinian state and for the right of the Arab citizens to self-identify as a *national* minority. In the case of feminists more specifically, "radical" means perceiving gender, ethnic, national, sexual, and class oppressions as mutually informing and inextricably entwined, and attempting to make the connections in all the protest and struggle activities.

Two other common expressions that I use regularly in the book, and which are less specifically *Israeli,* are "global" and "low-income women." By "global" I mean ideas, practices, and connections that extend beyond the political and symbolic borders of the state, and which are relevant in multiple cultural settings simultaneously. "Low-income" serves to describe the class situation of the women who are the addresses or clients of social economy projects. As is often the case with class terminology, this term is somewhat vague. As shown throughout the book, the implications of family income levels on people's quality of life, opportunities, and overall well-being are much too complex to be captured in a single term. Rather, "low-income women" is a minimalist expression that represents the official criterion for being included in the projects; I use thicker ethnographic descriptions to relate the complex realities of these women's lives.

Disguising the Identity of Research Participants

Throughout this book the three organizations that I researched extensively are given their real names—the Microentrepreneurship Study, the Bedouin Village Study, and Atida (both operated by the same organization)—and so are the Mahut Center Study and the Van Leer Research Group Survey. Also appearing under their real names are the various research assistants and colleagues with whom I collaborated. The identities of the different participants whom I met through the interviews and observations are disguised. My choice of pseudonyms was guided by the principle of concealing individuals' identities but keeping the ethnic or national markers of their names when such existed. In Israel, Jews and Palestinians can readily discern Ashkenazi, Mizrahi, and Arab names. Palestinians can usually also tell Christian, Muslim, and Bedouin names. Yet many Jewish names are Hebraized in ways that make their original ethnic identities untraceable. I, for example, only became Sa'ar at the age of twenty, when our family decided to Hebraize our original surname Sircovich. In contrast to this Eastern European name, Sa'ar is distinctly Hebrew (it means "storm") and ethnically neutral. So Jewish surnames in Israel may or may not be ethnically marked. First names on the other hand are mostly *un*-marked, except for those of people who immigrated to Israel as adults and kept their original names; this is characteristic of people who are now old or who arrived over the past twenty years, when the trend of Hebraizing names began to subside.[7] In choosing pseudonyms I have tried to keep these identifying/blurring markers as close as possible to the original.

Arguments

The Israeli field of social economy, like community economic development more generally, is a meeting place where actors from diverse subject positions come together in an effort to mitigate the rapacious effects of capitalism, yet without attempting to replace it altogether. These cross-sectorial partnerships yield a hybrid discourse on economic justice, social solidarity, and civic inclusion. I use the concept of economic citizenship to examine how these ideas form in a particular setting, at a particular moment in time. The notion that economic self-sufficiency is central to the fulfillment of civic entitlement originates in diverse—and very distinct—discursive fields. It means different things when spoken by grassroots feminist activists, who demand recognition of women's invisible economic contribution and claim the right of low-income women to be gainfully employed; by business philanthropists who promote corporate responsibility; by developers who aim to maximize the social capital of the poor; or by conservative politicians who opt to measure civic entitlement by the perceived fiscal productivity of individuals. On the ground, however, the notion of economic citizenship allows genuine dialogues that bridge these seemingly vast ideological distances. Besides travelling across social sectors, the idea of economic citizenship also travels across cultures. In the particular example of Israel, its localization entails an accommodation of seemingly incompatible emphases on the rights and duties of individuals to earn money, and on collective belonging and making a heroic contribution to the nation. Yet while it may sound idiosyncratic to local ears, the idea of economic citizenship begins to make sense as actors go hands-on into concrete economic empowerment projects. So it happens that alongside—not instead of—the loud narratives of essential differences and ethnonational exclusion emerge narratives of inclusion that appear to open up unfamiliar spaces for diversity. As members of the mainstream sectors of society make active attempts to reach out to those who until recently were seen merely as welfare subjects, if not outright hostile elements—passive, needy, abject—they refashion them as "self-entrepreneurs," hence active partners in the resurrection of a stronger civil society.

The grounded experiences of these newly admitted partners—low-income women of diverse ethnic, national, and linguistic backgrounds—reveal the role of gender in the adoption of the idea of economic citizenship. The ethnography shows that in handling the pressures to increase their income and become self-supportive, women are guided by the cultural schema of the gender contract, which expects them to participate in the workforce and earn money, but still keep domestic care work as their first priority and not become primary breadwinners. Of course the schema varies among different groups of low-income women, according to the particular gender regimes that dominate their lives. It depends on whether the organization of women's work is primarily domestic centered or public centered, on whether the available substitutes that allow them to seek out a paid job are primarily state based or market based, or on the implications for their lives of gender-specific legislation (issues of personal status, taxation, or employment contracts). In all the existing versions gender, as a structural and symbolic mechanism of distinction and domination, affects the degree to which women can actually respond to the discourse of economic self-sufficiency.

Lastly, analysis of the actual language that actors in the field use to make practical sense of economic citizenship shows the embedment of this idea in consumer capitalism. The ways participants talk about acquiring productive skills (learning to earn more money) are inextricably bound up with consumption practices. More specifically, they are drenched in the lingo of emotional capitalism. Here again the gender contract emerges as a constitutive framework, particularly in the tendency of participants in economic empowerment projects to make extensive use of a terminology of love when talking about work and about the task of becoming economically independent. The ethnography explores the manifold contradictions of this discourse: its apparently self-defeating effects for women whose care work is devalued to begin with; its seemingly unsophisticated ring as compared with emotional narratives of more successful economic actors; or the glaring disproportion of effusive love-care terminology as against deliberate avoidance of mentioning self-interest or commercial worth. At the same time, I point out the qualities of this discourse, which cannot be reduced to its "utility value." By using a terminology of love and care to talk about work, low-income women engage in an energetic recharging that makes them feel less alone in their daily struggles, gives them emotional relief and a sense of inherent worth, and allows them to experiment with middle-class cultural style, a not insignificant asset in and of itself. On a more theoretical level, in their persistent invocations of care in a discursive environment replete with tropes of success, individuality, and self-interest, the women are not simply being silly. Rather, the somewhat uncanny ring of their love-work talk brings the discourse of economic citizenship to bear on an aspect of attachment, in the universalistic, humane sense of the obligation to give personal support and to contain vulnerabilities, an aspect that it mostly tends to eclipse. As such, it therefore presents, if not in so many words, the visceral and awkward aspects of civil participation that the abstract, legalistic articulations of economic citizenship generally leave untouched.

Notes

1. For readers' convenience, I use a different font to distinguish the ethnographic sections from the main analytical text.
2. For a comprehensive review of this literature see Walby 1990.

3. Economic Empowerment for Women, accessed September 2013, http://www.womensown.org.il/en/template/?mainCatId=2&catId=34.
4. Al-Tufula Center, the Nazareth Nursery Institute, accessed September 2013, http://www.altufula.org/media-eng/.
5. "Atida, Your Gate to the Workforce," accessed September 2013, http://atida.altufula.org/articles.aspx?catid=1&id=1.
6. Mahut Center, Information and Training for Women, accessed September 2013, http://www.mahutcenter.org/index.php?tlng=english. See also http://mahutcenter-hebrew.blogspot.co.il/.
7. For several decades, Hebraizing names in Israel was common practice. It emanated from the Jewish exile complex, which led Israeli Jews of certain generations to attempt to reinvent themselves as the antithesis to their exilic ancestors. For many Ashkenazim, the motivation would have been primarily to disguise the marker that identified them with the generation of the Holocaust; for many Mizrahim, it would have been to disguise the marker that identified them as Arabs. In the early years of Israeli statehood, the absorbing authorities pressured or coerced new immigrants to change their first names too. Otherwise, new immigrants commonly chose—and continue to choose—modern Hebrew names for their newborn offspring, and young immigrants chose to change their own first and/or last names. In my family the initiative to Hebraize our surname was mine and my brother's, both of us Israeli-born. In recent years this trend has been subsiding, and sometimes even reversed as some people tend to resurrect their original non-Hebrew surnames.

PART I

Paradoxes of the Pursuit of Solidarity amid Polarizing Social Inequalities

CHAPTER 1

Social Economy
The Quest for Social Justice under Neoliberalism

The miracle of EEW is the tension that you see here between the business approach and the ideological attitudes. Women come to work here for ideological reasons and use business tools to promote their ideology. Here's an example: I was sitting with Amit[1] when she got a phone call from Phillip, one of our donors. He called to consult her on something that was not directly related to his support of EEW. There's this American billionaire who wants to invest in Israel and his representatives are now exploring the terrain to help him decide where to invest. So Phillip, who was preparing for his meeting with these representatives, invited Amit to give him tips on how to include the idea of women's empowerment in his recommendations, so that despite the fact that we are too small to get into the frame of this major investor, some of the money may eventually trickle down to us as well. I sat there listening to her and could hear how she led him, literally giving him words, to change the way he was thinking, all in a 15-minute conversation. She knows his world and understands that she needs to give him bonuses—to tell him what his foundation, and he personally, may get out of this. She used his business language to insert some of EEW's ideology into his narrative.

—Ya'el Toledano, a freelance business consultant at EEW.
(Interviewed by Amalia Sa'ar in 2003.)

This chapter describes the setting in which economic empowerment—as a practice and a vision—takes place, namely, the Israeli field of social economy. I portray encounters between actors with seemingly very different subject positions, such as the CEO of a philanthropic foundation and the feminist activist in the opening example, and the novel discursive tokens that are created as a result. I treat the accumulation of projects that aim to get low-income women out of poverty as a field of forces, in Bourdieu's sense (Harker, Mahar, and Wilkes 1990), in which actors struggle for positions using diverse strategies and negotiating the value of their assets by imbuing them with meaning. I set out the gaps and ideological inconsistencies among the people who operate the projects, as a precursor for the larger project of this book, which is how the idea of economic citizenship—the conditioning of civil inclusion on economic self-sufficiency—has come to make sense to people as remote from each other as radical feminists, minority rights activists, business philanthropists, and state agents.

I begin by outlining the history of structural inequalities in Israel and their culmination, at the present phase of aggressive economic liberalization, in extreme gaps and overlapping disadvantages. This review provides essential background for the stories of the women whose economic struggles are presented throughout the book, as well as for understanding the sense of urgency that fuels social economy initiatives. I then move to describe the new ideas that have emerged on how to restore social solidarity and social balance, starting with globally circulating notions of community economic development, and ultimately focusing on the local version that emerged in the process of adapting these notions to the Israeli context.

In the second part of the chapter I use ethnographic data to try to convey the spirit of the field. I do so by sketching its organizational structure, which is characterized by cross-sectorial partnerships, and by showing typical profiles of the actors who operate the projects, relating their motivations, their dilemmas, and their ideological perspectives. My intention is to communicate the unique beat of this field and the intriguing encounters and genuine dialogues that it creates among people who are grounded in very different social and ideological milieus.

In the opening excerpt, for example, a head of a middle-range philanthropic foundation, a Jewish-American man, was reaching out to the manager of a very small grassroots feminist organization, an Israeli-born woman, to consult her on how he may incorporate the idea of women's empowerment into a strategic discussion about the investments of a major Zionist-American donor. Although the parties of this conversation represent different constituencies, they share a passion for empowering minority and low-income women. And while their rationales may be very different—at the time of this conversation, EEW was only three years old and still very attached to the radical feminist circles from which it had emerged, whereas the donor, Phillip, worked for a mainstream Zionist foundation that was a regular strategic partner of several state ministries—they were trying to create a common language in which to talk about social justice. The chapter includes more stories like this one: I use the biographies of different actors to show the diversity of the field, as well as the captivating power of the idea of diversity itself. Lastly, I dwell on some key terms that recur in the actors' discourse and explore them in the specific context of structural inequalities to ask what is Israeli about this, or how this is a vernacular version of a global phenomenon.

Economic Liberalization and Social Inequalities in Israel

For the first three decades of its existence, Israel showed remarkable economic growth. State-led political economy combined a strong emphasis on nation-building and selective elements of social democracy. Centralist state control of capital, production, consumption, and labor was encouraged by the idea that the state's central roles were social and economic development, absorption of massive Jewish immigration, and the building of a solid defense system whatever the cost (Levi-Faur 1998; Shalev 1999; Maman and Rosenhek 2012). On the capital front, the state acted as the main redistributor of incoming capital—compensations from Germany, donations from world Jewry, or foreign aid from the US government—either directly or through several Zionist agencies, allowing very little room for private foreign capital. On the labor front, the Histadrut, the General Union of Hebrew Workers in the Land of Israel, played a key role in stabilizing labor relations by securing protected employment for Jewish workers. This organization was established in the early 1920s as a pillar of the Zionist labor movement and held uninterrupted political hegemony until the late 1970s. With the direct help of the state, it became a key actor in almost every sector of the economy, owning some of the largest industrial business groups in the country, the largest construction company, the largest commercial bank, the largest insurance company, and the largest retail chain, and developing a large institutional network. It thus acted, at one and the same time, as the biggest workers' union and the second major employer in the country, second only to the state itself (Maman and Rosenhek 2012; Grinberg 1993).

For the new state, close collaboration with the Histadrut was one of several tools utilized to fulfill its commitment to full employment for the Jewish population, together with massive investment in key economic sectors, notably industry, construction, infrastructure, and agriculture, and close supervision of import and export to protect local manufacturing. Particular attention was paid to the development of labor-intensive industries, notably textiles, metals, chemicals, construction, and agriculture (Levi-Faur 1998, 2001). Such occupations were deemed appropriate for the less-educated Jewish immigrants from Arab countries, the Mizrahim, and they seemed to achieve several goals at once: the immigrants would supply the necessary manpower for the rapid industrial development of the country (Levi-Faur 1995; Lavie 2006); in turn, steady employment of these immigrants, accompanied by subsidized housing, welfare, and standardized state education, would be the requisite channel to modernize them and thus enhance the future cohesion of Israeli society (Swirski 1989). Lastly, the geographic disposition of the new factories, agricultural communities, and construction jobs was strategically planned so that the demographic distribution of the Jewish population would prevent the return of the Palestinians, as well as severing territorial contiguity between the Palestinian communities that remained. The new towns built along Israel's southern and northern borders were called development towns. New immigrants, or those already residing in transit camps, were given jobs and housing to encourage them to settle there, and were penalized by losing these and other benefits if they refused (Kemp 2002). Thus Mizrahi Jews were assigned early on to the doubly subordinate position of being working class and residing in the social-geographic periphery (Tzfadia and Yiftachel 2004; Chetrit 2004).

Newcomer Ashkenazi Jews too were sent to transit camps and development towns. Many of them were Holocaust survivors who reached the new state destitute and traumatized. Yet many among them managed eventually to get better jobs than the Mizrahim, and ultimately also to get closer to the center—of the country and of the political establishment. According to Bernstein and Swirski (1982), the better paid and better connected sectors in the newly developing workforce consisted mostly of Ashkenazim, both veterans and new immigrants. These formed the governmental entrepreneurial-managerial apparatus, a sizeable stratum of industrialists, bankers, and other entrepreneurs who received the investment capital obtained by the government, and an even thicker stratum of engineers, technicians, and skilled workers. Mizrahim, by contrast, found themselves mainly in the large stratum of semiskilled or unskilled laborers. This class positioning, as mentioned, often went hand in hand with their geographic marginalization. It was also accompanied by their routine framing as "culturally backward" (e.g., Dominguez 1989), with far-reaching implications throughout the state apparatus, notably in the healthcare system, or in the schools system, where second-generation Mizrahi children were systematically tracked to vocational occupations (Swirski 1999; Yonah and Saporta 2002b; Chetrit 2004). Still, their inclusion in the Zionist project meant that by and large they were embraced by the Histadrut, which made them eligible for health insurance, subsidized housing, welfare benefits, and other entitlements.

The outermost of these concentric circles of belonging, namely, the secondary workforce, consisted of the weakest: Mizrahim and Palestinians. Although the Palestinians who remained within the 1948 borders were granted nominal citizenship from the start, for the first decade and a half of Israeli statehood they were ruled by military government, which effectively segregated them in homogeneous communities and strictly limited their entry into the Jewish areas. The imposition of military government directly and adversely affected their capacity to generate livelihood, either through agriculture or paid work. With most of their lands confiscated following the 1948 war, and their being effectively prevented from cultivating the plots they still kept, the Palestinians who remained in Israel underwent rapid transformation from *fellahi* or small-scale agriculturalists to day-laborers (Rosenfeld 1978). Since their previous cultural and commercial connections were brought to an abrupt halt and no new economic venues were made viable within their communities, their only recourse was to work in the Jewish economy. This channel, in turn, was regulated closely by the military government, which rationed the provision of transit permits to protect the employment of unskilled Jewish immigrants (Rosenhek 2003). Thus in times of high unemployment during the 1950s, restrictions on the movement of Israeli Palestinians were tightened, whereas in the early 1960s, when full employment was attained and there was still a demand for cheap and unskilled labor in construction and agriculture, they were admitted in growing numbers. However, they were excluded from the Histadrut (Rosenhek 2003), which effectively kept them outside organized labor. So until 1967 the Palestinian citizens comprised a reserve army of commuter laborers, employed as temporary and casual workers in jobs with low wages, poor work conditions, frequent violations of workers' rights, and high occupational insecurity (Rosenhek 2003; Semyonov and Lewin Epstein 1987).

An important turning point occurred in 1967 following the Six-Day War and the Israeli occupation of the West Bank and Gaza Strip. Having gone through a short-term recession in the mid-1960s, in the years immediately after the war the Israeli economy enjoyed a renewed boom, buttressed by the entry of a large reservoir of unprotected and cheap workers from the newly occupied territories and by a substantial growth in military industries. Concomitantly, the dual composition of the labor force was deepening. Like Israeli Palestinians, noncitizen Palestinians commuted daily to their places of employment, returning at night or at weekends to their families and communities. But unlike Palestinian Israelis, who by now enjoyed greater freedom of movement and some basic, if limited, state services, the noncitizens had no political or social rights. For the next twenty years, until the outbreak of the first intifada in 1987, large-scale employment of noncitizen Palestinians remained largely unregulated despite some attempts to change this; their routine border crossings arguably served the political interest of the state to naturalize the territorial continuity of Israel with the occupied territories (Rosenhek 1999). More directly, they served the demand of Israeli employers, including the Histadrut in its capacity as a major employer, for cheap, unprotected labor. Noncitizen Palestinian commuters replaced the dwindling supply of Israeli menial workers and helped keep in check the wages of workers in the primary sector. Under conditions of full employment in the aftermath of the 1967 war (Rosenhek 1999) younger generations of Mizrahi Jews were now aiming for less precarious and more rewarding employment. Israeli Palestinians too were boosted by the entry of their noncitizen brethren and, with the annulment of the military rule and later also their gradual admission to the Histradrut, they started to enjoy better job selection and better employment conditions.

Less than a decade later, in the aftermath of the following war in October 1973, the economy started to slow down. Local production was not meeting the state's rising military expenditure, and global economic restructuring also started to exert its effect. Four years after the war the Labor party lost power, for the first time in the state's history. Stagnation deepened during the late 1970s and early 1980s, inflation was rising rapidly and threatened political stability; meanwhile the big banks and conglomerates were actually getting richer (Shalev 1999).

Finally, in 1985 a national unity government signed an emergency economic stabilization program. That year marks the starting point of a far-reaching process of economic liberalization and deregulation, which continues ever more vigorously today. It includes a transition of the major business groups from the ownership of the state and the Histadrut to private capital, downsizing factories and outsourcing production to poorer countries, and selling mega-concerns to private hands, thus generating massive pressure to liquidate organized labor in them. Instead of the labor-intensive industries, which were the hallmark of the Israeli economy in the early decades, the state has taken to investing in high-tech industries, often in close association with the military industries, and to making it a priority to attract private foreign investments.

All this has led to a swelling volume of unorganized labor, accompanied by an increase in individual employment contracts, greater fragmentation among workers between and within different economic sectors, ever-widening wage gaps, growing numbers of workers who are employed through manpower agencies and subcontractors, more part-time workers, and diminishing legal labor safeguards (Maman and Rosenhek 2012; Filc 2004). Parallel to the progressive weakening of labor rights for citizens, the Israeli economy has incorporated a huge number of migrant workers.

In 1993, in an attempt to reduce its dependence on noncitizen Palestinians and despite its official commitment to allow the labor movement to be part of the peace process, the state started recruiting large numbers of migrant workers, primarily from Thailand, Romania, and the Philippines to work in agriculture, construction, and nursing, respectively (Bartram 1998; Raijman and Kemp 2004). This trend, which started small, grew dramatically in the following two decades. For example, between 1992 and 1996 the number of licenses for migrant workers increased from 10,000 to 95,000; this figure was nearly doubled by unauthorized workers, who in 1999 were estimated to number about 80,000 (Rosenhek 1999). By 2010 the estimated number of authorized and unauthorized migrant workers combined was 211,500, or 10 percent of the local labor force. This placed Israel at the top of the industrialized economies most heavily dependent on foreign labor (Raijman and Kushnirovich 2012). Officially authorized or not, migrant workers have been subject to a high degree of regulations and atypical employment relations. Fixed-term contracts, the binding system enforcing the migrants' direct dependence on manpower agencies and employers, and the threat of automatic deportation have made for a particularly harsh system that sometimes even degenerates into a human trafficking industry (Raijman and Kemp 2011). Besides introducing into the local labor force a large group of particularly cheap, flexible, exploitable, and expendable workers, this state of affairs has created shock waves that have left their mark on citizen workers as well.

A direct outcome of the economic developments over the last three decades is a huge increase in social inequalities. While Israeli society has never been egalitarian, the rising living standards of the population as a whole and the extraordinary affluence that economic liberalization has brought for a small, select group have opened yawning socioeconomic gaps. The following indications, taken from the Adva Center's annual report (Swirski and Konor-Attias 2012), are unambiguous: the Gini index, which measures inequalities in income distribution, has risen by almost 14 percent since the mid-1980s, so that Israel now scores fifth highest among member states of the Organization for Economic Co-operation and Development (OECD). The middle class has shrunk even faster than in other postindustrial countries. In 2011, top senior executives average wage was about sixty times higher (!) than the national average wage. The incidence of poverty has been steadily on the rise, placing Israel next to worst in the OECD club, above only Mexico. Its incidence among Arabs is almost three times higher than among Jews; other marked groups, notably the ultra-Orthodox, old people, and women, are also particularly vulnerable.

This brings us to the issue of welfare. Israel has been known as a relatively strong welfare state, at least during the first four or five decades of its existence. Some observers (e.g., Doron 2007: 92) regard the Israeli welfare state as a universalistic distribution mechanism that "reflects the institutional expression of the modern state's commitment to the welfare of all its citizens and their integration into the national community." A similar presumption regarding the state's equalizing intentions is implied in other studies as well (Lewin-Epstein et al. 2003; Zehavi 2012). By contrast, critical scholars argue that the Israeli welfare system is an important stratificatory mechanism and has been so from its inception (Maman and Rosenhek 2012; Levi-Faur 1998). Rosenhek (1999) even goes so far as to argue that the role of Israeli welfare in buttressing social stratification is not an anomaly, noting that welfare states operating in capitalist societies exclude subordinate groups as part and parcel of their inner logic.

In Israel, total exclusion from the welfare state has applied to noncitizen workers, first Palestinians from the West Bank and Gaza, and later migrant workers. Palestinian citizens have been partially excluded, with some variations over time. In the earlier decades of the state this was done by channeling important benefits through nonstate Zionist agencies (notably the Histadrut),

Table 1.1 Selected Data on Social Inequalities in Israel

Discriminatory policy against Palestinian citizens	Gross cumulative investments in construction for industry, 2000–2009 (in billions of Shekels) Total 21.20 Jewish communities 20.06 Arab communities 1.14
Class polarization	The lowest five deciles get 24% of the national pie, compared to 76% that go to the top five deciles. Among self-employed, the lowest five deciles earned less than the average national wage. In 2007, deciles 1–9 made 1.9 billion shekels, as compared to 4.3 that were earned by the top decile, and **13.5 by the top one percent**.
	The Gini Index, measuring social inequalities, places Israel as fifth lowest among 27 highly industrialized countries
Shrinking middle class	Israeli middle class, defined as households with 75%–150% of the median income, is the third smallest among a selection of 22 industrialized countries, consisting of only 36% of the population.
Gender wage gaps	Women's monthly average wage is 66% of men's, and their average hourly wage is 83%–84% that of men's. These gaps are stable over more than a decade
Ethnic wage gaps among Jews (2011)	– Ashkenazi urban employees' average monthly income was **33% above** the average monthly income of urban employees – Mizrahi urban employees' average monthly income was **7% above** that average, registering an improvement compared to the turn of the millennium, when their income was 5% below the average.
Wage gaps between Jews and Palestinians	Arab urban employees' average monthly income was **33% below** the average, registering a worsening of their situation, compared to 2004 when their income was 25% under the national average.
Soaring unemployment in the Palestinian communities	In some Arab communities, unemployment in 2011 was 4–5 times higher than the national average.

Adapted from Swirski, Shlomo and Etty Konor-Attias. 2012.

thus bypassing the ostensible commitment to universal attainment, or by physically preventing the Palestinian citizens from collecting benefits such as the child allowance, through restricting their movement under the military government (Rosenhek 1999). In later years some of these institutionalized forms of discrimination were eliminated or reduced;[2] still, the effectiveness of welfare benefits in getting people above the poverty line remains grossly biased in favor of the Jewish citizens.[3] Studies have shown consistent patterns of discrimination against the Palestinian citizens in the de facto transfer of welfare benefits, indicating that state welfare was and remains a major tool for ethnonational stratification (Rosenhek 1998, 1999, 2003; Lewin and Stier 2002, 2003; Lewin, Stier, and Caspi-Dror 2006).

One important exception here is the National Health Insurance Law of 1995, which set a precedent in terminating the hitherto binding connection between health insurance and membership of health funds. Prior to that law, membership in a health fund was voluntary and nonmembers had no health insurance. Health fees were collected by workers' unions, and the Histadrut's ownership of the largest health fund gave it enormous power. By ending this binding connection, the new law granted mandatory health insurance to approximately 1 million citizens, mostly Arabs and low-income Jews, who had not been covered under the previous arrangement. That said, the law's ability to generate universal health coverage eroded in the years after 1995, largely due to lack of a permanent mechanism to ensures an annual increase in government budget to meet population growth, aging, new technologies, and new medications (Horev and Keidar 2010). The government's share in financing health costs has decreased steadily while that of the health funds has increased, compelling them to operate complementary insurance programs to cover their rising costs. So for example, between 2001 and 2011 households' expenditure on complementary health insurances tripled, from 10 percent to 30 percent, with households in the top decile spending about ten times more than households in the second decile (Swirski and Konor-Atias 2012). In other areas too, notably education and crime prevention, the scope and quality of services have deteriorated. Many services have been outsourced to private companies, resulting invariably in higher costs for households and widening gaps in access to quality care, education, and personal safety.

Thus, contrary to the earlier version of Israeli welfare, recent privatization has had the effect of widening the gaps *within* the Jewish population, in addition to the gaps between Jews and Palestinians. It has also brought strikingly to the fore the interaction effect of class and gender, which entails significant advantages and substantial setbacks to upper-class men and lower-class women, respectively. Notably—and this feature of neoliberalism runs like a thread throughout the ethnography—the effects of the privatization of social services on low-income women are inconsistent, at once impoverishing and advantageous. On the one hand, it has worsened their job security as they are the prime employees of these systems. It has also often entailed a heavier burden of domestic care work, since it is they who now have to take care of their aging and sick relatives or keep their children busy during after-school hours. On the other hand, privatization of social services has facilitated the entry of migrant care workers, which has actually saved the day for many female citizens who would otherwise have to retreat from the job market to do care work at home. Then again, the advent of massive numbers of migrant workers has intensified the already existing orientation of a split labor market, which rendered low-income Mizrahi and Palestinian female citizens vulnerable to begin with.

Multiple Bases of Social Inequality

As this overview reveals clearly, the Israeli structure of social stratification has been organized along ethnic and national lines from the very beginning, and has remained consistent regardless of the dramatic economic and political changes over time. The initially hegemonic position of Ashkenazi Jews was shored up first through their dominance in the new state apparatus, in its Zionist subsidiary agencies, in the strong, highly connected economic sectors, and later through the military-industrial complex, the intellectual elites, and the high-tech and financial industries (Kimmerling 2001). Clearly, the ethnic labels *Ashkenazi* and *Mizrahi* are objectified forms of social distinctions that in reality are much more fluid and ambiguous (Dominguez 1989). Still, even considering changes over the years in educational, economic, and political attainments, the categories remain alive in local discourse. They retain tangible social implications, engender political organizing in and out of parliament, and stir heated identity debates (e.g., Hever, Shenhav, and Motzafi-Haller 2002; Levi 1999; Abutbul, Grinberg, and Motzafi-Haller 2005). Although Mizrahi Jews eventually also entered all the different elites, as well as the middle class, they nevertheless remain to this day overrepresented in development towns and peripheral neighborhoods, in low-wage jobs, and in the lower deciles. As shown in Table 1.1, in 2011, for example, the average wage of Ashkenazi employees residing in urban areas was 33 percent higher than the national average wage of urban employees, while that of Mizrahi employees was only 7 percent above the average. This, however, was mildly good news as it reflected improvement compared with ten years earlier, when their average wage was 5 percent below the national average (Swirski and Konor-Attias 2012). Mizrahim, furthermore, also remain more vulnerable to unemployment, poverty, and poor schooling (Swirski and Konor-Attias 2012). As of the 2010s, the complex picture of considerable number of Mizrahim at the centers of power and decision making while a critical mass still lingers in the periphery is a constant source of public debate on whether they are still the victims of racism and state discrimination. For the purpose of the present study, the long-lasting effects of structural discrimination may not be disregarded. They are discernible in the substantial presence of Mizrahi women among the participants, whose manifold vulnerabilities are related in the next chapter.

Table 1.2 Incidence of Poverty among Families by Population Groups (percentages)

	Income before transfer payments and taxes		Income after transfer payments and taxes		Rate of poverty reduction after deducing transfer payments and taxes	
	2012	2013	2012	2013	2012	2013
Total population	30.3	28.1	19.4	18.6	36.0	33.7
Jews	25.9	23.8	14.1	13.6	45.5	43.1
Arabs	59.2	52.4	54.3	47.4	8.4	9.5
New Immigrants	34.8	33.4	17.3	18.5	50.1	44.7
Ultraorthodox	62.2	63.6	46.7	52.1	24.9	18.1

(Table #8, the National Insurance Institute's Annual Poverty Report 2014)
http://www.btl.gov.il/Publications/oni_report/Documents/oni2013.pdf

As for the Palestinian citizens, they continue to suffer diverse forms of discrimination and structural violence (Torstrick 2000; Haidar 2005; Yiftachel 2006; Khamaisi 2009; Saban 2011; Abdo-Zubi 2011), and despite certain improvements their status has remained truncated, and some would say hopeless and inevitably crisis-ridden (Rouhana and Ghanem 1998). On the optimistic side, I mentioned the moderate widening of job opportunities, greater freedom of movement, and greater access to state welfare; to these I may add increasingly autonomous political participation, some successful instances of collective bargaining,[4] improving living standards for many, growing rates of education, and burgeoning cultural production. Against these, periodic surveys show many indications that the status of the Palestinian citizens has become fixed or has even deteriorated. While political protest has been allowed and has taken place continuously since the 1970s or even earlier, on several occasions—notably the first Land Day in 1976, the demonstrations at the outbreak of the second intifada in October 2000, and the protests at the Gaza in-

Table 1.3 Wage Gaps in Israel, by Ethnonationality and Gender, 2012 (in Israeli New Shekel)

	Women		Men	
	Average Monthly Wage	Average Hourly Wage	Average Monthly Wage	Average Hourly Wage
Arabs	4,952	38	6,383	35.2
Jews and others	7,414	49.8	11,833	66.3

Adapted from Dagan-Buzaglo, Hasson, and Ophir. 2014

vasion in 2009—it has instigated violent crackdowns that included the killing of protesters, mass arrests including minors, and heavy surveillance. Excessive police aggression against Palestinian citizens has been registered also during routine crime patrols. For example, according to a 2004 report of Mossawa (Arabic, "equality"), the Advocacy Center for Arab Citizens in Israel, in the three years following the killing by police forces of thirteen citizens during the Galilee protests of October 2000, sixteen more citizens were killed in various incidents, nine by the police and six by the army or the border police.[5] Hate attacks against Arabs, whether verbal, physical, or symbolic, are prevalent.[6] They largely go unpunished even when the anti-incitement law has clearly been violated, and they are actively and explicitly encouraged by numerous public figures, including rabbis and members of the Knesset. Between 2009 and 2013 the Netanyahu government was particularly active in legislating a series of laws expressly designed to curtail the Palestinian citizens' civil rights; most notable among them is the citizenship law, which bans entrance of Palestinians from the Palestinian Authority for purposes of family unification (Barak-Erez 2008). Adala (Arabic, "justice"), the Legal Center for the Arab Minority Rights in Israel, enumerates seventeen new laws or amendments to existing laws since 2009, designed unambiguously to restrict political self-expression, rights of residency, and land rights of Palestinian citizens, or the activity of NGOs that support such rights.[7]

Ethnic and national divisions are readily identified in local discourse as two of the major cleavages in Israeli society, alongside the religious-secular and the right-left divides. However, a comprehensive analysis of social inequalities, which takes into account citizenship, social class, and gender as structural mechanisms of stratification, has been much less tolerable in the local public discourse. Citizenship, for example, is widely regarded as the legitimate boundary of entitlement and belonging. Noncitizens' rights, or more specifically the human rights violations and the overall plight of noncitizens residing in Israel for lengthy periods, have come increasingly to the fore since the early 2000s, with the swelling influx of migrant workers and asylum seekers over the past two decades or so. Besides widening the already existing split in the labor market, the presence of noncitizens has had a direct bearing on social inequalities by eroding public standards of dignified existence, spurring xenophobic sentiments, and stoking up the mood favoring annulling or setting conditions on the citizenship of Palestinian-Israelis. But so far, public debates on noncitizens' rights have immediately turned the spotlight onto the identity of Israel as a Jewish state, rather than the all-Israeli structure of social inequalities.

Social class has been somewhat more admissible in the local discourse, but still limited. Although the rising rates of poverty have become a very popular topic for the media (Doron 2004), there is no readily available vocabulary to talk about "class," which continues to be vaguely articulated as a "social" issue.

As I show shortly, the discourse developing in the social-economy field seeks to understand class structure differently, its polarizing effect gradually overtaking ethnic and national divisions in importance. The popular social protest of summer 2011, which was led by and oriented precisely to the middle-class and mainstream political circles, gave this interpretation a further boost. However, as I discuss in the epilogue to this chapter and show in more detail in Chapter 5, this nascent discourse on economic citizenship and the right to dignified livelihood has been forming largely within, not against, the hegemonic ethnonational framework of belonging.

Gender, lastly, is probably the most difficult to pin down as an autonomous power mechanism. Despite some mainstreaming of public discussions about wage and other gender inequalities, gender is popularly perceived as "a women's issue" and as secondary to the major divisions of Israeli society; it is generally seen as narrower and less explosive—the lingering legacy of inequality rather than a core mechanism with present implications. Several reasons may explain the evasiveness of gender as a structure of power in itself: one is that regardless of the many forms of discrimination against women in Israel, they are not unilaterally "oppressed." Another is that gender cuts across all other social divisions: Mizrahim and Ashkenazim, Palestinians and Jews, religious, secular, right- and left-wingers, poor and rich ... all involve women and men together. Last but not least, the inscription of gender onto the most intimate layer of self-identity—the construction and experience of femininity and masculinity as natural and personal—effectively disguises its systemic aspects. In contrast to this popular impression, this book treats gender not merely a marker of personal identities, but as a power mechanism that informs all the major institutions of society, and draws on feminist intersectionality theory (Crenshaw 1989; Anthias 1998; Yuval-Davis 2006) to trace the multiple articulations of gender with other bases of exclusion and stratification. In the following chapters I look at various aspects of these intersections: the multiple vulnerabilities of low-income women (Chapter 2); their immersion in emotional capitalism and their agency in utilizing the opportunities afforded them in the field of social economy (Chapter 3); their approaches to wage labor (Chapter 4); and finally, in Chapter 5, their integration into emerging discourses on economic citizenship.

Adapting Ideas of Social Justice and Social Responsibility

Since the end of the twentieth century, poverty reduction initiatives in high-GDP countries, particularly in large urban areas, have taken a clear community-oriented, participatory turn, combined with a growing focus on enhancing poor people's capacity for economic self-sufficiency. In direct response to globalization and economic restructuring, large numbers of programs, commonly termed *community economic development* (CED), have emerged, which draw on the shared efforts of community organizations, public agencies, local businesses, and private actors. These initiatives offer comprehensive strategies that combine social and economic objectives (Morin and Hanley 2004).

Capitalistic-Bound Responses to Growing Social Gaps, the Idea of Community Economic Development

According to Alison Mathie and Gord Cunningham (2003), the evolution of CED theory represents a confluence of three different development paradigms: developing or improving economic systems and infrastructure, developing the economic capacities of individuals, and developing the economic capacities of groups to undertake community economic development. The first perspective sees CED as akin to the old concept of development-as-economic-growth, but taking place at the community level. The community is seen merely as a geographic location and has no theoretical importance. This perspective also sees development as a primarily exogenous process: the initiatives employed tend to involve technological improvements and infrastructure development, in the hope of attracting investment and industry from outside. The second perspective, individual capacity building, sees CED as the by-product of the economic success of individuals. "Community" tends to refer to a target group of individuals rather than to a geographic locality. Collective action may be employed not as an end in itself, so the main actors in the development process may be external NGOs and donors or local organizations. Lastly, the group capacity-building perspective sees collective action as an end in itself. Collective action enables individuals who lack the resources to independently improve their well-being to work together to achieve this end. This perspective defines CED as an endogenous process. The main participants are the members of marginalized groups who undertake collective action. In practice, though, as Mathie and Cunningham observe, all three perspectives are often present in initiatives of economic development. This has also been the case in the Israeli version documented in this book. CED then is initially a hybrid approach, and its implementations in effect condition it to retain this quality, since they invariably bring together groups, individuals, and stakeholders with very diverse subject positions. As we shall see later in the chapter, this characteristic is of central importance to understanding the cultural production that occurs through and around CED initiatives.

Another prominent characteristic of CED programs, besides their inherent hybridity, is their openness to feminist discourse and action, an openness that owes to their strong egalitarian, localized, and hands-on emphases. Since feminist approaches to women's economic empowerment are central also to the Israeli case, I have chosen to borrow, for the purpose of this brief outline of CED, the definitions of Canadian feminist activists. In their study of young women in two inner-city Winnipeg neighborhoods, Molly McCracken and her partners (McCracken et al. 2005) define CED as follows: Community Economic Development is a bottom-up rather than top-down route to economic development that takes a capacity-building approach to poverty, and considers individual and community assets as starting places for building local communities' capacity and economy. Community economic development aims to go beyond problem solving and build healthy and economically viable communities. It is an alternative to conventional approaches to economic development, founded on the belief that problems before communities—unemployment, poverty, job loss, environmental degradation, and loss of community control—need to be addressed in a holistic and participatory way. It can be defined as action by people locally to create economic opportunities and enhance social conditions in their communities on a sustainable and inclusive basis, particularly for those who are most disadvantaged. Along similar lines, with a slightly more focused emphasis on employment, the Canadian Women's Foundation (2010) defines women's economic development and sustainable livelihood as enhancing their employability, exploring and consolidating their economic possibilities, and facilitating their gradual passage from survival to asset building.

Community economic development then, proffers a very contemporary formulation of development that aims to combine growth with justice, through applying both socialist and capitalist ideas. While many CED initiatives are an evident continuation of the mid-twentieth-century movements against urban poverty, the close collaboration between grassroots activists, private businesses, and state agencies inevitably imbues them with pragmatic and mainstream political-economic ideas. Unlike the older social democratic emphases on the state as a benevolent redistributor of welfare, CED gives more credit to poor people's economic agency by replacing their depiction as endemically needy and highlighting their "assets" and "capacities." But—and this point will recur throughout the book—reorienting the discourse on economic justice to poor people's *assets* is a potentially thorny move. While such focus celebrates their ingenuity, recognizes the value of their cultural knowledge, and ultimately underscores their humanity, at the same time it serves as a convenient token for drawing them straight into the neoliberal logics of self-sufficiency. One of the most widely discussed examples, to which I return in my discussion of empowerment later in the book, is the co-optation of traditional women's saving circles by microlending conglomerates. Still, despite the emphasis on paid work as a major, if not *the* major source of dignified livelihood, the discourse of community economic development rejects extreme versions of neoliberal individualism. As indicated by its name, it aims to shift responsibility for poor people's well-being back to the community. Also in contrast to the unilateral emphasis on growth, as appears in more extreme versions of neoliberalism, this discourse emphasizes balance among the diverse components of human communities, and between economic and environmental development. Lastly, despite its immersion in global webs of discourses, resources, and powers, it aims to cushion the crushing effects of globalization by taking a decisive stand against unlimited economic growth in favor of more balanced local economies.

Social Economy: The Israeli Version of Community Economic Development

In Israel too the structural changes that accompanied economic liberalization have created a need for a new discourse on social justice. Against surging social and economic inequalities, worsening job insecurity, shrinking state welfare, and continuous stalemate in the peace process, ideas of sustainable economic growth and a more balanced approach to social, ethnic, and environmental forces are gaining in popularity. The term "community economic development" itself, however, has not entered the local discourse. Instead, ideas generally associated with CED in other parts of the world are more commonly identified with the Hebrew term "social economy" (*kalkala hevratit*) (Levy 2004; Ilany 2005).

The appearance of "social" in the Hebrew version of CED is not coincidental. As I show in my previous work (Sa'ar 1998, 2006a), in Israeli public discourse attempts to tackle contentious issues, primarily those related to ethnic, national, or class relations, almost invariably spark quarrels on whether the issue at hand is "political" or "social." Labeling an issue "political" is generally regarded locally as highlighting its conflictive components. By calling controversial issues political, speakers habitually communicate their belief that efficient civil action must acknowledge issues of power and domination. The counter-argument is usually that anything "political" is tainted with interests, and that a constructive approach to touchy subjects must frame them as "social" or "apolitical," so as to create consensus rather than deepen divisions (see also Simchai 2009).

Two implied meanings in particular are often associated with "the social." First, "social" is a common euphemistic reference to tensions involving lower-class Mizrahi Jews. As mentioned earlier, despite their numerical majority Mizrahi Jews have been a sociological minority for several decades, and are still overrepresented in the lower socioeconomic echelons. The fact that many Mizrahim are highly educated, that they figure in the different elite groups, and that interethnic (but intra-Jewish) marriages have become commonplace, has not eliminated old grudges against the deep-rooted and practically institutionalized Ashkenazi racism. Quite the reverse: these resentments have been politicized—in parliamentary politics, in intellectual production, or in the actions of civil society groups working to resurrect Mizrahi cultural production and quick to make loud protests at the periodic racist slippages of public figures. Then again, this kind of Mizrahi identity politics has itself caused substantial resentment. Many Israeli Jews, Ashkenazi and Mizrahi alike, reckon that it aggravates historical injustices unnecessarily and unjustifiably because, as noted, things have improved significantly for large numbers of Mizrahim. In this touchy discursive terrain, those wishing to skirt ethnic tensions tend to replace explicit mention of the topic by talking about "the social issue."

The other common implied meaning of "social" concerns intra-Israeli Jewish-Arab relations. Here the major tension revolves around the dual Jewish-cum-democratic definition of the state, two components that the Palestinian citizens generally regard as irreconcilable while the Jewish citizens generally consider as reasonably compatible, even if not perfectly so (see, e.g., Smooha 2002).[8] Under the democratic heading, the Arab citizens are entitled to certain important individual civil rights but their exclusion from the Jewish national component means that their collective rights, notably the right to identify as Palestinians, to exercise cultural autonomy, or to have collective land ownership, are severely curtailed. Moreover, as I explained earlier, even rights that are seemingly not controversial, such as access to education, healthcare, police protection, or defense against discrimination in the workforce, are very poorly fulfilled. This multifaceted exclusion provokes civil society groups to protest, litigate, and organize in order to claim the rights of the Arab citizens. Among the Jews, responses to such actions and discourses range from meek justification through ambiguity and suspicion to outright hostility, depending on how these acts are interpreted. If they are considered "political" they are all too likely to generate suspicion and hostility. But if they are successfully framed as "social," then tolerance is claimed under the justification that these are legitimate democratic practices/discourses (see also Al-Haj 1995).

Given this semantic resonance, one may understand why the local version of community economic development is called *social* economy. As I show in the following sections, the incorporation of CED-related ideas into the Israeli context has been filtered through the intricate intersections of ethnic, national, class, and gender hierarchies. The attempts to mainstream potentially radical ideas about social justice and better integration of marginalized populations have required delicate packaging and sophisticated negotiation. Against this background, the calming timbre of "the social" is a good indication of the shape this new discourse of civic entitlement and economic justice is taking.

The Israeli Field of Social Economy

Social economy, then, can be said to stand for bottom-up poverty-reducing efforts that offer an alternative to routine state-centered approaches to economic development. Contrary to the old socialism, the discourse taking shape around social economy can accommodate collective ideas of social justice with individual desires for well-being. It sees enterprise and business development as a lever for growth, not as an inevitable source of social malfunction. It fosters work *with* and not *against* the economic sector, *with* and not *against* the government. It contains ideas of success, happiness, and wealth for everyone. It also gives greater weight than the old socialism to individuals' agency, wishes, and responsibility.

Projects and the People Who Operate Them

Since the late 1990s and increasingly in the 2000s, Israel started to fill up with semiprivatized, NGO-led programs aiming to better the economic situation of groups in the social and geographical periphery, with particular, though not exclusive, emphasis on women.[9] The projects commonly target women from marked populations, notably Arab, Jewish ultra-Orthodox, migrants from Ethiopia or the former USSR, as well as Mizrahi women from poor neighborhoods. Far fewer projects target men (primarily Jewish ultra-Orthodox, Arab, or new immigrants) and youth. The overarching aim of most projects is to enhance the economic situation of members of these groups, by giving them occupational training, either specific or general, boosting their self-confidence, and increasing their overall ability to negotiate their way in the workforce. By my estimate, in 2015 economic empowerment projects across Israel number several hundreds. They range from very localized and small-scale courses to well-oiled and heavily financed projects that train hundreds and even thousands of participants yearly and operate in several locations simultaneously. Some programs are sectorial, targeting women from particular ethnic, religious, or language groups, while others are more inclusive. Adriana Kemp and Nitza Berkovitch (2013) estimate the number of low-income women who participated in the various projects in the field so far at 17,000.

Training courses are by far the most popular form of action in these projects. Themes usually include computer skills, marketing, product development, writing CVs, and Hebrew. These may then be supplemented by more specific branch-related topics, such as training as an assistant in tender-age education or as a secretary at insurance agencies, acquiring particular technical skills, or marketing and business management (in microentrepreneurship projects). Along with this teaching component all the programs without exception have a component called "dynamic" (short for group dynamics). This is moderated group discussion, in which the trainees are invited to reveal their feelings, fears, and innermost dreams, as they stand at the threshold of becoming income-generating, "productive" members of society. As I discuss at length in Chapter 3, this effort to boost the participants' self-esteem, generally referred to as "empowerment," is at once a key scenario in the social-economy field and the locus of some of its major paradoxes. Other types of activities taking place in the field, in addition to training and empowerment courses, are litigation, protest, unionizing, legal and professional counseling for low-income employees, cross-sectorial and international networking, and producing professional and academic knowledge about women and work.

A particularly popular component in the projects is entrepreneurship. To clarify, unlike the UN-supported development industry, in the Israeli social-economy field, microenterprise, while popular, is not the only or even the most prevalent form of action. For example, of the sixteen programs reported on the website of the Special Projects Fund of Israel's National Insurance Institute in 2013, under the rubric "integrating women in the workforce" only seven had "entrepreneurship" in their title (I explain the role of this institution in the next section). A higher proportion, fifteen out of thirty projects, emerged in the Van Leer Research Group Survey, one of the five primary sources of this book, where we explicitly sought out projects that did entrepreneurship. The scope of micro*lending*, moreover, is smaller still, with one important agency, the Koret Israel Economic Development Funds (KIEDF), which works primarily with Bedouins and new immigrants, and a handful of much smaller projects that operate among asylum seekers and work migrants. According to Kemp and Berkovitch (2013), between 2006 and 2009 KIEDF provided a total of 2,280 microloans, of them more than half to Bedouin women. Other existing foundations, by contrast, set requirements and charge costs, which are too high for typical women microentrepreneurs, the result being that women comprise only a third of their clientele (Kemp and Berkovitch 2013). Nevertheless, the idea of entrepreneurship has come to be perceived as an important general work skill, even in projects that focus on helping women find paid employment, communicating the message that whether salaried or self-employed, people must be able continuously to rebrand and market themselves to succeed in today's dynamic workforce.

Characteristically, the personnel operating the projects include project managers, coordinators, fundraisers, and women whose main occupation is to teach the courses. A relatively high proportion among them are Palestinian and Mizrahi women, and some men, for whom the social-economy field offers new and exciting career paths. Typically, the lecturers, group moderators, and economic consultants who do the actual teaching of the courses, and who subsequently accompany their low-income clients in their business ventures, are freelancers with two major types of expertise. They have a background in finance, accountancy, business management, human resource management, and related themes; or they have worked as facilitators of group-dynamics sessions in feminist circles, Arab-Jewish dialogue programs, or support groups for welfare recipients. Another important type of expertise is legal knowledge, sought particularly in organizations that engage in lobbying, policy initiatives, and legal support. Last but not least, the field also engages actors whose main expertise is knowledge production, to develop operational models and evaluate impact, or to work as action researchers.

Cross-sectorial Partnerships

Organizationally, the projects commonly operate as partnerships of several bodies, often combining nonprofit civil society organizations, state or municipal agencies, private philanthropists, and representatives from the business community. So at the grassroots level, the partners are often nongovernmental organizations firmly rooted in the arena of women's rights, minority rights, and social change activism. Alternatively, they may be less ideological nonprofit organizations affiliated with local or national establishments, with previous experience in tender-age education, women's health, and the like, who have directed some or most of their activity to the economic empowerment of women. These organizations raise funds for each project, and the type of funding dictates the degree to which they operate alone or in collaboration. Usually projects are operated through dense networks of local and national partners, with funding from international donors or national benefactors, or both. Typical partners are local municipalities and their various subsidiaries (community centers, welfare bureaus, Neighborhood Renewal agencies), state ministries (notably the Ministry of Industry, Trade and Labor [MITL], the Welfare, and the Immigration Absorption Ministries), other state agencies (Special Project Fund of the National Insurance Institute, Authority for Small and Middle-Size Businesses, Centers for Fostering Entrepreneurship called MATI, or several authorities within the Prime Minister's Office), actors from the business community, and large Zionist foundations that function as semiprivate extensions of the state.

Since the establishment of Israel, large Zionist foundations have played a major role in the development and operation of the state's social and economic infrastructure. Actors such as the Jewish Agency, the Joint Distribution Committee (JDC), the Jewish National Fund, the Rothschild Foundation, the Rashi Foundation, and others have been heavily involved in the development of new communities around the country. This longstanding outsourcing of state responsibilities to such bodies, which are explicitly committed to enhance Jewish and Zionist goals, and which as private bodies are not bound by the criteria of universal redistribution, has been strongly criticized as an institutional form of state discrimination (Kretzmer 1990). However, these lines of national exclusion seem to have loosened somewhat with the recent involvement of these bodies in economic empowerment and antipoverty schemes. Having rearticulated their interpretation of "democratic strength" to include reducing inequalities between Jews and Arabs, these foundations have become important partners in projects that target Palestinian citizens.

One prominent characteristic of the involvement of large Zionist foundations in the social-economy field is their tendency to be active partners, as opposed to detached donors. For this purpose, some of them establish large nonprofit organizations that work in close collaboration with state ministries on the one hand, and with civil society organizations on the other. One such organization, which fits the description of what Ardhana Sharma (2006) called a government organized NGO (GONGO), is Tevet (Hebrew acronym for *tnufa be-ta'asuka*, "momentum in employment"). Established in 2005 as a joint project of JDC Israel and the MITL, Tevet aims to increase the workforce participation of men and women from five socially vulnerable categories in particular: young people with no family support, new immigrants, Arabs, ultra-Orthodox Jews, and people with mental disabilities. Tevet's main mission is to enhance expert knowledge on workforce participation of such populations, through developing courses, textbooks, and operational models, and then training personnel in different civil society organizations on how to implement it. In the present research, Tevet figured repeatedly in its capacity as senior partner in several of the projects that I studied and as a highly influential actor in the field generally.

Another important actor of a slightly different character is the Special Projects Fund of the National Insurance Institute, the central state agency responsible for all social benefits. This fund, which defines itself as a future social hothouse, "aims to support and encourage experimental welfare services for at-risk groups and people with particular needs, such as battered women, dysfunctional families, released prisoners … job seekers, street dwellers, and more."[10] In 2013 the Special Project Fund, which acted as a strategic partner in two of the projects in which I did fieldwork for this study, reported twenty-one active welfare-to-work programs, all addressing women or adolescent girls—again, over a wide range of "disempowered" groups.

As mentioned, a different source of funding in the field is the business community, which has shown increasing interest in social entrepreneurship. Several recent millionaires from the high-tech, financial, and industrial sectors have established foundations, sometimes forming attached nonprofit organizations (NPOs) or channeling the funds directly to existing NPOs, to combat poverty and social inequalities through promoting education, employment, and well-being in the periphery. These tycoons characteristically see themselves as working for the national good, and they have a sense of obvious entitlement to talk directly to policy and decision makers inside the state system as well as among Zionist donors, offering generous matching if the government agrees to invest in enterprises they deem important. They are just as keen to work directly with grassroots actors on account of their presumed hands-on experience and because they are perceived as a way to bypass the ponderous state bureaucracy.

An example of a business-organized nonprofit organization (BONPO) is Be'atsmi (Hebrew, "By Myself"). This organization, established in 1995, is supported primarily by private businesses (including a bank, several large industrial and financial concerns, and middle-range and small firms) and philanthropic foundations, and receives matching funds in cash or kind from several government ministries, state agencies, and local municipalities. Be'atsmi's declared goal, as stated on its website, is to help low-opportunity people of diverse backgrounds—women and men, Jews and Arabs, ultra-Orthodox Jews, new immigrants, and former prisoners—find sustainable and fair employment to match their skills and ambitions. In 2012 it reported operating forty-one projects in thirty-three communities across Israel, with a cumulative total of 7,500 participants.[11] Over the years, Be'atsmi has won tenders to operate projects that had been developed by Tevet-JDC. One of these, whose operation was divided between Be'atsmi and the Women's Lobby, was Eshet Hayil (Hebrew, "Woman of Valor").

In 2010, research assistant Liraz Sapir held telephone interviews with representatives of Be'atsmi and the Women's Lobby, as part of the Van Leer Research Group Survey, to map the involvement of civil society organizations in the field of social economy. In her interview, the Be'atsmi representative reported Eshet Hayil as the main project of that organization. Designed "for women from Ethiopia, the Caucasus, Bukhara, Arabs and locally born Israelis on welfare … Very weak, with hardly any education … ," Eshet Hayil reportedly operated slightly over thirty groups in a wide variety of localities across the country. Each of the two representatives (of Be'atsmi and of the Women's Lobby) gave a similar estimate of 1,500 trainees per year and over thirty employees, most of them working part time. The Be'atsmi representative also said, "Soon there will be a new tender from the Welfare Ministry and we'll start operating on their behalf," and noted, "It's a great success for the program that a government ministry wants to adopt it."

As it turned out, both organizations eventually lost their franchise to operate the project. In 2013, Tevet's website reported that Eshet Hayil was operated by the Association for Encouraging and Advancing Community Centers in Israel, together with the MITL, the Ministry of Housing/Neighborhood Renewal, the Ministry of Immigration Absorption, and local municipalities. Yet while this particular program moved entirely to the domain of the state and local municipalities, the two above NPOs continued to be active through other programs. As of 2013, Be'atsmi reported a different large-scale project, Mifne (Hebrew, "Change"). Another product of Tevet, Mifne offers "intensive individual and group escort in order to create an occupational change in people's lives."[12] As for the Women's Lobby, this veteran liberal-feminist organization continues its general cause of promoting women's rights. Since its franchise to operate Eshet Hayil ended, it has continued its ongoing activities of lobbying, producing indexes and data analyses, and doing empowerment work with women and girls. For this feminist organization, like others that we shall meet in Chapter 3, getting into a large-scale project in the specific field of employment made sense considering the momentum that gathered around this topic. Yet because its basic agenda is more general, it could afford to "lose" it and stay active.

As the idea of corporate responsibility began to gain popularity, so did the attempts to standardize and regulate "social giving" (*netina hevratit*), as Israelis like to call this type of philanthropy. For example, in 1995 a group led by businessman Ronny Douek established Zionism 2000, which aims to promote active citizenship by standardizing social philanthropy and creating collaborations of the business community, the government, and civil society. Designating three target populations—children and youth at risk, residents of Israel's periphery, and the business/private sector, Zionism 2000 involves "thousands of volunteers, educators, social leaders, philanthropists, and business corporations" in "promoting a new and improved social agenda."[13] In 2006 it established Shitufim (Hebrew, "Sharing"), together with three other philanthropic foundations. Shitufim's declared goals are to further the establishment of "effective" [using the English word] and meaningful Israeli charity, to promote third-sector organizations, and to foster active dialogue among NGOs, businesses, and government. To achieve these goals it organizes intersectorial round tables and creates knowledge: it produces databases, publishes reports, and popularizes catchy terms such as "social capital" and "diversity."

Zionism 2000 with Shitufim, like JDC Israel with Tevet, in their capacity to mobilize substantial funding, engage decision makers and high-profile politicians, execute ambitious projects, and exert significant influence on the agenda and discourse of social responsibility, are strategic actors in the field of social economy. Eitan Shani, a social analyst I interviewed in 2013, who has been evaluating the impact of social economy projects since 2008, counted them as "infrastructure organizations," together with about ten others. Beyond immersion in particular projects, these organizations aspire to plan and organize philanthropy and corporate responsibility better, to develop standardized measurements of social impact, promote transparency and accountability, professionalize NGOs' financial and organizational management, and develop a language in which ideas of social sustainability can be communicated across the full spectrum of government, businesses, and civil society.

Grassroots Grounded Projects

Despite the heavy involvement of the business and government sectors, grassroots organizations have played an important part in shaping and operating the field of social economy. These are human rights, minority rights, and feminist organizations, which in the late 1990s began to shift their focus toward the domain of economic rights and launched pioneering initiatives in that direction, taking inspiration from CED initiatives in other countries. These groups sprang up from the legacy of human rights, so when they started working on the economic empowerment of women and minorities they were ill-equipped, ideologically and organizationally, to collaborate with the business, state, or municipal sectors. For example, when Economic Empowerment for Women, one of the grassroots organizations in which I did fieldwork for this research, launched its first microentrepreneurship course in 1999, its representatives were laughed out of the offices of MATI, an agency of the MITL that gives consultancy services for small businesses, to which they applied for collaboration. Less than a decade later, this same organization had become a regular partner of MATI and a prominent participant in forums on women's economic empowerment, along with high officials in state agencies, municipal welfare bureaus, large philanthropic foundations, and BONPOs. Other social change and feminist organizations likewise continue to play an important role in the ongoing development of the field.

Hence the field of social economy produces somewhat unexpected encounters of actors with very different subject positions and identifications. A clear ideological and institutional opposition exists between people who are identified with the dominant political and economic systems and those who have made it their vocation to criticize and oppose these systems; nevertheless, individuals across the board have reason to engage each other in their quest to promote their projects. The distances between them therefore widen and narrow as they engage in overt disagreements or, conversely, as they discover social, professional, and sometimes even political affinities, or as personal careers carry individuals across from one arena to another.

As for funding, grassroots social-change organizations direct much of their fundraising efforts to private and public foundations outside the GONGOs and BONPOs, so that in at least part of their projects they may remain the sole visionaries, operators, and representatives. Characteristically, these are progressive Zionist foundations such as the New Israel Fund or particular Jewish federations, which define their mission as supporting human rights and a democratic culture, or non-Jewish international bodies that support minorities, women, workers' unions, and the like. I mention some of these projects in Chapter 3, in a brief review of radical feminist initiatives that do not explicitly center on the economic issue. This pattern, moreover, is particularly characteristic of Palestinian organizations, which are less likely to receive support from state and related mainstream agencies. Although the target populations of such bodies now tend to include Arabs, their entitlement is limited to issues distinctly considered "apolitical," a serious qualification as many of these Palestinian organizations have an explicitly political discourse and orientation.

However, when they operate projects in the more specific field of social economy, the vast majority of grassroots organizations work in close collaboration with larger, more mainstream bodies. Projects typically are run by clusters of partners, with one NGO usually acting as the main operator and the others varying in their degree of involvement. Thus one partner, say the local welfare bureau, may be active at the stage of recruiting participants; another (a community center or some other public institution) may provide the room in which classes and conferences actually take place, perhaps with some secretarial services included, while a third partner may pay for the lecturers and moderators. In other cases collaboration among the partners may be much closer and active, with the more mainstream partners keeping a close eye on progress through participation in steering committees, demanding detailed interim reports, or paying routine visits to the field.

The Tapestry of the Field

In the course of this study I conducted and recorded focused conversations with forty-two people, thirty-five women and seven men, who were directly involved in the field as project managers, lecturers, group moderators, impact evaluators, consultants, or representatives of foundations and ministerial agencies. I interviewed thirty-one of these people myself, and the rest through research assistants. A few of them also participated in a focus group that I held in Haifa in 2009. For the rest of this chapter I draw on these conversations to outline some of the prominent features of the field—discursive motifs, biographies, strategies, motivations, and dilemmas—as seen from the perspective of the people who operate the projects.

Overwhelming Encounters across Class and Ideological Divides

Rivka Shamir was about sixty years old when I interviewed her in 2003 in her office at the private accountancy firm where she was an associate. Two years earlier she had joined an NGO that works with low-income women as a freelance lecturer in their business training courses. Rivka opened her interview with me with a statement: "FemiBiz [pseudonym] has fulfilled a dream for many women, and also for me." Then she continued:

> For years, I've dreamed of teaching economics to women. I contacted a bank and offered to teach for them, and then MATI [the agency of the MITL that gives consultancy services for small businesses] but I didn't get any response. Why do I want

to teach women? Because a woman cannot be independent who depends on her husband's purse strings ...

Then one day I was invited to give a talk at the women's club at this regional council [names the council] and I titled it "What do economics and feminism have in common?" In my ignorance I knew nothing about feminist activity here in the north and I drove all the way to the Women's Lobby in Jerusalem to collect material. Anyway, after my talk the organizer talked about me to someone from FemiBiz, who had also given a talk there, and they called me to ask if I'd work with them. I was so happy that I shouted "I want to!" ... The beginning was very exciting. In the first few meetings of the course that I taught I was so nervous. I expected the women to say that the material was too difficult. But no, they said it was very interesting and that I was being very respectful. Now, I've taken many courses in my life and attended many lectures, I never paid any thought to whether the lecturer was being respectful. Respect didn't come into it because I simply took it for granted ... Then I got similar reactions also in the second course [taught in a different city] ... Women said that not all the lecturers had treated them with respect.

Later in the interview Rivka talked about the learning difficulties of women who attend the classes when they are preoccupied with pressing problems at home:

Disempowered women do not just suffer from low energy. The opposite is also true. They can be very stormy. Any slight comment that someone makes might start a fire. Sometimes this made teaching really difficult. I think it is possible that other lecturers, whom the women experienced as disrespectful, were not necessarily offensive. They were simply reacting to the personal disquiet of some of the participants ... [And later], Their distress was so overwhelming that it was very difficult for me to listen to them. So I actually didn't tell them that I was also a volunteer at the hotline for battered women. I didn't want to encourage them to share with me more than I was prepared to take in.

A complete stranger to the world of organized feminism, Rivka lacked both the conceptual and the institutional framework to implement her dream to impart her economic knowledge on other women. Her early attempts to offer a course were rejected because they were made in a void. In the early 2000s FemiBiz and other grassroots organizations were only just beginning to communicate their message beyond the confines of feminist circles. Meanwhile, outside the "social world"—as we shall also see in the following interview with Noa Golan—sentiments were starting to brew about the need to "do something" and reach out to people in the periphery. The world of social activism provided access to such people, which seemed fresh and unmediated. It also seemed to offer compelling narratives, albeit, as interviewee Omar Azayza (below) put it, somewhat too sharp or "radical."

Another topic arising from Rivka's interview is her overwhelming experience of actually encountering low-income women. As another business lecturer, Nira Bergman, put it in her interview with me around the same time, "These are battered women. They have had so much agony in their lives. They barely have the energy to open a business." Thus the projects conceived and implemented in the social-economy field provide a unique opportunity for direct engagements between people radically different in their class positions. Like the two upper-middle-class Ashkenazi-Jewish women cited here, actors of diverse social backgrounds are attracted to enter into such engagements; so are the women on the receiving end. Chapters 2 and 3, respectively, present a comprehensive description of the multiple vulnerabilities of the low-income women who enroll in the projects, and document *their* agency in utilizing the new opportunities to network and associate beyond the boundaries of their social class.

"Diversity" and the Surprising Embrace of the Palestinian Citizens

Noa Golan, fiftyish, and a manager of a BONPO, was interviewed for this study by Noor Falah in 2010.

> I worked as a lawyer and then spent many years doing strategic planning and marketing consultancy, so I can say that I grew up in the business world. Then one day, when I already had status and money, I got up, left everything and went to look for the social world. Heaven knows why. I haven't a clue. I just had this gut feeling. So I took a position in a company that promotes corporate responsibility and also did some consultancy for partnerships between businesses and civil society organizations. Five years down the line I left to establish a new organization that promotes such partnerships, and two years later I was recruited by [names a well-known magnate] to do this new project that helps integrate Arabs into the business world. When we started it was clear to us that we needed to generate a sea change in the attitudes of the business world to diversity [Noa uses the English word] in general, and to Arab university graduates in particular. There was nothing in the country back then in the field of diversity. So we started developing knowledge and tools for businesses; started piling up a directory and reaching out for businesses that would be willing to give Arab candidates a chance.

Later in the interview Noa says:

> We have come [into existence] for a limited time—I would like to say seven years. I now know that it's more realistic to talk about fifteen years. However, we are merely a mediating factor. We want to ripen the conditions for change and then leave ... The large manpower agencies, such as Manpower and Hever, we consider them our partners, not our competitors. We pass on to them all the knowledge that we accumulate and develop, because we don't really want to be doing placements for long. We'd rather they did that, just as they do with Jewish job seekers.

This excerpt touches on at least two issues that characterize the social-economy field more generally: the resonance of a high-tech logic in the new discourse on economic empowerment, and the elaborate symbolic work that goes into framing Palestinian citizens as a legitimate target group for "social" investments. To start with the latter, the inclusion of the Palestinian—or "Arab," as most Israeli Jews prefer to call them—citizens among the target populations of the social-economy field, and the framing of their well-being as critical for the Israeli *national* well-being, is quite a recent development. The term "diversity," which in the United States for example is so popular that it may be regarded as a key symbol of American culture, is very new to the Israeli discourse. Although diversity may be translated literally into Hebrew (*givvun*) or Arabic (*tanawu'*), it has no *emic* parallel; the insertion of these or similar words into daily speech does not have the effect of a nonantagonistic evocation of social divisions, which the English "diversity" does. That is why Noa, like other actors I spoke to in the business, philanthropy, and government sectors, used the English word and not any Hebrew equivalent. Grassroots activists, by contrast, used it only very rarely, when in their communications with high-power officials they sensed that their message might come across as too radical.

The inclusion of the Palestinian citizens in BONPO- and GONGO-led projects of social economy is striking considering the centrality of Zionist money and Zionist discourses in these projects. As presented in the background section of this chapter, in the early decades of Israeli statehood the large Zionist foundations were used precisely to bypass the state's nominal commitment to universal redistribution and to actively oust the Palestinian citizens from the sphere of economic development and social integration. This does not mean that the mechanisms of ethnonational exclusion have been reversed or annulled. Arguably, as I pointed out earlier, marginalization of the Palestinian citizens remains solid and in some important respects has even worsened: poverty among them has deepened, their relative deprivation has increased parallel to the relative rise in their living standards, and judging by the recent series of racist laws and vocal expressions of anti-Arab feeling, their alienation seems to have even become more blatant. That said, it is noteworthy that their inclusion in the recent initiatives of social economy is not limited to the radical margins of grassroots activism. The Palestinians are in fact taken into account by the full range of partners operating in the field. Among them is the Prime Minister's Office, where a special authority was created in 2008 to "maximize the economic potential of the Arab, Druze and Circassian populations by encouraging their integration into the national economy."[14] Similarly, economic development projects fostered by the Jewish Agency now explicitly place the advancement of Arab citizens on their agenda, including projects specifically designed to develop the Negev and Galilee, two regions that have been the emblems of state Judaization.[15]

This development, whereby the Arab minority is declaratively and actively brought under the wings of the Zionist apparatus, does not necessarily indicate a weakening of the hegemonic perception of Israel as the state of the Jewish people, or a shift towards the state-of-all-its-citizens position upheld by the non-Zionist left. Rather, it signifies a sense of urgency in the mainstream, secular Ashkenazi-Jewish elites to reduce social inequalities as a means of strengthening the democratic component of the state, which they perceive as complementary to its Jewish component.

Several forces concurrently are responsible for this twist in the historical course of ethnonational exclusion. One, as just mentioned, is the old elites reacting to the rising tide of religious fundamentalism by clinging to the liberal component of democracy and cultivating an image of civil society as a space for apolitical pluralism. The connection between "diversity," social strength, and economic strength is traceable back to the early 1990s, with the Rabin-led peace process that culminated in the 1993 Oslo Accords. Guy Ben-Porat (2004) documents the sweeping support among the leaders of the business community of the idea of a New Middle East as an engine of economic prosperity, and their commitment to invest billions of dollars in regional economic initiatives out of the conviction that "the war industry has run its course and peace is a better investment" (cited in Ben-Porat 2004: 190). The heads of the business organizations remained vocal in their support for the peace process even after the assassination of Yitzhak Rabin in 1995, publicly expressing their concern that stopping the peace process would have terrible implications for Israel's economic future. This optimistic vision of peace and economic prosperity notwithstanding, Israeli public support for the peace process was and remains bound by ethnic and class lines. Ben-Porat notes that besides the traditional identification of the religious and the Mizrahi populations with the political right, their estrangement from the idea of a New Middle East was rooted in their realization that the anticipated fruits of economic growth would not trickle down to the lower classes and the social peripheries. Thus the collaboration between the business elite and the Labor Party, which is traditionally identified as Ashkenazi, marked the peace process as an interest of the elites, not the rank-and-file. Instead of winning hearts for peace, the business investments in regional economic enterprises served mostly to solidify the overlap of ethnic, class, and political divisions. Be that as it may, by the end of the 2000s no one was talking any longer about regional economic enterprises. Still, in the circles of the leading business elite, the link had been forged between minimizing political conflict and enhancing economic sustainability.

Another major force behind the new motivation to include Palestinian citizens in social economy initiatives is economic liberalization, which has made global connections and discourses an important part of the local business culture. In 2010 Israel finally joined the Organization for Economic Co-operation and Development (OECD). The negotiations leading to its admission, as well as its eventual membership, have created pressures to abide by the organization's standards of economic governance. Among other things, these dictate that the government must take direct action to reduce poverty, foster the periphery, and protect minority rights. A particularly conspicuous example of such influences is the surging preoccupation with the low labor force participation of Arab women, which as I document elsewhere (Sa'ar forthcoming) has rapidly become a consensual concern of government officials, grassroots activists, and experts of all sorts.

Indicative of the deeply paradoxical nature of the social-economy field, this sudden openness on the part of the bureaucratic and business elites to Palestinian citizens, and their consequent immersion into economic empowerment projects, have brought them into close contact with social change activists, who therefore constitute a third important source of influence. As shown throughout the book, and particularly in my discussion of civic entitlement and economic citizenship in Chapter 5, the collaborations in the projects of actors with very different subject positions make for strange bedfellows. Admittedly, the impact of the neoliberal logic on all participants in these encounters is enormous; but nor does the critical counterdiscourse of the grassroots activists go unnoticed by their more mainstream partners.

Going back to Noa's narrative, another interesting motif, which reflects the mood in the field more generally, is the spirit of dynamism, creativity, and ambitiousness as essential elements of economic success. When Noa talks about the organization that she represents, which she was recruited to establish, she points to its anticipated dissolution (ideally within seven years) as the ultimate measurement of its success. In a similar vein, in my field diary I recorded several times the term "exit" (in English) spoken by NPO directors and representatives of foundations to whom I listened as they envisioned their involvement in particular projects. The idea of "exit" resonates strongly with the high-tech logic of success. Israeli popular culture is full of legendary stories of bright young men who started up a company with merely an idea and some seed money; then a few years later they managed to sell it to a global conglomerate, which brought about the demise of their original company and made them multimillionaires. This, of course, is not the experience of most high-tech workers, nor is the pick-up-and-go a feasible option for the average woman in the business world. Yet the possibility is believed to be there, and deemed to be reserved for those who have the additional spark, and the courage to listen to their innermost voice and follow it even before they know where it is leading them. These elements, reflected in Noa's narrative of her personal career path, are central in Israeli neoliberal discourses of success. To varying degrees they are also popular throughout the field of social economy—among those who conceive, finance, and operate the projects, as well as among some of the low-income women who enroll in them.

A Bottom-Up, Radical Approach to Social Economy

The next excerpt is taken from an interview I conducted in 2003 with Ofra Gonen, a woman in her mid-fifties who worked as a coordinator and group moderator in an economic empowerment project. Ofra's background was very different from Rivka's and Noa's. In important respects her life history actually resembled that of many of the projects' clients. Her brief biography, as she told me on that occasion, reflects vividly the sense of growth that some women have experienced through their involvement in the field.

> I grew up in a poor neighborhood, but I didn't know that until I was accepted at a good high school in a different area, after I passed the state exam, the *seker*. Only after I joined the new school did I become aware of the enormous gap between the few of us who came from there and the majority who came from the more affluent neighborhoods. I had academic difficulties but refused to get assistance, even though I was eligible. I found it insulting, me being a good student and all. So I left, and at fifteen, after only one year in high school, I was already working. I did office work and worked as a cashier at a stall at the food market. I was always very strong in math. On this kind of job you have to work out large numbers really fast. Think how it is in the market. You don't have time to write things down. You need to have a good brain and a good memory. I was very good at it and the boss liked me a lot. He'd send my parents complimentary boxes full of fruits and vegetables to show his gratitude. I did that until I was drafted to the army [at eighteen], and I stayed in the army for four years, instead of two, because I didn't want to go back home. After four years I left and immediately found a job in a factory. I worked there for two years until they went bankrupt; then the man who bought the company took it on himself to teach me accountancy. I managed all the accounts of the factory and the shops, and took night classes to complete my matriculation certificate. I stayed on that job until I was about thirty, except for a year and a half, aged about twenty-five, which I spent in London. Eventually I decided that I wasn't getting much there. I wanted to find myself, maybe study. I've never stopped wanting to.
>
> After I left the factory I found a job as a caretaker at the shelter for battered women. The pay was less. By the way, the guy who took my job at the factory immediately got a salary that was double what I had. When I pointed that out they said that he was a breadwinner, married with kids, and that if I stayed they'd give me the same. Not that I hadn't tried to get a raise before. Anyway, I worked part time at the shelter, which got me right into the feminist "business." A year later I already got arrested in a proabortion demonstration. I also found a job doing interviews for a study on Mizrahi disenfranchisement. That got me onto the Mizrahi issue. We had that NGO [names the NGO and some well-known Mizrahi activists]. The next stage was studying how to moderate Jewish-Arab dialogue groups.

Around the mid-1980s a guy who had worked with me in the factory asked me to do part-time accountancy in his new business, so I started doing that, and my salary for working a few afternoons a week was the same as what I got in the shelter. So I left the shelter and made that company my main place of employment. My job there grew with the years and I stayed until 1998. All that time I volunteered for feminist activities, did consciousness-raising groups in poor neighborhoods, went to demonstrations, and became more and more active. In the late 1990s I went to study senior business management in a program at the university. They accepted me even though I didn't have the credentials, because I had good recommendations and they saw my record at the company. Now I've finally left my job as an accountant and I work only in NGOs, doing several part-time jobs.

Ofra's narrative affords us the perspective of grassroots social-change activists in the social-economy field. In her case, preoccupation with the *economic* or class situation of women in the periphery is but one stopping point in a continuous collective engagement in discrimination, oppression, and social injustice. Like the narratives of grassroots activists generally, Ofra's is first and foremost political: the economic plight of the women is related to their ethnic and national marginalization, which are in turn magnified by the gender power structure; it is impossible to tackle the one without the other, or to choose to focus on internal inequalities without taking a stand on the Israeli occupation of the Palestinian territories. While in this particular excerpt she mentions a proabortion demonstration (a gender/sexuality issue) and Mizrahi activism, Ofra, like many of her partners in the civil society organizations in the social economy field, is also a core member of the feminist peace movement.

The sense of multiple overlaps between class, ethnic, national, and gender issues, as reflected in the personal biographies of many activists of Ofra's generation, provides the ideological setting of the challenges at hand. This is very different from the liberal—indeed the neoliberal—framing of the problems of social inequalities as "social," in the emic Israeli sense of apolitical. For many of these activists' more mainstream partners, such positioning of social inequalities is radical and potentially disconcerting.

One of the fascinating things that happen in the field of social economy is a subtle dialogue on justice and entitlement among people who are located quite far apart on the Israeli-Palestinian political map. In part, the dialogue is made possible through mitigating terms, such as "diversity" or "empowerment," which lend themselves to contradictory interpretations while still allowing conversation. Or else it proceeds "without words," through the routine, day-to-day practical operation of the projects, and the genuine care and passion shared by many of the actors to make Israeli society less greedy and more compassionate. Nevertheless, the intractable nature of the ethnic and national conflicts, the high level of violence, the harsh terms of the political discourse, and the periodic outbreak of Israeli-Arab hostilities put the delicate weave of the dialogue under great strain.

As in workplaces more generally, the cross-sectorial collaboration in social-economy projects becomes fragile during the periodic political crises that erupt in painful succession. For example, in 2008 an organization I call here Essentially Independent won the Knesset Chairperson's Award for its contribution to women's well-being. On hearing the announcement the members of the organization were happy and proud. But two months later, when a delegation of them were due to travel to Jerusalem to attend the award ceremony, Israeli troops had just pulled out of Gaza after a three-week bloody invasion that galvanized sweeping support among a majority of the Jewish citizens and bitter protests by the Palestinians and the Jewish-Palestinian peace circles. Some members of Essentially Independent were beside themselves, feeling that they could not, under any circumstances, shake the hand of the Knesset chairperson, who had been openly supportive of the invasion led by her party. However, they knew that rejecting the prize would carry the dire consequence of blacklisting them for a host of mainstream business, government, and Zionist foundations, which they could not afford. An open rejection of the award, moreover, would also offend some of the volunteers and freelance employees of their own organization who did not belong to the feminist-radical-left circles, as well as many of the clients of the courses, who were traditional right-wing voters. During the invasion some core Essentially Independent employees and volunteers participated in demonstrations and signed petitions, but they spontaneously avoided discussing their opinions with other members, whom they knew did not share them. This is common practice in Israeli society, where family members, work colleagues, and neighbors take the greatest care to avoid explicit articulation of differences they experience as unbridgeable, particularly if they are part of a political minority.

Eventually, after intense deliberations, the board of Essentially Independent sent a bus with twenty-five women, about half the number who had originally registered for the journey; the absentees included two core employees and two board members. There were no public statements, but the director, who begrudgingly decided to travel, refused to go onto the stage and shake the hand of the Knesset chairperson. One of the board members, a peace activist herself, volunteered to replace her. This move too was kept low-key, and when the acting chair of the board expressed her bewilderment at the director's not receiving the prize in person, it was off-handedly explained away as personal shyness. In this organization, the board of about six volunteers who rotate every two or three years is generally made up of women with a background in grassroots feminism and women rooted in the business, financial, or academic sectors. As a third feminist-peace activist board member confided in me during the visit, she had spent the days preceding the event in long conversations with two other, business-sector board members, trying to assuage their agitation at the very idea that Essentially Independent might take a political position on an issue that in their opinion was not at all part of its platform.

Going back from the ideological to the structural, another interesting characteristic of the field of social economy is an ongoing movement of actors within, and to a lesser degree between, institutional spheres. We saw this in Noa Golan's account of her career path, and in a different way also in the life course of Ofra Gonen, who has moved among various organizations as an activist, and who, throughout her working life, has alternated between combining and separating her activism and her paid employment. This dynamism entails an active, ongoing exchange of people, ideas, strategies, knowledge, and other resources within and across the different sectors involved in the field. More subtly, it also implies intriguing articulations of "work" on continuums of payment, volunteerism, and moral investment. For understandable reasons, the inclination to use social economy or related human-rights/social-change activism as a source of livelihood, or even as the ground from which to launch a career, is more prevalent among Mizrahim and Palestinians, whose opportunities are significantly limited from the start. Still, in their interviews many of these actors stressed that their employment in social economy contained a significant component of choice.

New, If Limited Career Opportunities for Women from the Social Peripheries

Of the various groups that operate in the social-economy field, the Palestinian citizens, and particularly university-educated Palestinian women, seem to be they who stand to profit the most. The rapid growth of the field has created new jobs, which are high quality in that they include a fairly large degree of autonomy, authority, and personal and ideological self-expression, although all in all civil society organizations still comprise a very small occupational sector. According to Hagai Katz and Hila Yogev-Keren (2013), in 2009 civil society organizations in Israel offered just over 2,500 jobs, less than 1 percent of the total number of jobs offered in the third sector that year. The salaries are not very high but still promising compared with the average salaries of Palestinian-Israeli women. The official salaries tend to be close to the national average wage and higher than the median wage, which as Swirski, Konor-Attias, and Arian (2013) point out is the wage of most people of the social peripheries. This is good news then, particularly considering the high unemployment rates among university-educated Palestinian-Israeli women, and the extreme difficulties of Palestinian-Israeli women in general finding steady, gainful, and rewarding employment (Sa'ar, forthcoming). Yet in practice, many if not most of the jobs that are available are part time, hence the actual salaries are much lower. So despite their decent *theoretical* level, in 2009 the reported average salary in civil society organizations was exactly half the national average wage (Katz and Yogev-Keren 2013). Moreover, as many of my interviewees testified, the overwhelming nature of the work often entails investment of time stretching beyond the official job description. This is a built-in imbalance that unwittingly duplicates the typical overworked/underpaid nature of feminine work, and ironically echoes the situation of many of the low-income women that these projects aim to empower.

Civil society organizations in Israel, including those in the field of social economy, are vulnerable because of their dependence on philanthropy and because the tenders to operate projects are characteristically short term. This adds endemic job insecurity to their employees' low salaries. The generally low budgets of the projects and donors' reluctance to cover overhead or permanent positions put pressure on NGOs to cut their expenses. Most of them maneuver by dividing each position among several employees (hence the part-time jobs), and by outsourcing much of the work to freelancers, as in the case of the lecturers and moderators who teach the empowerment courses. The results are the high prevalence of seasonal employment, high levels of personnel turnover, and a small number of positions that include basic social benefits (Katz and Yogev-Keren 2013).

Thus follows a second irony: this sector, whose primary goal is to improve the economic situation of the people in the secondary job market, unintentionally creates precarious conditions for its own employees. According to Katz and Yogev-Keren (2013), 68 percent of employees in civil society organizations, like the third sector more generally, are women, and they are more dependent on these jobs than the men in this sector, for whom employment in NGOs tends to be a complementary rather than a primary source of livelihood. Complementing this list of problematic characteristics, civil society organizations, in their capacity as employers, tend to duplicate the patterns of discrimination that characterize the workforce more generally: women on average earn only about 68 percent of what men do; Palestinians earn 85 percent of what Jews do, which is actually a relatively moderate deprivation compared with other sectors; and Ashkenazim earn an average of 62 percent more than all others (Katz and Yogev-Keren 2013).

Still, as indicated in the following excerpt, the rewarding aspects of the field are far from insignificant. Nibal Khouri was forty-odd years old and a holder of a masters' degree in social work in 2009, when Nisreen Mazzawi interviewed her in her capacity as full-time program manager of an economic empowerment project for Palestinian women. When asked about her background, she said:

I worked for about ten to twelve years doing training and empowerment work with women in different NGOs, and this is how I have built my career. In addition, [I want to say that working with] women is something that I like doing irrespective of the fact that I find my livelihood in it. It has to do with my opinions and convictions regarding femininity and all that. So I've been very satisfied with my work ... All the employees in the different NGOs that I worked in have been feminist, and so was the work itself. The people I've worked with have been [that way inclined] personally and professionally. It has made networking [in my present position as program manager] really easy. Not only have I had no problem cooperating with other NGOs, but my professional knowledge also helped me achieve my goals quite fast ...

My feminist thinking and my interest in the topic go beyond my work.... If I compare my feminism today to my feminism when I just started working in the field, it's really different. I used to think that feminism was just about achieving equality between men and women. Today I can see how my thinking has developed from simple liberal feminism to a more comprehensive understanding of social liberation. I aspire for a society that will be enlightened and liberated in all respects, and women as an oppressed group are of particular interest to me. [Feminism] is also a political issue. I care about the Palestinian minority. I go to demonstrations. I have a general interest in the fate of the Palestinian population. I like to participate in all kinds of activities that might bring about change. This is so in both my personal and professional life.

Partly, I applied for this job of doing project development for microbusinesses because I wanted a change and I wanted something new. I told them already in the interview that I didn't have any economic background. That didn't bother them. They said that they were looking for the feminist outlook, and that they already had people who knew about economics. And since I began working here I have discovered a new field. I used to think that economics was numbers, accounting. I didn't really understand the connection between the social and the economic. It has been a slow process. I feel that this new economic topic that I'm getting into is a [good] challenge for me. I'm fed up doing the same feminist empowerment all the time. Sure, it's important. But I want to be doing something new about it ... I'm hoping that this way we can reach out for many families and women, and that the economic movement will become something tangible. Today everyone is working on it, but you don't feel it yet.

Networking, Coalition Work, and Competition

Besides a high level of satisfaction and ideological identification, Nibal's narrative conveys the importance of networking. Networking takes place within the civil society sector, as in Nibal's description, and outside it, across sectorial, class, ethnonational, and international boundaries. Professionals like Nibal often move between different NGOs, some all-Palestinian, others dominated by Jews. Noa Golan, for example, in the interview cited above, talked about her past relationships with two other project managers, one Arab and one Jewish, with whom she was collaborating on the project discussed in the interview. She had met the Arab partner previously when the latter was working for JDC Israel. Similar exchanges occur throughout the field. Within the sphere of Arabic-speaking NGOs, people generally know each other very well as they have mostly worked together on more than one occasion; they also meet socially, either as personal friends or as acquaintances, and tend to belong to the same or similar political circles. Jewish actors move in concentric circles of familiarity, and the longer they work in the field the more their circles become diverse and their relationships deeper. Through their associations in the field, some of the veteran Jewish actors get access to individuals in power positions in the business, government, and philanthropy sectors. The veteran Arab and Jewish actors commonly have friends and acquaintances in each other's national group, with whom they have a history of collaborative work. Yet invariably the Arab actors, as members of the minority, know more Jews than the reverse; all of them speak fluent Hebrew and are intimately familiar with Israeli-Jewish culture and society. The vast majority of the Jewish actors, by contrast, speak no Arabic and only a small number of them are familiar with Palestinian culture and society. On a much smaller scale, lastly, networking of actors in the field spreads internationally too, through their meetings with feminist, peace, or labor-rights activists in other countries at international conferences, shared workshops, and mutual visits. Besides personal acquaintances, international networking also entails maintaining active familiarity with globally circulating discourses of rights, entitlements, and justice.[16]

A common type of activity emanating from networking is coalition work. Unlike economic empowerment *projects,* which as described earlier are practical and involve formal partnerships of organizations from the civil society, the business community, and the government sector, activities to pressure policy makers, influence public opinions, and create an alternative discourse are also featured in the social-economy field. Usually confined to grassroots organizations, they include lobbying, advocacy, producing reports and policy papers, launching media campaigns, and initiating appeals to the Supreme Court of Justice. Because such activities are typically underbudgeted (most of the budget of grassroots NGOs is earmarked for the projects that they have committed to), organizations commonly try to advance them by joining forces and pooling resources.

Omar Azayza, a director of a Palestinian NGO for workers' rights, was in his late forties in 2009 when Nisreen Mazzawi interviewed him for this research. Holder of a law degree, he had worked as a journalist before taking up his position at that organization in 2000. In his description of his organization's platform and activities he used an emphatically ideological language; he and his team were there to support, represent, and fight for the rights of Palestinian workers. The following excerpt intimates the importance many social activists ascribe to framing their work as politically and ideologically motivated, and therefore better than the work of comparable organizations in the civil society sector that have made pragmatic compromises that presumably make them less effective. His words below refer to the compulsory, government-initiated welfare-to-work program Mahalev (Hebrew acronym for "From income support to secure employment"), or the Wisconsin Plan, as it was more popularly known, which was implemented as a pilot in four regions in Israel from 2005 to 2010 (Helman 2013; Maron and Helman 2015). Highly contentious among the public at large, and with mixed reviews from professional evaluators, the program was eventually dropped and did not go beyond the pilot stage.

> In our organization we tell it as it is, whatever the cost. Even if it makes us look radical, we still stick to our truth. Here's an example: when they launched the Wisconsin Plan, I think that no NGO did what we did [to stop it]. True, the position that we took impoverished us financially, but we managed to make a difference. Our position regarding the Wisconsin Plan was unambiguously negative, and when I say "our" I mean the Palestinian NGO [names his organization]. We refused to take it upon us [to be within the cluster of local organizations that collaborated with the operator] because we didn't believe that this government project was the answer to unemployment in the Arab population ...
>
> There are some women's organizations that do [economic empowerment] projects [mentions a few organizations]. But unlike us, employment is not their primary field. So they tackle issues of legal rights of women employees, or unemployment of university graduates. That's good. But in my opinion confronting this issue should not be limited to writing reports and submitting them to the Knesset. If you can't achieve something in the state of Israel, [you should try to achieve it] without the state. This method of submitting reports has not advanced the employment of even one single woman. We too tried to prepare reports and send them to the Knesset. It got us nowhere. I'm talking generally here about all the organizations. If you don't begin to do real work you won't see any change, be it for women, students, farmers, university graduates ... anyone. I'm not saying that it's not important to stimulate public opinion on women's problems. But I think that many women's organizations have failed to understand that they need to make a switch. That it is not helping. Like, I can convince international organizations that I'm being discriminated against and [try to get them to put pressure on the state] that they should build more factories and force them to employ Arabs. But I also need to stand up and protest, and I need to be consistent and persistent. Because experience has taught us that the only way to accomplish something is by fighting for it ourselves. Writing reports is not a substitute for fighting for your rights. Arab women with university education are unemployed. There are no jobs for them. State ministries are closed to them. We must translate these reports to real action. For example, bring university graduates, put them on a bus, and protest in front of the Knesset.

The tension between action and "mere talk" that emerges from Omar's words is very familiar in both Palestinian and Israeli public cultures. This semantic opposition is a common rhetorical token used to claim moral superiority in debates on the right way to tackle social problems. This rhetoric, as I have shown in my previous work on Jewish-Arab activism in Jaffa (Sa'ar 2006a), often goes hand in hand with the aforementioned semantic opposition of political vs. social, and similarly reflects the dilemmas of people who know they are treading contentious ground when they try to rally support for issues that they feel strongly about. It is highly typical for people in such situations to debate over a practical and a confrontational course of action, knowing full well that each choice they make will have its repercussions. Whatever their inclination in specific situations, the debating parties commonly justify their choice by presenting it as either more courageous and truthful (proper action as opposed to "mere talk") or wiser: thoughtful and responsible "talk" that might generate change as opposed to impulsive action liable to backfire. In practice, all civil society organizations without exception take both courses of action. They all reach out for collaborations with partners in other sectors; they all make detailed work plans and fill out tedious reports; they all struggle to match the latest outlines issued by the different foundations; and they all make compromises. At the same time, all of them also resist the pressures to conform, and toil endlessly to reassert the boundaries of their ideological and political integrity.

Epilogue

In the summer of 2011 Israel witnessed a wave of social protest of unprecedented size. The movement, which took the form of tent encampments and spread from the center to the periphery, started with protests against the soaring prices of housing and basic foodstuffs (for a while it was dubbed "the cottage-cheese protest"), and developed into a general cry to redirect national priorities to remedy the polarizing effects of economic liberalization. Hundreds of thousands of protesters—some say over a million—marched wave upon wave under the slogan "The People Demand Social Justice." These were accompanied by an avalanche of public debates—round tables, dialogue circles, newspaper articles, talk shows, blogging, conferences—about the social implications of the neoliberal policies of the previous few decades. Particular focus was put on the difficulties of young people, notably, in this familistic society, young couples, in making ends meet, on the deteriorating state of education, health, housing, and welfare, and on the unwarranted affinity between capital and government. Echoing similar events in the Middle East, Europe, North America, and elsewhere, the Israeli social protest of summer 2011 nevertheless had its particular local significance.

In complete contrast to previous protests against the rising cost of living, the core leaders of this movement were young, middle-class, not-yet-married, predominantly educated, Jewish, secular, and Ashkenazi: hardly the familiar Israeli face of economic deprivation. Of course, the demographics were quite different in the many tent cities that sprang around the periphery, where one would find mostly weary, hard-up single moms with their small children, unemployed men, some drug addicts, and deep despair. Moreover, the young, healthy, educated, center-based leaders of the 2011 movement were not there merely to support the poor and the miserable as in the past; this time they felt that it was *their* protest. They demanded greater economic opportunity to grow and prosper, not just to survive; they believed that this could be attained with, not at the expense of, greater social solidarity and more generous state subsidies for health, education, and housing; and the activists here demanded a say in the big economic policies. They wanted stronger state regulation of economic monopolies, more rigorous progressive taxation, and a generally more responsive government.

A second factor of major significance in the summer 2011 protest movement was that its leaders pointedly distanced themselves from the traditional Israeli label of "left." Contrary to the familiar position of the Israeli left that "the occupation corrupts" and that "oppression is oppression is oppression," namely, that any struggle for social justice inside Israel must be linked to the struggle to end the Palestinian occupation, these young leaders insisted on keeping their message strictly "social," in the emic sense of the term, as presented earlier in the chapter. Palestinian citizens by and large remained marginal to the movement, but when they did join in (primarily in mixed cities like Haifa or Jaffa, and in a handful of Palestinian localities) they were generally made welcome, albeit as a "social"—not a "political"—constituency; explicit expressions of Palestinian national sentiments were not invited for display on the movement's central stage. Nor was the Mizrahi-Ashkenazi issue explicitly discussed. Activists never appealed directly to the discrimination of Mizrahim. Instead, they offered solidarity with the lower classes, a term that skirted the ethnic issue, neither ignoring it entirely nor admitting it explicitly. A third glaring issue that was left unspoken was gender. The public face of the movement included several young women who were undisputedly among its core leaders. These strong, outspoken, unapologetic individuals bore an unmistakable feminist imprint. For example, Dafni Leaf, in one of her many interviews, mentioned her being overweight and also a rape victim as factual parts of her autobiography, not worth hiding or apologizing for, nor dwelling on; these were presented as matter-of-fact parts of her public persona, just like the health condition that had prevented her being drafted into the army. Yet none of them ever assumed the explicit title "feminist," listed gender politics as part of her agenda, or allied herself with any particular feminist group.

Arguably, the movement leaders' refusal to take on the "political" label and their persistent avoidance of linking their struggle to the Mizrahi/Ashkenazi or the feminist causes were critical to their successful rallying widespread support. However, judging by their speeches and the eventual parliamentary affiliations of some of them, this was more than a mere tactic. In sticking to the imaginary middle line of "the social," they were operating firmly within the local cultural scenario that I have outlined throughout the chapter in respect of the social-economy field. This key scenario dictates that the right way to address potentially destructive social divisions is by accommodating them in the hegemonic looking-glass, namely, adjusting the dominant definition of reality without replacing it. With the demise of the old hegemonic Zionist order and its moral terminology of justice and belonging, the present neoliberal order dictates a different vocabulary of civic entitlement. Admitting "diversity" without yielding power to subalterns in any profound way reflects the adjustability of this order. As shown throughout this book, neoliberalism offers emotional experiences of mass participation. The social protest was one such opportunity. Consuming empowerment (Chapters 3 and 4) is another. It likewise allows a continuous trickle of individuals from periphery to center and into the old elites. In the 2013 parliamentary elections, forty-eight new members, including some of the 2011 movement's leaders, entered into the Knesset, comprising a 40 percent turnout of House members. And it erects stages on which actors of diverse backgrounds can perform together in the "new spirit of capitalism," which, as Luc Boltanski and Eve Chiapello (2005) explain, at once identifies with capitalist logic and criticizes it.

Notes

1. The names of all informants have been changed. See the Introduction for an explanation of my rationale in choosing the pseudonyms.
2. For example, since 1976 claims for child allowances have been submitted directly to the National Insurance Institute through the registration of newborns in the hospital (Rosenhek 1999).
3. Israel, National Insurance Institute, "The Scope of Poverty and Social Inequalities, an Annual Report," accessed September 2013, http://www.btl.gov.il/Publications/oni_re port/Documents/DohOni2012.pdf.
4. In 1992, the Arab parties in the parliament successfully negotiated an agreement with Prime Minister Rabin to guarantee their support of his government from the opposition in return for his commitment to take active steps toward improving the status of the Arab citizens. As shown in the annual reports of Sikkuy (Hebrew, "chance") an Organization for Advancing Civil Equality, successive governments from that time on have indeed drafted and budgeted concrete plans, although implementation has been very partial. Sikkuy, the Association for the Advancement of Civil Equality report, resource distribution report, accessed April 20, 2013, http://www.sikkuy.org.il/english/reports.html.
5. Mossawa Center, the Advocacy Center for Arab Citizens in Israel "Racism Report," accessed 20 April 2013, http://www.mossawacenter.org/my_documents/publication/AR_Racism_Report_2004.pdf.

6. Mossawa Center Annual Racism Report 2012, accessed April 20, 2013, http://www.mossawacenter.org/en/item.asp?aid=919. Mada al-Carmel, Palestinian Research and Information Center. 2012 Israel and the Palestinian Minority Political Monitoring Report 16, accessed 8 May 2013, http://mada-research.org/en/category/reports/.
7. Adala, the Legal Center for Arab Minority Rights in Israel, report on discriminatory laws and bills, accessed 20 April 2013, http://adalah.org/Public/files/English/Legal_Advocacy/Discriminatory_Laws/Discriminatory-Laws-in-Israel-October-2012-Update.pdf.
8. See also Smooha (2010) on the debate between the mutual alienation and rapprochement theses regarding relations between Jews and Palestinians inside Israel.
9. For an overview of civil society organizations providing services to women as part of the creation of an alternative women's welfare sphere in Israel in recent years see Almog-Bar and Ajzenstadt (2010).
10. National Insurance Institute Special Projects Fund, website accessed 13 April 2013, http://www.btl.gov.il/Funds/Special%20Activities/Pages/default.aspx.
11. Be-atzmi, an NGO that assists underprivileged Israelis integrate on their own into stable and appropriate jobs, website accessed 13 April 2013, http://www.be-atzmi.org.il/team.asp.
12. Ibid.
13. Zionism 2000, a businessmen-led association committed to social responsibility and the promotion of active citizenship in Israel, website accessed 30 April 2013, http://www.zionut2000.org.il/site/front/showcategory.aspx?ItemId=350.
14. Authority for Economic Development of the Arab, Druze, and Circassian Populations at the Prime Minister's Office, website accessed 1 May 2013, http://www.pmo.gov.il/English/PrimeMinistersOffice/DivisionsAndAuthorities/Pages/AuthorityfortheEconomicDevelopment.aspx.
15. The Tsafona and Daroma (Hebrew, "Northwards" and "Southwards") development plans, two BONPOs supported by the Jewish Agency, are a case in point, website accessed 4 April 2013, http://www.jewishagency.org/JewishAgency/Hebrew/Israel/PriorityRegions/DaromaAndTzafona.
16. More on transnational feminist networks, see Moghadam (2005a).

PART II

Women Making Sense of the Demand to Make Money

CHAPTER 2

Vulnerability

"Everywhere she goes, a woman in poverty encounters the fantasy of her disappearance," said Ayelet Ilany (2012), formerly of Economic Empowerment for Women, reflecting on the common complaint that the Arabs and the ultra-Orthodox Jews skew Israel's scores on the OECD and similar international indexes. "Couldn't we just drop them from the statistics?" she cited a well-known TV talk-show host. Against this crushing fantasy, she continued, feminists tell women, "We are with you. We see you. We respect you. We stand by you and will do everything in our power to make you stronger. The very position of acting *together with* women in poverty is an act of resistance against the economic policy of this government."

This chapter draws a collective portrait of low-income women in Israel. Its frame is "intersectionality," in which gender articulates in multiple ways with other mechanisms of power and exclusion, notably class, ethnicity, and in the case at hand, ethnonationality. I explore the similar and the different among various subgroups, paying special attention to the interplay of structural barriers, particular locations, and personal agency. The low-income women who enrolled in this study were widely heterogeneous, of diverse ethnic, national, linguistic, and religious backgrounds. The Jewish and Palestinian participants differed significantly in the environmental, structural, and historical roots of their marginality, but so did the subgroups in each of the two national categories. They varied also in their personal and family histories of poverty, in their human-capital resources and their involvement in productive labor, in the scope and severity of their emotional scars, and in their capacity to maintain intimacy and develop trust. Here I attempt to keep this diversity close to the surface as I depict their vulnerabilities and their overt and covert capacities. This will lay the foundation for our understanding, in later chapters, of the attempts to resuscitate these capacities.

Vulnerabilities

"In your report, it is important that you write about how the complexity of women's disempowerment affects the nature of business consultancy." Wafa Khouri, a self-employed business consultant told me in an interview in 2003.

> For the graduates of EEW, business consultancy must include also legal and personal matters, because their business problems are inextricably entwined with their personal status, their health, and so on. For example, Suheila [one of the graduates of the course I observed] recently discovered that her ex-husband got her into terrible debt by forging her signature on two check books that he had stolen without her even noticing. He gave away checks for a cumulative sum of nearly NIS 40,000 [US$10,000], mainly to one supermarket in Upper Nazareth, where his girlfriend lives, and to the Ford garage that does the maintenance of his truck. Prior to that he got her into another debt, of NIS 11,000, for which she recently received "debt unification" [a court order that requires her to pay set monthly installments, and which entails a long-term bond, high interest, and restrictions on her bank account]. I explained to her the severity of this arrangement and stressed that she should do all she could to avoid getting another debt unification. She should take a lawyer and also consider paying a graphologist to prove that the signature had been forged.

To understand the effect of empowerment let us first consider the multilayered vulnerability of the women in question. For one thing, low-income women are highly susceptible to violence of different sorts. To start with the most commonly acknowledged form, about 24 percent of the women in the Microentrepreneurship Study were victims of domestic and/or sexual abuse. This is a cautious estimate, possibly optimistic, since many women did not think it was relevant, or felt uncomfortable sharing such information, in a study on business entrepreneurship. While the standardized questionnaire handed out to the full sample of 239 women did not contain a direct question on domestic or sexual violence, we did ask whether there had been a difficult event that affected the woman's capacity to work and earn money. Only 4 percent of the interviewees checked that question, explaining that they were referring to the violent behavior of their husbands or ex-husbands. In the life-histories that were collected from fifty-eight of these same women, however, 21 percent related distressing stories of violence at the hands of their spouses, fathers, or both; two of these women reported being abandoned by their mothers in childhood. Two other women (an additional 3 percent) mentioned ongoing violence at the hands of their sisters. Strikingly, none of these women checked the "difficult event" question when they completed the standardized questionnaire, even though it was clear beyond doubt from their detailed life histories that these experiences had had an immense impact on every aspect of their lives, including their ability to work and earn money. In all these cases, moreover, the overwhelming effect of the violence was aggravated still more by the women's need to contain the direct or indirect victimization of their children as well.

Irena Yaplonsky, a divorced Jewish immigrant from Ukraine, was in her early fifties and living in Jerusalem when Xenia Gurbachevich interviewed her in 2003. Her husband for thirty years and the father of her two children, by then young adults, began acting violently towards her several years into their marriage, as his drinking problem deteriorated. It started with swearing and developed into beating, "until I was black and blue all over," with occasional assaults with a knife. The first time he pulled a knife on her he tried to force her to jump off the balcony. On later occasions he cut her back and her arm; finally, when the children were in their late teens, she filed for divorce. In their ten years in Israel, Irena's husband never brought in any income, and her own earnings were never sufficient for the family's needs. When asked to describe what at last convinced her to join the entrepreneurship course, Irena said:

> I don't know, I was alone, alone. Then I got up and thought, "No, I've got to go somewhere." I bought a subscription to a swimming pool. I registered for a women's group at the community center ... I forced myself to get up. I thought, "No one is going to lift me up, I must lift myself." The children as well. They're busy with themselves. The children want me to smile and help them, to give them presents. Who cares how miserable I am?

Suheila 'Eilabouni, a recently divorced Muslim mother of four and the woman that Wafa was referring to above, was thirty-seven when I interviewed her in Haifa in 2003. At the time of the interview, her ex-husband of eighteen years was serving a jail sentence on charges of violent assaults against her, several of his lovers, and the two policemen who came to arrest him. He had been violent toward her already during their engagement, when she was only sixteen. During the years of their marriage he beat her up regularly, and on a few occasions he even held a knife to her throat and threatened to kill her. Although she testified that he had never been directly aggressive to the children, he did hit their son at least once, when the boy was trying to defend his mother. Besides his physical violence, Suheila's husband was unreliable in providing for her and their children. Yet he refused to allow her to work outside the house, "because only prostitutes do that." At the same time, he would lavishly and openly spend money on his occasional lovers.

While domestic and sexual violence are known to exist across the class spectrum, their effects are often exacerbated by racism, sexism, and class inequalities (e.g., Marsh 1993; Anitha 2011; Dalal and Lindqvist 2012). Examples are high crime rates in poor neighborhoods, prejudices of welfare and law-enforcement officials against members of minority groups (Shalhoub-Kevorkian 2004), and of course the attrition of the continuous struggle to make do on a very low budget. For example, in a study by Dalia Sachs, Sarai Aharoni, and myself on the impact on Israeli women of the armed Israeli-Palestinian conflict (Sachs et al. 2007) the levels of post-traumatic stress disorder following exposure to terrorist attacks proved significantly and consistently higher among women who experienced multiple forms of marginality (e.g., if they belonged to a minority group and were also old, low-income, or living on the periphery).

Back to the Microentrepreneurship Study: Shoshana Attiyas, fifty-odd, Jewish, from a small periphery town in the north, testified to having been brought up in a loving and supportive family. She spoke about the neighborhood where she lived, and had been born and raised: "Well, you can see the area here … the socio economics, I won't go into details." Her deceased husband and the father of her six children had been a drug addict who served jail sentences totaling ten years, and afterwards was murdered in front of two of their children.

> My husband was murdered and so was my brother in law … and in between the tragedies I have had to cope all on my own … Two of my children were there when it happened and saw it … There were times when I would stand in the kitchen and simply not function. I didn't cook or clean. The kids just managed somehow. Until one day I realized what I was doing to them, that they needed me, they needed to see me in the kitchen … I said to myself, "This can't be helped. I must be there for the kids …" There were times when I really fell apart, but I decided not to sink. I'm more focused now, thank God.

Even without direct exposure to crime or abuse, living through years of economic hardship is a major source of disempowerment. The constant anxiety, the never-ending calculations, and the panic—or despair—each time they face an exceptional financial expense that cannot be postponed—all were heavily abrasive on women. Many felt weakened by such an ongoing experience. Some said that it made them lose their self-confidence. Many reported adverse effects on their mental and physical health. The vast majority of the women whose life histories are the basis of this book, close to a hundred altogether, related such experiences. Often these were stories without drama. Ayala Cohen, forty, Jewish, an Israeli-born mother of three, had recently separated from her husband when Ya'ara Buksbaum interviewed her in Haifa in 2006.

Having left school three years before graduation, at her father's insistence and against her will, she had no profession and her only occupational experience was occasional caretaking of other women's children in her own home. When her children were small she stayed home with them, and since her husband's salary was not enough, the parents of both of them supplemented it through gifts. With no independent income, now separated, and with her children at school, she wanted to find a job but had neither formal qualifications nor occupational experience. She was considered too old even for simple jobs, so the dozens of applications she sent through Mahut Center did not yield even a single job interview.

Shirin Nabulsi, a 28-year-old Christian Arab divorcee, was living in Haifa with her two small boys when I interviewed her in 2004 as part of the Microentrepreneurship Study. Her ex-husband, a drunk and a gambler whom she had left three years after they married, paid no child support and in fact had never even seen his younger boy. Getting in-kind assistance from her parents, who were unable to give her any financial support, she was trying to come up with ideas to transform some of her talents into a small business. Unlike Ayala, Shirin actually had a full matriculation certificate from an expensive private high school, and ten years earlier she was considered a promising candidate for university studies. Yet by the time of our meeting she was calculating every penny. So when the teacher told her that her son's sports shoes were too tight and he couldn't participate in gym class until he got a new pair, she decided to keep him home for the week, until her next social benefit check came through. Similar calculations came up recurrently in nearly all the interviews. They made women feel depressed, ashamed, and angry. Ayala, for example, said:

> I feel that the situation is getting harder and harder. The price of a [subsidized] loaf has just gone up to seven shekels. I went crazy the last time I went to the grocery store. It's absurd! My entire monthly allowance is 2,500 shekels that I get from the National Insurance as income supplement. (Q: So how do you manage?) It makes me mad. (Q: Really, how do you manage?) I'm heavily overdrawn at the bank, but with great difficulty I get by somehow. You learn to live with what there is. I don't know how to explain it exactly. It means never buying anything for myself, only for the children. Never going out with a friend, never buying myself new clothes ...

Besides not buying themselves new clothes or going out with friends, some women also reported much more drastic sacrifices, including cutting down on their food consumption and skipping medical and dental treatment. But even the seemingly more benign cutbacks had a price. Quite a few women supplemented their income with handouts of used clothes and food products from charities. For many, this was stigmatizing and humiliating, although we also met a few women who integrated the products obtained through charities into elaborate networks of exchange utilized to meet their social obligations.

Not surprisingly, the continuous juggling of diminishing resources takes its toll on women's health and well-being. In the Microentrepreneurship Study, 44 percent of the respondents reported being constantly tired, and close to 30 percent defined their state of health as middling. Of the Arab respondents, 35 percent had sick persons or very young children who demanded their intensive care; for the Jewish respondents the figure was 15 percent, a statistic that reflects the gap between the two populations in access to daycare and supportive services. A negligible number of women reported that their male partners assisted them in the caretaking. Also, even when external assistance was available, the women felt that caring for the needy dependents was their own primary responsibility. The oversized burden of domestic care-work among low-income women is not unique to the women of this study. In our abovementioned study on the effects of the Israeli-Palestinian conflict on women in Israel (Sachs et al. 2007) we found significantly higher stress levels, poorer health, and lower satisfaction with personal well-being among women living in poverty than in middle- and upper-middle-class women. Last but not least, 38 percent of respondents in the Microentrepreneurship Study reported having gone through a difficult event in recent years, detailing loss of a close person, sickness, accident, domestic violence, or depression. Exposure to such harrowing events is of course not necessarily limited to low-income women. However, their effects may be aggravated by meager access to mental and material help, although here too there are important variations. As shown below, some communities, notably ultra-Orthodox Jews and rural Palestinian communities, have supporting cultural institutions that are not found in more heterogeneous urban settings. But then, such communities also have tighter control mechanisms.

Vulnerabilities Related to Work

A major source of vulnerability that affects low-income women is the job market. The overlapping disadvantages of gender, class, and ethnicity (or ethnonationality) directly influence the types of jobs they get and propel them onto what Orly Benjamin (2006) has called "the downslopes of the work market." The jobs of the women who participated in this study included entry-level office work, employment in the lower echelons of the retail industry, teaching, caretaking, menial jobs in factory assembly lines, agriculture, and cleaning. Some of these branches had a higher incidence of informal employment than others, and nonstandard employment—part-time, seasonal, and hourly—was highly likely. Wages were almost invariably very low, so much so that women who made the minimum wage considered themselves lucky. Most of the women were employees who for reasons explained below worked intermittently for various employers. Some had microbusinesses, which they usually operated from home, or were trying to get such businesses going after they despaired of finding a regular job.

Entry-level pink-collar workers were mostly clerks, receptionists, and part-time secretaries. In the retail industry women worked as cashiers and general employees at supermarkets and department stores; as saleswomen in small shops or retail chains, where they occasionally were promoted to junior managerial positions; or as cosmetics saleswomen paid by the hour. Caretakers worked with children, the elderly, or people with disabilities in institutions or in private homes. These women were generally employed on an hourly or daily basis, through the National Insurance Institute or temping agencies, or directly by families. In this branch, as in cleaning work, informal employment was common. Women also worked as cooks and cleaners in various institutions, and self-contracted cleaning work in homes and offices. All these jobs were performed by Jewish and Palestinian women (Bernstein, Benjamin, and Motzafi-Haller 2011). Palestinian women also did menial work in agriculture and on assembly lines. Although in Israel as a whole factory work—textiles in particular—actually has more Jewish than Palestinian workers, in this study only the Palestinian participants did this type of work.

Inconvenient Location on the Care-Cash Continuum

Noy Avni was a divorced 47-year-old mother of two children, aged twenty and sixteen, when Ya'ara Buksbaum interviewed her in Haifa in 2007. Throughout the eight years since her divorce she received income supplement from the National Insurance, which compensated for her husband's not paying child support. This allowance was cut by half when her older daughter turned eighteen. Prior to her marriage Noy had worked for seven years in three different places, always through manpower agencies, and was laid off from all three due to the companies' downsizing. She then left the job market on the birth of her daughter and stayed home with her children for twelve years. When asked to describe her decision to stay home, she said:

> My husband was self-employed and he had enough hours to allow me not to work. And since I couldn't really help him in his business, I shouldered all the [household] netel [Hebrew, "burden"]. I raised them and really tried to give them everything they needed when their father was not at home.
> Ya'ara: Do you remember this as a good experience?
> Noy: Of course. It's happiness, real fun. Absolutely (laughs) ... It's like, I loved every minute.

Noy went back to work right after her divorce, doing temporary part-time jobs in retail. Adding her wages to the National Insurance income supplement and sporadic small sums of money that she got from her siblings, she managed well enough. However, in the year prior to the interview she had no longer been able to find work. As mentioned, her income supplement was halved, and was expected to end altogether two years later, when her son turned eighteen.

Noy's work history was a typical story among the women who enrolled in the Haifa-based Mahut Center project, both Jewish and Palestinian,[1] and with some variation it was prevalent also among the Palestinian women in the Atida project in Nazareth.

Framed as a choice, the lesser evil or an obligatory act, women's temporary retreat from the job market to take care of their families is more likely than not to set them on a course of precarious employment for the rest of their working years (Sambol and Benjamin 2006). This is particularly true for women of the middle class or lower, who operate within very narrow economic margins; the implications are graver still for lower-class women who are also part of minority groups, divorced, and older. Women's constant passages between unpaid domestic and paid public work conveniently frame them as "bad employees." The histories of their workforce participation are typically discontinuous, so that they appear unreliable and not up to date, which feeds back into an already existing image of women, particularly nonprofessionals and mothers of young children, as semivoluntary workers. Several women testified that employers refused to hire them because they anticipated that their motherhood would interfere with their job performance. But when their children were older, they were rejected for being too old.

In their report on ageism in the labor force, Buksbaum and Dagan (2010: 23) give the following quote from an interview with a Palestinian-Israeli woman:

> Salma: Today I am not [looking for work] since my grandchildren stay with me and I look after them. All my children are employed and they leave their children with me … Even if I wanted to look for a job, I have a more important job at the moment … I prefer to focus on rearing and educating my grandchildren, which is better than leaving them with a nanny or someone. This is what made me sit at home.

Dora Babayof, another client of Mahut Center, who migrated from the former Soviet Union (FSU) fifteen years prior to her interview with Ya'ara Buksbaum in 2007, explained why she chose to leave her place of employment for eight years:

> I left for family reasons. I wanted to help my daughter. She gave birth and I wanted her to get a job so I stayed with the baby … Now my job is to take care of my grandchildren and I'm actually pleased because I have found … well let's say that this too is a job. I have found satisfaction in this job and I get a lot from staying with my grandchildren. And considering my age [mid-fifties], I'm done … There was a time that I did look for another job, but I was not very satisfied with what I found, so I ended up staying with the grandchildren.

In these and similar cases, women were aware that their domestic care work had *economic* value even though it was unpaid. Their decision to prioritize this work, moreover, made sense if we think, as these women seemed to, of families as income-pooling entities (Wallerstein and Smith 1991). The irony is that such a contribution does not necessarily give the women the esteem that may be expected when we consider the high value placed on motherly care-work and that, for the most part, it also leaves the women themselves dependent and vulnerable; all the more so when women are required to care for the elderly and/or when their position within the family is weak. Nardin, a Palestinian-Israeli woman quoted in Buksbaum and Dagan (2010: 23), said:

> My mother-in-law has no caretaker at the moment. So I take care of her and do all the work despite the fact that we have constant disagreements. My son too stops me getting a job at the moment. I run nonstop. I sit with my mother-in-law two to three hours each morning, and I'm with her also at noon and in the evening. I take care of her 24/7. I dash home to manage to clean and arrange the house fast — before my son comes home from school, so that I can be available for him, and when I'm done with him my husband and his children come home and I need to attend to them. So I don't have enough time.

There are several reasons for low-income women tending periodically to enter and exit paid employment, all directly related to their particular location on the care-cash continuum. All too often the demands for their domestic work by their spouses, children, and at times extended relatives are matched by factors in the official workforce that repeatedly push them out of it. As members of minority groups with little or no official credentials, they inevitably land in one bad job after the other (Kalleberg, Reskin, and Hudson 2000). Such jobs imply not only very low wages, frequent redundancies, and diminished social benefits. They also mean widespread encroachment on their labor rights, including not getting paid for overtime or alternatively having their paid hours reduced or even their job periodically suspended, bonuses and travel expenses or even entire months' wages kept in arrears, when their employers need to balance their budget. Lastly, they also mean very little or no defense against bullying and sexual and racial harassment. In a truly vicious circle, the irregular employment pattern of women from marginal groups at once reinforces their image as unreliable, slovenly workers and damages their own self-esteem and self-confidence. These effects grow worse with the years, as women's cumulative physical and emotional exhaustion becomes paired with ageist attitudes.

Class B Employees

Temporary employment arrangements have been on the rise for almost three decades now, as part of the ongoing shift of the Israeli economy to a dual labor market structure: some workers, habitually referred to as "class A," enjoy job security, social benefits, legal protection, and the right to unionize, while others working by their side ("class B") are deprived of such rights, which allows their employers greater flexibility to increase their profits and survive in globally competitive markets. The Law of Employing Workers through Manpower Agencies 1996 permits employers to extend the status of their "temporary" employees indefinitely, as long as the employing company has signed a collective agreement with the Histradrut, which most manpower agencies have (Benjamin 2002). This has facilitated the employment on unfavorable terms of rising numbers of clerks in public-sector institutions, including universities, local municipalities, large companies such as the National Shipping Company or the Electricity Corporation, as well as government bureaucracies, for years on end, sometimes decades. This arrangement adversely affects their wages, social benefits, and job security. These large public institutions commonly turn a blind eye when the manpower companies violate the rights of the workers they supply, which they persist in doing despite recurrent attempts by the courts, the Knesset, and public activists to sanction and regulate them (Farminger 2010; Filc 2004).

By most estimates, the number of people employed on a temporary basis is somewhere between 4 percent and 10 percent of the Israeli labor force.[2] Ronit Nadiv, who conducted a survey for the Ministry of Industry, Trade, and Labor on employees working through manpower agencies, reports that 60 percent of them are employed in the public sector in retail, services, and clerking jobs. Women are twice as liable as men to be employed through such agencies, and the rate of people earning the minimum wage or less among such employees is twice the rate among other employees (Nadiv 2003). An amendment to a law of 2000 that forced employers to limit the period of temporary employment to nine months, after which they were required to absorb those employees as class A workers, took eight years to go into effect. Concomitantly, the protective labor laws and the harsh sanctions on illegal actions by manpower companies are very poorly applied. The following extended excerpt from the narrative of one of the Mahut Center interviewees gives a graphic depiction of temporary employment and the vulnerabilities that come with it.

Sara Shabtay was forty-five, a separated mother of four, when Ya'ara Buksbaum interviewed her in 2007 as part of the Mahut Center Study. Sara started working during her high school vacations as an assistant secretary at an auto shop where her father was the manager. At age eighteen, in the five-month stretch between her high school graduation and the start of military service, she worked as a substitute secretary in the (national) Electricity Corporation and then in ZIM, the national shipping company. She then did two years of military service, where she again worked mostly as a secretary and telephone operator, and went back to the workforce promptly upon her demobilization. She worked continuously for fifteen years as a secretary, always on a temporary basis.

> I remember working as a substitute secretary for the Electricity Corporation. Imagine. Such a company, and I got in without any problem. Because back then the Histradrut had lots of work places and the employment bureau was connected to these places. It was not privatized yet. They were the only ones who would refer

people to these work places. Manpower, which as I recall was the first manpower company in the market, already existed, but that was only for cases when [employers] really needed someone urgently or for people who wanted to avoid the employment bureau. But generally, if you needed a job, the employment bureau was the only place to go. They were the ones who sent me to the Electricity Corporation and then to ZIM.

Sara here mentions two large companies, the Electricity Corporation and the shipping company ZIM, which were government-owned for many decades. The employees of such companies had automatic membership of the Histadrut, which assured them job security, a pension, social benefits, and a battery of additional bonuses. Although unregulated employment was introduced into the Israeli job market in the early 1970s (Sambol and Benjamin 2007), it remained marginal until the late 1980s. Then, as described in Chapter 1, the state embarked on economic liberalization, which, however slow and controversial at first, got into full swing from 2000. Whereas in 1994 the ten largest government-owned companies employed about 87 percent of the workers in the government companies sector, by the mid-2000s most of these companies were fully privatized, and only about 10 percent of the sector's employees still worked in government-owned companies (Hasson 2006). Privatized companies include the telephone company, the airport authority, the seaport authority, the national mail, El-Al national airlines, Koor Industries (previously the owner of over 100 plants throughout the country), the Electricity Corporation, the Gas and Oil Refineries, Israel Chemicals, and the Mekorot water company.

> Sara continues: After the army I worked in many places, but it was always temporary. My last job was with an American company that had a factory here, which supplied the Electricity Corporation with some material that reduced the soot in the chimneys [of the power stations]. This American company had signed a five-year contract with the (Israeli) Electricity Corporation, and every five years they would decide whether or not to extend it. So after I had been there for seven and a half years, the Electricity Corporation opened a new international tender and got a much cheaper deal from a Greek company. And although the American company did stay in Israel for another few years, because it worked with other local factories, they had to fire many people. At that point [I discovered that] there was no longer an employment bureau, and since then I have been unemployed. It's been twelve years now.
> Ya'ara: What do you mean, there's no employment bureau? Did you go there?
> Sara: No employment bureau. Do you know why the bureau is still there? For the statistics. So that people will come and register if they can prove that they've worked for six months [to be entitled to unemployment benefits]. They never get work through the bureau because it has no work to give. They browse the newspapers for want ads, just like you and me. They can't make any employer take the people that they send because 90 percent [of the work places] today

are private and no one is obliged to take in people that the bureau sends. There's no Histadrut anymore [i.e., the Histadrut has lost its control over the large employers]. Not like before, when work places belonged to the Histadrut. Today almost everything is privatized.

I'll tell you what's happening now. Once I answered an ad in the newspaper for someone who needed a secretary. It turned out to be a manpower agency. The woman took my CV, all my data, sat and talked to me. And at the end she said that she didn't have anything to offer me and that she'd call me. So I said what about that ad in the newspaper? No, it's a fiction. Just to make people come and register with them. I never managed to get a job through a manpower agency and I've registered with all of them …

Ya'ara: What other jobs did you have?

Sara: I always worked as a secretary. It was always through the bureau and always for short periods, as a substitute for someone who went on maternity leave or sick leave, or on a special contract. Apart for that long job that I told you about I worked for half a year here or a year there, or for shorter periods.

Ya'ara: And during the past twelve years, did you have any jobs?

Sara: It's been hell, I'll tell you that. At first, after I was sacked I thought, I'll have a little time off. During those fifteen years that I worked I had the children. I had my first son when I was twenty-four. The last job that I had [with the American company] was part time. I worked from 12 noon to 4 pm, Fridays off. And it was alright. I was married then and my husband had a job … So I stayed at home for about two years—my youngest daughter was in preschool when I left that job. The employment bureau sent me to do an accounting course. But it was useless, because wherever I'd go [applying for an accounting job] they wanted experience, and I had none. So the courses of the bureau are good for nothing. You study and study … and their teachers are lousy too. And then when you finish no one will hire you because you have no experience. I remember that they took new immigrants, people with university education, they put them through the advanced course, the bureau and the state that is, gave employers incentives to take them in. The state would pay their first three salaries or something, so that they'd have a job. But no, [employers] used them and then dumped them.

About seven years ago I found a job in the water department at the municipality, but through a manpower company. My husband called them up and said that his wife was a secretary looking for a job. So they said fine, but she should register with the manpower company first and then come to them. They had a backlog of letters that needed typing. Their [tenured] secretary was a prima donna, so they needed someone from outside to do her work … The chair was really uncomfortable but it was forbidden to get up, and there were no breaks. I worked like that for a few days. Then they said I needed to type faster and get through more letters. I was shocked. I said, "What are you looking for? A robot?" I also pointed out that the regular secretary grabbed the shortest letters so no wonder she appeared to get more letters typed than me. Well, the manager didn't like my attitude so she brought in another woman and sacked me. Soon afterwards she sacked her too.

Then my husband found me a job as a secretary in an insurance office, through a friend of his, even though we were already separated. There too there was a young secretary who had come before me. She started giving me trouble. There was I, being efficient and polite to the clients, while she was messy and would spend half the time on the phone with her husband and daughter and then get up and take breaks just when we had pressure of callers. It was clear that my presence there threatened her. Once or twice she even took her lunch break when it was my turn and didn't return, so I couldn't take my lunch break. When I complained to the boss, he didn't like it so he called my husband and notified him that I was fired. I was there barely a week. I was shocked. What, to sack me just like that? One complaint and you're out? And I was the one doing the better job! ... After that I gave up. I've been buying the newspapers every week, marking all the ads, but not making any phone calls. I can't bear to hear another "No" or think that I'll get into a new place and then be fired without any reason. It's a trauma.

Ya'ara: Tell me about other jobs that you had.

Sara: Now this hostel [a cooking job that was set up through Mahut Center], after so many years ... They wanted me to work only four hours a day three times a week, and during that time to manage to cook for forty people for the whole week. Each working day they wanted me to prepare four meals that would last them for two days. And toward the weekend I had to cook for three days and also prepare all kind of extras, salads and stuff, all again in four hours. There was like no difference between [cooking for] weekdays and for weekends. So on the first day it took me seven hours, because I also had to do the dishes and tidy up ... I always needed more time but they wouldn't pay overtime, which was really annoying. My entire monthly salary was 1,900 shekels [approximately $450; the monthly minimum wage that year was NIS 3,585]. And let me remind you that before that I had worked a short time in that community center, and there they did pay overtime. So I asked at the Histadrut and they explained to me that there was no overtime because it was a part-time job. If you work less than eight hours a day there's no overtime, they told me. This has to be wrong, but that's what they told me at the Histadrut. So anyway, I really worked more hours because there was so much to do, the salads and the chicken and that. Now during the week the manager was there and she could see that everything was alright. But on weekends she was not, and they'd use the opportunity [to make me look bad]. They would call her from the hostel to complain that the food was too salty, or raw, or whatever, and she'd call and tell me. On several occasions when I came on Sunday I'd ask to taste that dish they'd complained about, and they'd say "Oh, we threw it away." Since when do they throw away food so easily?

I worked there for seven months until suddenly this talk began. Then gradually the workers [employees who run activities with the inmates] started cooking with the inmates, because they didn't have much to do with them anyway. And I started getting phone calls telling me, "Don't come today, we have too much food already." And I was like, "Excuse me, this is my livelihood!" but no, they already had food. It went on like that until one day she came and told me

> that they had to cut down on expenses and they could have the other workers do the cooking because they didn't have too much to do ... Then listen to this—they had to give me a month's notice. So during that last month that I worked there, all of a sudden there were no complaints whatsoever. The food stopped being too salty or too sour ... everything was 100 percent that last month there.

Besides the frequent redundancies, Sara's narrative discloses other elements that contribute to the disrupted employment pattern characteristic of women on the margins of the labor force. Recurrent experiences of unseemly and often outright humiliating treatment combined with insultingly low pay and disregard of their labor rights do not greatly encourage these women to stick to a job. Besides the exclusion of such workers from protection and benefits available to class A workers, we see here the unapologetic refusal of the Histadrut to stand by them even upon a direct appeal to defend their labor rights. Furthermore, Sara's example in the last job she talks about, management using employees to isolate others and mark them as inefficient so as to create a pretext for their dismissal, was by no means unique. Several other interviewees described a stressful and competitive atmosphere among co-workers when they worked in places such as apparel chain stores, supermarkets, or small offices.

Sexual Harassment

While it is hard to estimate the scope of sexual harassment among low-income women,[3] direct testimonies came up in interviews, particularly in the Atida and the Mahut Center studies where women were asked directly about their work histories. For example, Mali, of the Mahut project, told Ya'ara Buksbaum the following:

> There was another reason for quitting my job. It was sexual harassment. Our supervisor, he would keep me there for overtime, and although the other cashiers came to replace me, he would keep me working in the warehouse, writing what needed to go on the shelves and stuff. Later I realized he kept me working late so he could drop me off at home, and once he told me, "Let's go to my place and not to yours." I acted stupid and I never answered him. I didn't fight with him. I didn't even talk to him, nothing, until it came to the point that I couldn't stand him. He told me, "Either you do it this way or you're out." He gave me my notice that very moment.[4]

Ayelet Ilani, formerly of EEW, relates a particular type of sexual harassment that women talked about in workshops that she conducted. Potential employers to whom they were referred by the employment bureau demanded their sexual submission in return for signing a waiver that would allow them to continue collecting their unemployment benefits.[5] Like sexual abuse at home, sexual harassment is the lot of women on all rungs of the class ladder. Yet in the case of low-income women, their insecure status from the outset makes it even more difficult to fight back. Many women therefore feel that their only defense is to leave the job. This reaction is particularly common among Palestinian women, in whose case, as I discuss in Chapter 5, the legitimacy for participating in the workforce is itself shaky to begin with.

Ageism

The discontinuous employment pattern gets particularly detrimental as women (and men) grow older. As Sara put it in another part of her interview, "Since I stopped working at the age of thirty-eight, I'm old. I'm nothing." The problem of ageism in the Israeli workforce commands increasing attention thanks to the advocacy of civil society organizations such as the Mahut Center. A report prepared for the Ministry of Industry, Trade, and Employment in 2010 found that 48 percent of job seekers older than forty-five reported being turned down on account of their age, and that self-perceived age-based discrimination was more prevalent than discrimination on any other basis, including discrimination for being Arab, a woman, or a mother of young children (in Buksbaum and Dagan 2010: 9). Research conducted by Buksbaum and Dagan for the Mahut Center in 2010 indicates that gender inequalities in the labor force, such as wage gaps or the scope and length of unemployment, worsen among people older than forty-five. These inequalities are particularly acute among women of groups on the social periphery. The general view that "the (work) world belongs to the young" is so prevalent, write Buksbaum and Dagan, that actors all across the job-hunt scene—employers, manpower agencies, and even some job seekers—fall prey to the notion that people above forty-five are old and useless. The women who participated in this study testified that job interviewers had no qualms telling them to their faces that they were too old for the job even though they were directly violating the Law of Equal Opportunities at Work. Some of the women in their forties who exclaimed, like Sara, "I'm old and useless" were clearly protesting what they felt a gross injustice; others seemed to have internalized this conviction. Such women rationalized their inability to find employment with notions such as "the mind of old people becomes like the mind of babies" or "it's like when the Israelites came out of Egypt, [you know how the saying goes that] they needed to bring Egypt out of the Israelites? We need to have our generation brought out of us" (Suheir and Ayelet, respectively, in Buksbaum and Dagan 2010: 40).

Still, Women Long to Have a Job

To sum up thus far before discussing particular subgroups, I should note that despite the manifold impediments that they faced in the official workforce, the participants in this study continued to attribute enormous importance to paid employment. By and large, women believed that employment, apart from providing them with much-needed cash, would offer an opportunity to gain social respect, self-fulfillment, and a sociable setting to spend their days. In the words of Ayala Cohen, "The working environment that I imagine is an office with a few nice girls, young, each sitting at her desk, each with her paperwork. I see myself in that office, with my cup of coffee and the telephone, doing my work. This is my fantasy. The secretary fantasy, as Rinat [the moderator from the Mahut Center] calls it." The secretary fantasy came up persistently in many interviews, particularly with participants in the Atida and the Mahut Center projects that were geared to integrating women as paid employees. It appeared much less in the interviews with participants in the Microentrepreneurship Study, which trained women to be self-employed, although there too quite a few women hinted that they would drop their business entrepreneurship and opt for a pink-collar job if they could find one. It did not arise at all in the Bedouin Village Study, where women were far more marginalized and far less educated. There, women's ideal jobs were those of assistant or caretaker in tender-age education, although in practice most of them worked in agriculture, cleaning, or assembly lines. I will return to this longing for a position that is meaningful and fulfilling in my discussion of women's perceptions of work and in my analysis of the deeply paradoxical nature of economic citizenship, in the concluding two sections of the book.

Subgroups

Low-income people in Israel are overwhelmingly Mizrahi Jews—they are the largest group—and Palestinians, who are grossly overrepresented in poverty although their actual number is smaller. Mizrahim, descendants of immigrants from Arab or Muslim countries, are overrepresented in periphery towns and low-income neighborhoods. They are particularly susceptible to being caught up in the vicious circle of nonstandard jobs, unemployment, and income instability. Mizrahi women, likewise, are a majority among single mothers and poor women generally (e.g., Swirski et al. 2002). In my research too, Mizrahi women were the majority among the Jewish interviewees as well as among those who attended the workshops. In effect, many of the vulnerabilities described thus far in the chapter tend to coalesce with the experiences of being Mizrahi women, as portrayed, for example, in the ethnographies of Pnina Motzafi-Haller (2012) and Smadar Lavie (2014). In the following detailed description of subgroups, however, I do not treat Mizrahi women *as a group* because, despite their history of collective discrimination (the fact that their parents were trucked to the periphery and that they were denied high-quality education), being part of the majority ethnic group, the practical implications of their living on low incomes are predominantly class-bound. It is important to note, however, that Mizrahi women figure in all three non-Palestinian subgroups below, including ultra-Orthodox and new immigrants, and of course single mothers.

Palestinian Arab Women

Before outlining the vulnerabilities of Palestinian Israeli women, it is important to note that the segment of Palestinian society that remained in Israel after the 1948 war has developed into a complex society with its unique features. Despite political and structural discrimination—which have created numerous disadvantages, including stalled urbanization, blocked economic opportunities, and very high rates of poverty—new generations, new technologies, and growing regional and global connections have yielded diversification in lifestyles and innovative cultural production, and women have been important partners in these processes (Kannaneh 2002; Stewart 2012). The ethnography in Chapters 3 and 4 provides ample insight into the inventive and resourceful aspects of Palestinian women's strategies. I start, however, with description of the harsh economic conditions that is the lot of many of them.

The Palestinian citizens of Israel are overrepresented in poverty, and are steadily becoming more so. Roughly 20 percent of the state's population,[6] the Palestinians comprise 38.9 percent of its poor (Endeweld, Barkali, Gottlieb, and Fruman 2012). Also among *working* families, the increase in the incidence of poverty in recent years has been nearly twice greater for Arab than for Jewish families (Israel, NII 2012). Poverty is associated first and foremost with a large average number of persons per household and low levels of family income, which in turn are traceable to endemic problems in the occupational structure. Longstanding discrimination and blocked opportunities in the national labor market have yielded narrow occupational diversity, very high unemployment rates among men older than forty-five (Sa'di and Lewin-Epstein 2001), and a tendency to concentrate in the ethnonational enclave, where income levels are low due to stalled development and low purchasing power.

This situation was reflected directly in the three main data sets of the present research. In the Microentrepreneurship Study, the income levels in the households of the Arab participants were consistently lower than those of the Jewish participants, even though most of the former were married whereas nearly half of the latter were divorced or widowed. Only one third of the Arab participants in this study reported having a wage income when they entered the project. In the other two studies, which included smaller samples and qualitative data (interviews and participant observations) but not statistics, many of the women reported that their husbands were unemployed for long spells or that their ability to provide their families with cash income was inconsistent. Alternatively, husbands' salaries were too low to cover the family's expenses,

Table 2.1 Arabs Aged 15 and Over, by Labor Force Characteristics, Sex, and Selected Characteristics, 2013

Percentage in labor force of people over 15 years of age:

	Women	Men	Total
Religion			
Muslims	22.9	64.2	43.7
Christians	47.9	68.4	57.8
Druzes	33.3	68.0	50.7
Age			
15–17	1.3	7.2	4.3
18–24	27.4	68.5	48.7
25–34	42.2	83.5	63.0
35–44	36.0	84.7	60.7
45–54	26.8	76.3	51.5
55–64	13.3	52.5	32.6
65+	…	10.5	5.0
Years of Schooling			
0–4	3.0	21.7	8.5
5–8	12.1	53.9	33.0
9–12	21.0	66.7	46.1
13–15	39.4	69.1	52.9
16+	70.2	83.5	76.6

Adapted from Israel, Central Bureau of Statistics, *Statistical Abstracts of Israel 2014*, table 12.10

particularly when these included school fees—the exceedingly low level of the Arab public schools obliges Palestinian citizens to use private schools in larger numbers than the Jewish citizens—and higher education tuition. One noticeable difference between the Arab and the Jewish women, however, was that the former tended overwhelmingly to live in apartments owned outright by their husbands, and even if they lived on the premises of their extended families they did not need to pay rent and generally were not bound by large mortgage payments. This was the case particularly among women in rural communities, where it is customary to postpone marriage until the groom can provide his bride with an apartment, although, as was revealed in the interviews, in many cases it was the women's earnings that made the actual construction possible.

In terms of women's employment, the rate of Palestinian-Israeli women's labor force participation (LFP) is notoriously low. On average, only about 22.5

percent (as against 71.3 percent of Jewish-Israeli women) were employed in 2006. The situation is slightly better for women with thirteen to fifteen years of schooling (34 percent LFP) and much better for women with more than sixteen years of schooling, 65 percent of whom were employed that year (King et al. 2009). Moreover, for professionals and women with university degrees, employment rates have actually been on the rise, largely due to expanding opportunities in the social services sector (Shalev and Lazarus, 2013). Still, for the majority of women the situation is quite gloomy. In 2006, 46.5 percent of Palestinian-Israeli women had a high school education or lower (including 10 percent with very little or no schooling), and among these, employment rates have been on the decline (King et al. 2009). Another factor that affects the statistics is the overrepresentation of Christian women, whose employment rate of 38 percent is nearly four times higher than their proportion in the Palestinian population. Christian women tend to be better educated than Muslim women, their fertility rate is significantly lower (it is the lowest of all Israeli subgroups, including Jewish women), and they are less likely than Muslim women to leave work after marriage and childbearing (Khattab 2002). By contrast, among the 80 percent Muslim majority, only 15.6 percent of the women were registered as employed in 2006 (King et al. 2009). At the extreme end of the spectrum, Bedouin women are grossly underrepresented in the official work force.[7] They have limited access to schooling, healthcare, and transportation, and are also highly liable to enter into polygamous marriages.[8]

When employed, Palestinian women are susceptible to discrimination. In 2006, the salaries of Palestinian-Israeli women were on average 68 percent of those of Jewish women and 74 percent of those of Arab men (King et al. 2009: 43), two groups that themselves suffer from wage discrimination. In reality, the actual income of most employed Palestinian women is lower still, considering that at least a third are employed part time (31.7 percent, as against 27.7 percent of Jewish-Israeli women; King et al. 2009: 35).[9] Also, women employees tend to concentrate in the ethnonational enclave even more than men. This is the combined outcome of blocked opportunities in the Jewish-dominated national economy and the preference of most women to commute shorter distances to work, partly due to insufficient daycare services and public transportation, and partly because their paid employment continues to be framed as secondary to their unpaid domestic care work (more on this in Chapter 4). Within the enclave, pay is often much lower than the legal minimum wage. Alternatively, employers report higher salaries than those actually paid. Besides this, female employees in the ethnonational enclave are susceptible to similar types of maltreatment that characterize the downslopes of the workforce more generally, namely, humiliating treatment, arbitrary dismissal, withholding wages and bonuses, nonpayment for overtime, and sexual harassment. These offenses, which came up vividly in the interviews conducted as part of the

Atida and the Microentrepreneurship studies, are confirmed also in a field survey conducted by the Arab feminist organization Kayan (Shtewi 2014).

Menial Work—Cleaning, Agriculture, and Textiles

Low-educated Palestinian women are particularly prone to do menial work in cleaning, textiles, and agriculture. Of these three branches, cleaning emerged as the most readily available solution for women, Palestinian and Jewish alike, who needed cash and could not find other jobs. In the case of Palestinian women, all three branches were mediated by middlemen, who often worked with larger manpower agencies, thus adding yet another link to the chain of those who profited by their labor. While some cleaners did manage to be directly employed by private homeowners, the physical and social distance from Jewish communities made such arrangements rarer among Palestinian than among Jewish workers. According to Deborah Bernstein, Orly Benjamin, and Pnina Motzafi-Haller (2011), whose work on Mizrahi, Palestinian, and immigrant cleaning women is one of the rare studies of cleaning work in Israel, direct employment in private homes is the most profitable in terms of wages. The hourly pay for cleaning work done under direct employment of homeowners tends to be one and a half times or even double the minimum hourly pay. However, such arrangements are often unreported, hence unprotected; they may be abruptly terminated, and usually include a low number of hours per month. By contrast, working for an institution (through a subcontractor), yields a rate just above the minimum wage, but has the security of a full-time job and job-related benefits. Lastly, private homeowners seeking cleaners through cleaning agencies is a relatively new feature in Israel, and Benjamin and colleagues do not provide ordered data of this arrangement.

In agriculture in particular, wages are among the lowest in the entire economy. According to a study by the Knesset Center for Research and Information (Nathan 2010), the official average wage in agriculture is about 60 percent of the average wage in the national economy, but the actual wage is significantly lower, because employers systematically tend to pay their workers less than the minimum wage. Other exploitative characteristics are hourly or daily pay as opposed to monthly, systematic withholding of social benefits, and nonentitlement of seasonal employees to unemployment benefits (Nathan 2010). It is difficult to obtain reliable data on the number of Palestinian-Israeli women who work in agriculture. Official data distinguish Israeli workers, foreign workers, and Palestinians from the Palestinian Authority (PA) and Gaza. According to the Central Bureau of Statistics, in winter 2012 the number of Israeli women employed in this branch was 10,000, compared with about 44,000 Israeli men (about 23 percent). It is likely that many if not the vast majority of these women were Palestinian.[10]

Although employers in agriculture, packing, and textiles are obliged by law to pay no less than the minimum wage, to issue a pay slip, and to pay full social benefits, most ignore the law, with the full knowledge of the relevant ministries and the police. As reported by Nathan (2010), in 2008 the Ministry of Industry, Trade, and Labor employed only 35 inspectors, a number far too small to enforce the law. Additional impinging on workers' rights comes through the institution of middlemen, which predominates in the agriculture, textiles, and cleaning branches. In the case of Palestinian women, the middlemen are typically neighbors or relatives, who contract the work from employers, recruit women, drive them from the village to the work site, and collect their salaries. Michal Schwartz, of the Workers' Advice Center Maan, which can claim some achievements organizing agricultural workers, writes:

> In agriculture one finds the worst kind of exploitation. The young women are bussed to work collectively by a male responsible for them (the *ra'is*), who often is a family member. He gets the money from the employer and divides it among the workers, skimming some 40 percent for himself. The women workers are paid NIS 80 to 100 per day [US$ 23–29], although the minimum daily wage is NIS 165 [approximately US$ 55]. The farm owner does not consider himself responsible for his workers, and often does not give them a wage slip. That means that the workers do not enjoy any social benefits; in case of injury, for example, they must fend for themselves. (2011: 59)

In Hseiniyye, the Bedouin village where Nisreen Mazzawi and I did fieldwork in 2010, about 25 percent of the village women joined the waged workforce during the 2000s for the first time in the history of this community. The vast majority of these women found employment as menial workers, in agriculture (most of them), cleaning, and packing. Agricultural workers typically begin their day between 4 and 5 a.m. After a solitary morning prayer they prepare breakfast and school snacks, and then leave for work. Around 7 a.m. they may call their children to wake them up and make sure that they get ready for school. At the end of a working day, which typically lasts until midday or 4 p.m. (depending on whether the crew decides to do a single or a double shift), they return to continue their domestic chores. These include home maintenance, cooking, and visiting, as well as supervising their children and driving them around. One of our older interviewees, a woman in her early fifties who still keeps a few sheep, reported rising at 3 a.m., praying, then tending to the sheep before she goes out with the work crew. In the winter she also takes the sheep out to graze for two hours in the evening. Once a year, at lambing time, she spends another hour and a half every day boiling milk and making dairy produce for sale.

The Israeli textiles industry, formerly among the largest branches of Israeli industrial production, has shrunk rapidly over the past two decades. In the

1950s and 1960s the state initiated the opening of large textile plants in remote towns on the country's northern and southern peripheries. While the original ethnic-gender-class composition of the industry was distinctly designed to buttress the Zionist goals of absorbing immigration and settling the borderlands, the social mobility of some of these immigrants gradually made way for the entry of Palestinian citizens. Noa Lavie (2006) calculated that in 1979 Palestinian-Israeli women comprised 15 percent of the industry's workers; by 2000 the figure was 33 percent. At the same time, the relative numbers of Jewish women originating from the Middle East and North Africa among the industry's workers declined during those years. A still more dramatic decline was registered among Jewish women of European or North American origin, who constituted 32 percent of the workers in 1979 but only 10 percent in 2000. Then again, new immigrants from the FSU and Ethiopia, who arrived in Israel in growing numbers during the 1990s, were pushed into textile work, such that their rate of participation in the industry rose from 12 percent to 31 percent, with a peak in 1997, when 38 percent of the workers were recent FSU immigrants.

Since the 1990s a new shift occurred, with Israel signing international trade agreements that allowed it to outsource the most labor-intensive components of production to countries in south Asia, the Far East, and Eastern Europe. Shortly afterwards, the "economic peace agreements" with Jordan, the PA, and Egypt paved the way to similar outsourcing much closer to home, merely a few hours' drive across the border.[11] Concomitantly, during the 1990s "security collaboration" with the South Lebanese Army allowed the daily bussing of workers from Lebanese border villages to plants in Palestinian villages in northern Galilee (Drori 2000). For Israeli workers, this shift entailed painful downsizing that hit hard those small towns and villages that had become "plant towns." By 2000, more than 7,000 Israeli workers had lost their jobs in this industry (Lavie 2006) and more than 10,000 others were made redundant over the following decade.[12]

As for textile workers, Israel Drori (2000) documented the operation of eight textile factories in Galilee during the 1990s, which together employed some 1,500 people. Most of them were Arab or Druze women who worked on the assembly line, and a very small minority were men, primarily Jewish, who worked as managers and technicians. Although he does not give ordered data about wages, social benefits, pay checks, and sick leaves, Drori's detailed ethnographic descriptions reveal unequivocally that workers received less than the minimum wage and that they did not get sick leave. He mentions, for example, a job interview in which an experienced supervisor was offered NIS 2,000 a month. Considering that a supervisor, who as Drori asserts was in demand at the time, was offered a wage lower than the legal minimum (which in 1998 was NIS 2,622), rank-and-file sewing workers obviously received less than that. Drori also mentions that some workers were as young as sixteen when they started, and in some cases much younger still (he relates one case of a twelve-year-old who worked for four years in the same workshop under the identity of her older sister). That said, it is important to bear in mind that even a low estimate of NIS 70 per working day, while the legal minimum wage was NIS 120, was double what Palestinian textile workers in the PA reportedly earned in approximately the same period (Bornstein 2002). Hence despite social stigma and the overall exploitation in the industry, textiles were an important source of employment for Palestinian women in Galilee. In the late 1990s, the above reversal in state policy also hit the plants in Galilee, obliging managements to take what Drori (2000) calls a "high tex" turn. The bulk of the production was outsourced to countries where labor was cheaper while the local plants opted to retain only the more technologically sophisticated components. As a result, four of the eight plants in Galilee closed down and hundreds of sewing workers were laid off (Drori 2000).

A common characteristic of the different branches of menial work described here is the overt immersion in patriarchal relations. Characteristically, the middlemen, who are the women's relatives or neighbors, assume the personae of benevolent mediators who are also self-appointed moral supervisors. Since women have no direct knowledge of the sum paid by the farmer whose field they are harvesting or the by the institution they clean, their only bargaining possibilities are with that middleman. For example, some of the interviewees in the Bedouin Village Study who worked as seasonal agricultural laborers prided themselves on the middleman's raising their daily pay when they proved that they had worked hard enough. Paradoxically, activists of the Workers' Advice Center who try to unionize such workers testify that the women often feel indebted to the middleman, and as frustrated as they may become over their employment conditions, they tend to remain oblivious to his role in the chain of their exploitation.[13]

Diversity

Despite this bleak depiction, it is important to note that the low-income Palestinian-Israeli women who participated in the projects actually formed an extremely heterogeneous category. The economic empowerment courses held in the cities of Haifa and Nazareth assembled women with very diverse levels of education. While some participants had barely ten years of schooling, others had full high school diplomas, post–high school vocational training, and a few even university degrees. In the Bedouin women's group the gaps were even more striking, as two women with university degrees participated in the empowerment meetings together with illiterate women, whom one of the educated women then engaged in literacy classes. A striking characteristic in these groups was the short social distance between the different participants, but also between women who were struggling with deep poverty and others (sometimes their immediate relatives, neighbors, or schoolmates) who were leading normative lives, going on vacation, renovating their homes, sending their children to study abroad and doing all things done by prosperous members of their community. To varying degrees these successful, normative people were not exempt from the structural and political barriers imposed on the Palestinian citizens. They too were potentially susceptible to discrimination at work or to racist offenses in the public space. They too might have found themselves or their dear ones subjected to severe limitations on their freedom of movement and of expression. Still, they were living full, complex lives in a very narrow social space where comfortable success is closely shadowed by potential marginalization with all its vulnerabilities.

Another striking aspect of diversity among Palestinian-Israeli women, besides education and degree of leisure consumption, was the glaring gaps in the living conditions of Bedouin women, women of other rural communities, and women who lived in the cities. Somewhat ironically, although urban women have easier access to employment and higher education, and are generally regarded as more sophisticated, they actually tend to be worse off than rural women in terms of home ownership and area of domestic space. Apartments in the city are smaller and must be fully paid for upon purchase. By contrast, apartments in rural communities are larger and fancier, yet nevertheless more affordable: they are built by pooling the labor of brothers and sons, and the process can stretch over years, actually when the family is already living within. On the other hand, women in rural communities often complain about lack of privacy and poor community infrastructure, which impinges on their employment opportunities and increases their dependence on cars. In the case of Bedouin women, the precarious legal status of their communities often aggravates the drawbacks of rural life without the compensation of urban conditions. As described in the Introduction, some of the Bedouin women who participated in this research were barely emerging from a life in shacks, where they had to manage households with no running water or electricity, and raise children in a village with no clinics or schools and virtually no public transportation. Here are some descriptions that came up in the interviews. Jamalat, thirty-nine, a mother of ten who was interviewed in 2010, describes to research assistant Nisreen Mazzawi her life before the construction of their new house:

> I would cry all the time ... I was pregnant with my first child and had to go to draw water to wash the floor. Then I had to go again if I wanted to shower ... (I could only carry) one bucket at a time. My husband did not have a license for a tractor that would have allowed him to go and bring water ... My father-in-law let us use

the water (from the well) in his house only for drinking, but for washing and cleaning we had to fetch water from the farther well.

And Umaima, thirty-five, said:

> After I got married I lived in one room for twelve years. There was no water or electricity. Everything was in the same room: the kitchen, the bathroom ... No one ever came to visit me because I couldn't entertain guests inside the house. Can you imagine how difficult it was for me? Now that we've built [a house] that's it, [I consider] this the sweetest and happiest point of my life. Thank God.

While the village of Hseiniyye where these women live eventually obtained recognition in the mid-1990s, whereupon people were allowed to build comfortable houses, these descriptions still hold true for dozens of other Bedouin villages in Israel. Yet even in Hseiniyye, the newly constructed homes, some built by the women with their own hands, were still not legalized in 2012. Because in the absence of a ratified master plan for the village, the authorities refused to issue building permits even when they did not dispute families' private ownership of the plots on which these houses were built. So alongside their boundless joy at the new and comfortable houses, the women also reported high levels of stress as a result of demolition threats, huge expenses in fines and lawyers' fees, and a whole new bureaucratic front that they needed quickly to learn to handle (see Sa'ar 2012).

Palestinian women then, even those in the lowest income brackets, are quite a diverse category. Despite their manifold vulnerabilities, they too have high hopes and great expectations of paid employment. In Hseiniyye, to take the weakest link as it were, the women we interviewed were actually very happy and proud to be employed. They took great pleasure in their newly found access to cash, in their ability to share together with their husbands the heavy economic weight of the transition to the new lifestyle, and in their ability to give their children a better educational head start. The younger women also contemplated finding easier venues. Alongside the "double shift" of paid work and domestic work, they also invested time and money in acquiring new skills. Almost all of them were learning to drive and planning to buy cars. Some also toyed with the idea of vocational training, primarily as caretakers and kindergarten assistants, which would allow them to open a certified daycare service at home or be employed as assistants in others.

Immigrant Women

Beside the Palestinian citizens, descendants of the local indigenous population of the land who managed to remain after the establishment of the state of Israel and today comprise about 20 percent of its citizens, large numbers of Israelis are immigrants—primarily Jews but not always—who have arrived to Palestine/Israel in continuous waves throughout the twentieth century and into the twenty-first. In many important respects, the situation of recent immigrants is radically different from and much better than that of the Palestinian citizens. Under the Law of Return, Jewish immigrants are granted citizenship automatically. They are entitled to far-reaching economic benefits, and are very likely to be put on a fast track to the heart, sometimes even directly to the elites, of the dominant national group. By contrast, the Palestinian citizens are positioned at the opposite extreme in terms of belonging, and also of social, economic, and political opportunities. While the former are often given special state benefits and special absorption grants, the latter, as detailed in Chapter 1, are marginalized even within the system of universal, standardized state benefits. Still, recent immigrants and Palestinian Arabs have something in common: members of both categories are highly susceptible to poverty, social marginality, and unemployment. Importantly, the relative figures are very different. For example, in 2011, 40 percent of recent immigrants, as against 60 percent of the Arab citizens, were poor. The proportions changed dramatically, however, after the transfer of state benefits, which lifted 60 percent of the recent immigrant poor—but only 11 percent of the Arab poor—above the poverty line, leaving the incidence of poverty among these two groups at 16.3 percent and 53.5 percent respectively.[14]

Despite the significant contribution of state benefits to alleviate poverty among recent immigrants, the stories of immigrant women in Israel reveal a sharp sense of disruption and dislocation. The chances of falling into poverty largely depend on the women's countries of origin, the types of cultural and human capital they carry with them, the scope of their local connections, or the number of years since their arrival. It is striking that all but one of the fifty-odd recent immigrants who participated in the different phases of the study, or of the numerous others who had arrived as small children but still felt that their parents' immigration crises affected their life course, came from Middle Eastern, African, or Central Asian countries; the exception was a descendant of Holocaust survivors. In fact, immigrants to Israel who are vulnerable to poverty and social marginalization are primarily people from Arab countries and in the past three decades from the FSU or Ethiopia. Indirectly, immigration was also represented in this study in the narratives of middle-aged Jewish participants who were born in Israel to immigrant parents or had arrived as small children, and talked about the deep crisis that immigration created in their parents' lives. More directly, the topic came up in the narratives of recent immigrants from the FSU and in much smaller numbers from Ethiopia too.

A small group of fifteen women of Ethiopian origin participated in the Microentrepreneurship Study. Unlike the participants in most other groups in that project, these women attended the course somewhat irregularly and never actually completed it or opened businesses. Their knowledge of Hebrew was poor and the organization failed to hire an Amharic-speaking moderator. Perplexed by their inability to communicate with the women, the staff of the EEW, which was in charge of the project, classified them as not yet ready to start up independent businesses and decided to reduce the business training part of the course. Instead, the meetings focused on general empowerment and on helping the women find immediate employment. Nor could the research team manage to conduct orderly observations and interviews with the participants, or to administer the standardized questionnaires. Instead, I held one group conversation with eight of the women and interviewed their moderator; my research assistant Chava Nishri held open individual conversations with the other seven. Apart for the fact that five of the fifteen were single mothers (four divorced and one widowed), the group was actually notably heterogeneous: prior to their immigration, one woman made a living by cultivating a small plot of land, while another had been preparing for medical school. A third woman came from a well-to-do urban business family, while yet others came from remote rural regions. In Israel, however, most of them experienced severe economic hardship. They all expressed an urgent need to earn money, but poor Hebrew skills and having small children made it very difficult for them to do so. Besides the economic hardship, the women told us of their sense of loneliness and the racism they faced on a daily basis; several spoke of the violence of their ex-husbands. All were keen to enroll in vocational training that would improve their chances of employment.

Recent immigrants from the FSU had a very different profile. About 40 such women were among the 239 participants in the Microentrepreneurship Study. Nine of these were also included in the life-histories sample, and another four were interviewed as part of the Mahut Center study. Many of these women had acquired university degrees or vocational training in their countries of origin but for various reasons they were unable to work in their professions after the immigration. Consequently they experienced a steep drop in their occupational status and self-esteem.

Xenia Vinocur, for example, a 42-year-old divorced mother of two, who was interviewed by Ya'ara Buksbaum in 2007, migrated to Israel from Ukraine in the early 1990s. Although she had a master's degree in Russian language and literature and five years' experience as a teacher, she could not find work in her profession after she arrived. Instead, she worked on an assembly line at a packaging plant for two years, and thereafter mostly cleaned private homes. She had initially migrated to Israel because her husband's parents decided to do so and he did not want to separate from them. Not Jewish herself, Xenia had no other relatives in Israel. After her divorce she lived for a few years with another man, the father of her second daughter, but he treated her with great violence. Finally she escaped, and moved north. Her mother came to stay with her for a while and help her with the baby. But she was unable to extend her visa, and when she returned to Ukraine Xenia was left all alone. She says:

> Since I came to Israel I haven't stopped working even for one week. After they dismissed me from the factory I didn't wait for unemployment [benefits]. I just couldn't afford to. I went straight out to look for a cleaning job. Now my older daughter is thirteen and she is very embarrassed that her mother is a cleaner. She doesn't tell any of her friends. Never in a million years. She is ashamed to wear clothes that other people give us. She wants to have nice things. I really want to move on for her sake, I just don't know how.

Another example is Ravit Babayof, who was interviewed by Adi Romano in 2004.

> Born in a villa in a small resort town in the Soviet Union to a successful exporter of dyes and yarns, Ravit described beginning her life in an affluent family. "My mother, who by the way couldn't read or write, used to be driven to the market by the chauffeur. After selecting the fruits that she liked she would take a wad of banknotes out of her bag, hand it over to the salesman and say, 'Take whatever I owe you.'" It all collapsed, however, with her father's death in the mid-1960s, when she was only four years old. Her mother did not know how to manage her financial affairs, and a decade later, as her situation continued to deteriorate, she decided to sell whatever was left of the property and smuggle herself and her two youngest children out of the Soviet Union, leaving her married older daughters behind. En route they were robbed of all their money and arrived in Israel destitute. So it happened that at age fourteen Ravit had to go out to work, forfeiting the chance of learning to read and write Hebrew. Thus, in the course of a single generation, this daughter of an affluent, educated, and urbane man, whose older sisters in the Soviet Union had university degrees, spent her early adult years practically illiterate. She became a hairdresser, and succeeded in her trade. Only in her mid-twenties did she finally manage to teach herself to read and write Hebrew. Yet despite her ingenuity, as a sole provider for her mother and younger brother, she was unable to continue her education. At the time of the interview she was forty-two, twice divorced, with two sons and recovering from cancer, and still dreaming of going to university.

Ultra-Orthodox Jewish Women

Ultra-Orthodox Jews have the highest incidence of poverty of all subgroups in Israeli society, slightly exceeding Palestinian Arabs. In 2011 the figure was 66.9 percent (as against 60.4 percent for Arabs). After the remittance of state benefits, this percentage fell by 18.8 percent to 54.3 percent, and although state benefits impact much more deeply here than among the Arab citizens (Lewin and Stier 2002), they still remain the poorest group in the country. The two most decisive causes of this situation are the exceptionally large number of children per family and the low labor-force participation of working-age men. In 2008–9 the overall fertility rate (the average number of children that a woman is expected to bear in her lifetime) for women living in all-ultra-Orthodox neighborhoods or settlements was 6.8, as against 3.5 for Muslim women, 2.5 for Druze women, and 2.9 for all Jewish women.[15] In practice, many ultra-Orthodox women bear ten children or more, and it is not rare to find families of twelve and even fifteen children of one mother (Birenbaum-Carmeli 2008; Ivry, Teman, and Frumkin 2011). At the same time, a substantial majority of ultra-Orthodox men, as many as 60–70 percent according to some estimates (Blumen 2007), voluntarily retreat from the official workforce to dedicate themselves to a life of studying the holy books of Judaism. Besides the moral prestige of religious scholars, this norm is instigated by a longstanding government agreement (called "the status quo") to exempt yeshiva students from military conscription. Note, however, that many men who begin their married lives as full-time members of the so-called men's society of scholars (MSS) either drop out of the yeshivah/*kolel* (religious college) between their late twenties and early thirties, after they pass the age of mandatory military conscription, or work informally in the evenings to help meet their families' mounting economic needs. Then again, save for particular sects, such as the Gur, which has many successful merchants and businessmen (El-Or 1997), ultra-Orthodox men commonly lack the skills to integrate into high-paying, upwardly mobile jobs.

Poverty, however, is relative. A prevalent attitude to poverty among ultra-Orthodox Jews, which also came up in the interviews collected as part of this research, is that the calling, respectively, for women to bear a large number of children and for men to dedicate themselves to religious study, renders material want a relatively minor problem. In fact, in line with a strong rabbinical distaste for luxury goods, material poverty is often framed as a measurement of piety (El-Or 1997). Also, in the case of ultra-Orthodox Jews in particular, the actual level of their households' income is not represented accurately in the official figures since besides wage income and state benefits they make heavy use of local charities and exchange networks, a factor that remains entirely outside the official statistics.

In contrast to the other subgroups, notably the Palestinians, for ultra-Orthodox women employment is quite normative. The ideal of "A princess's honor lies inside the house" notwithstanding, and despite the burden of rearing numerous children, women are encouraged to earn money in order to free their husbands to join the prestigious MSS, a status that also carries a small stipend. Teaching is by far the most sought-after occupation, and many young women enroll in the local teachers' colleges. Yet as both El-Or (1997) and Kalekin-Fishman and Schneider (2007) report, because the available positions cannot accommodate the high number of qualified teachers, women also work as seamstresses, wig-makers, accountants, typists, secretaries, and caretakers, in their own family businesses or increasingly outside the ultra-Orthodox community. Alternatively, some women attempt to start up home-based small businesses, hoping to increase their income with minimal investment and presumably without interrupting their domestic care-work. The Microentrepreneurship Study included twenty-seven women who were trying to get on this track; numerous ultra-Orthodox women enroll in similar economic empowerment initiatives.

The wages of ultra-Orthodox women, like those of other women on the periphery, are generally low. And like other low-income women, they do not compensate for the loss of National Insurance income supplements, which automatically cease when wage income is reported.[16] As a result, besides opting to keep their paid employment informal, women become notably resourceful in utilizing handouts of leftover food, clothes, school appliances, furniture, etc. Because, as mentioned, poverty in this group is so prevalent and presumably not as stigmatic as in other groups, reliance on charity does not seem to incur shame. Its practicalities, however, become very tiring. Lea Banay, a married mother of nine from Benei Brak, was fifty when Adi Romano interviewed her in 2004 as part of the Microentrepreneurship Study. Her narrative offers a window into the complexities of the economic reality of many ultra-Orthodox women:

> We don't go out, neither adults nor children. Our children make do with few toys. Many children share the same room. We do our shopping in bulk ... Our lifestyle is oriented to much less consumption [although not to an extreme. For example], I have insisted on attending physical exercise classes all the years, and I sent one of my daughters to art classes. She is very talented but has a low self-esteem, and a class like that can help her and also contribute to her in the future professionally. So this is both to develop her talent and to enhance her future earnings. It is good, it builds her up, and the cost is minimal. But other than that I don't send them to extracurricular activities ... I stopped after nine [children] because of the expenses. We lived in a rented apartment. My husband worked as an electrician. Life was *keif* [Hebrew, "fun"] but not easy. It's fun to be together, to be Orthodox, to keep the Sabbath, to fulfill all the commandments of the woman, all the commandments of the man. But it was difficult economically. We needed to turn to the *gmah* [acronym for Gmilut Hasadim, a charity institution unique to ultra-Orthodox communities). And there's also someone here in this city that I didn't really care for, but still we applied and got financial help.
> Adi: What sort of help do they give?
> Lea: Financial, they give money, but also goods for the home.
> Adi: Do they give loans?

Lea: No. Never a loan. [They give] presents. There's a fund that gives to whoever is in need. Say for dental treatment. I received enormous help for that, for me and for the children. I got some help to pay for the groceries, and for our mortgage payments. That is, after we lived in rented apartments for sixteen years, the bank helped us [with a mortgage]. So for three years we had difficulties with the mortgage, because my husband had quit his job.... He decided that he wanted to study, and he quit just like that.... He had been employed about nine years and he never made more than [NIS]4,000 [a month]. And it was never easy. We would pay 1,800 for rent and the rest went on schools, *yeshivot* [for the older sons], religious schools [for the older daughters]. Not easy, but thank God. I wouldn't trade that for any hardship or for any other satisfaction.

Adi: In what way was it hard?

Lea: Making a living. It was very hard. So our relationship was wonderful, but there was no income ... the children would cry. It was hard. I wanted to give the children a little more than what I had received. The kids grew up in a home with no computer, no TV of course, and hardly any radio or tape recorder. No luxuries at all. Fruit we had on Shabbat. I have wonderful children. Their character [is wonderful]. No one ever took me to therapy. I didn't need that. None of us needed it and God willing none of us will ever need it in the future. So they didn't have and they didn't suffer from it. Everyone thinks that if you have many children they are deprived or lack. But no.

Adi: You said that you wanted to give them more than you had.

Lea: I mean in terms of nutrition. When I was a child we'd have chicken once a week and fish once a week. The rest of the week we'd eat *parve*, neither meat nor fish [sic], that is. I too cook a lot of *parve*.

Adi: Can you explain what you mean when you say financial hardship?

Lea: Financial hardship is that I feel awful when I can't pay the electricity bill on time, or the water bill. The telephone bill I never pay [on time]. I always wait until I receive a final warning and then go and take a loan. I've had difficulties with these payments throughout the twenty-four years of my marriage. Also with the mortgage. And my husband only works part time because he studies.

Adi: Didn't he quit his job?

Lea: Yes well, he can't really not work at all. So he works informally after the yeshiva hours. He worked in function halls washing dishes or doing electricity repairs. Today he drives people in his car in the afternoon. This brings in maybe 3,000 shekels a month. It's not easy. [This sum pays for] groceries, electricity, the water bill, and that's all. Right now I have to pay for the boys' *yeshivot*, that's 400 shekels for each one, and the monthly payment for the religious college for one daughter, that's another 1,000 shekels, and another 500 for the younger one's high school. Here we pay once a month. Seculars [both Adi and I are secular, and having met with me at an earlier stage of the research, Lea was clearly addressing her narrative to us] make one payment for the whole year, but we send the kids to private schools and we're required to pay every month. The budget of these schools is too low so the parents have to ... It can't be helped. A kid in school, I want him to study well.

Adi: So how do you manage?

Lea: We get help from friends with our mortgage payments. And then I also take from the *gmahim* [the religious charities]. Every woman here gets such help. Don't let anyone tell you otherwise. I'm not ashamed. I'll tell you, I'm entitled to 400 shekels a month, so I take it. And vegetables are distributed for free here. There are secular benefactors who give them to the Orthodox public instead of grinding them up.

Adi: What do you mean by grinding?

Lea: Food growers grind up the leftover fruit to keep the price up. So instead of doing that, some growers secretly bring it over here. Say, if they sell a tomato for 20 agorot it'll lose its value, right? So instead they bring it over to Benei Brak to give away for free. I'm one of the families that take fruits and vegetables. Now, if I could afford it … I'm totally not proud. My husband is more proud than me. If I could afford to, I wouldn't use all that. But reality shows me that I do need and so I don't act spoiled.

Adi: Do many people use that?

Lea: Lots. Most of them. I'd say 90 percent. There are maybe 10 percent who don't need. Here you're either high class or you're low class. There's no middle. Like, every home here has ten kids. In my neighborhood almost every home has fifteen kids. Both parents work. [Typically] the dad is a *melamed* [religious teacher] and the mom is a teacher. Many women here are teachers. And it's still hard so people seek out help. This stuff never gets to the press …

Adi: So what you're saying is that your economic situation has never really balanced?

Lea: Never. Some times were a little less difficult and others were really hard.

Adi: And now?

Lea: Now is a hard time. But I'm working outside. I take care of sick babies at the hospital. It's good money and not too strenuous. I work between eight and nine hours a night. Right now I have a secular family whose daughter was born sick. She needs constant care because she's at risk of choking. So they stay with her during the day and I replace them at night. It's convenient. My kids don't even feel that I'm gone. They sleep and I come home at 7 a.m.

Adi: And then you sleep during the day?

Lea: Sometimes I rest, because I'm sleep deprived. But the kids know that mom is earning some money to pay for their school and the *yeshivot*. I'd like to work at home and make a more serious living, but I don't have the conditions right now. I've got two and a half rooms. [As she explained in another part of the interview, Lea's business plan was to make clothes for sale among her neighbors. She waited until two other daughters married and moved out to have room for a table for her sewing machine.]

Adi: How many people live in the house?

Lea: Nine. One of my daughters is married and one son is in a [boarding] yeshiva.

Adi: All in two and a half rooms?

Lea: Yes. You can see that my daughters got an operation going on here. They get up every morning, wash the dishes. After that I do a round [of cleaning] …

I'm a very happy woman. I'm not desperate, God forbid. I won't lie to you, the economic situation does influence the person. I get really upset when I can't pay my debts. I pray to the Creator, and he helps whenever he helps.

As Lea herself points out, not all ultra-Orthodox families live in poverty. However, besides the thin stratum of self-sufficient and actually wealthy people that she mentions, there *is* also a middle-income stratum (Kalekin-Fishman and Schneider 2007), which she is not aware of probably because such people tend to live in newer towns and neighborhoods rather than in her immediate Benei Brak surroundings. And there are also other marks of distinction in the ultra-Orthodox society that evade the official statistics. Lea, for example, is Mizrahi and she is also formerly non-Orthodox. Both she and her husband grew up in observant families that nevertheless lived in largely secular neighborhoods, and their married siblings now lead secular lives. These siblings look down on them. They deride their decision to have so many children as primitive, and consider their poverty self-inflicted. So unlike the born ultra-Orthodox, Lea and her husband are isolated from their extended families. In a different way, the fact that they are not born ultra-Orthodox marginalizes them also within Benei Brak itself, where most of their friends and the prospective grooms and brides of their children are still, even after twenty-odd years, primarily other nonborn ultra-Orthodox.

Ultra-Orthodox society in Israel is markedly segregationist and hierarchical not only in its relations with its non-ultra-Orthodox surroundings, but also within. While it beckons secular Jews to "find religion" and join in its lifestyle, it rarely admits them to the innermost circles of the local elites. It is also ethnically segregated and often quite explicitly racist toward Mizrahim. The ethnic cleavage, for one, was a very visible element in the economic empowerment course in Benei Brak that was included in the Microentrepreneurship Study. Coincidentally or not, the most destitute in that group were Mizrahi women. And while the Ashkenazi women who participated in the study were similar to the Mizrahi in terms of objective measures—they had large families, very small cash income, sporadic or partial workforce participation of husbands—the tone of their interviews clearly revealed the self-assurance of women who considered themselves morally and socially successful. These women could name revered *talmidei hakhamim* (Hebrew, "outstanding scholars in Jewish religion") among their immediate relatives, and could realistically hope that their sons might become such too, or that their daughters might marry them; their parents and married siblings lived nearby and led identical lifestyles. They saw themselves as perfectly normative members of their community, even if they too were assisted by charities, never bought luxury goods, and never enrolled their children in fancy extracurricular activities.

Single Mothers

One last distinct category that emerged as relevant in the research is that of single mothers, who were primarily Jewish and non-ultra-Orthodox. While in

2011 single mothers comprised about 10 percent of households with children younger than seventeen in Israel overall,[17] the incidence of poverty among single-parent families was 30.8 percent.[18] In the Microentrepreneurship Study, almost half (48 percent) of the Jewish and about 10 percent of the Palestinian participants raised their children on their own, mostly due to divorce or separation. In Israel, unlike the United States for example, most single mothers actually start off married. Of the approximately 13 percent who have children out of wedlock, most are middle class and Jewish, that is, of a relatively strong socioeconomic background, which is again quite different from the image of "welfare mothers" commonly associated with such women in the United States (Ajzenstadt 2009; Sa'ar 2009b). By contrast, Mizrahi single mothers have a particularly high propensity to become poor (Motzafi-Haller 2012; Lavie 2014).

In more than one respect, raising children without the support of fathers makes the repercussions of poverty particularly acute for women. The level of child-support payment by low-income men in Israel ranges between very low

Table 2.2 Single Mothers—Selected Data

Numbers and national background	119,261 Jewish. They comprise 92.4% of single moms	9,788 are non-Jews.* They comprise 7.6% of single moms.
Age	80% are above 34 years of age 33% are 44 year-old or older Average age: 41	
Employment	Single moms have higher employment rates than married mothers (76% compared to 59%, respectively)	
Welfare benefits	In 2010 30% of single parent families received welfare benefits, a drop of 43% during the decade, following policy change in 2001 that defined stricter criteria	
Welfare benefits by national background	Entitlement to welfare benefits among Arab single mothers is twice as much as that of Jewish single moms (61% compared to 29%), reflecting their respective labor-force participation patterns. In 2008, 76.3% of Jewish single moms were employed, compared to 33.5% of Palestinian single moms.	

* Official state publications have had a strong propensity to use the category "non-Jews," and to minimize or avoid the use of the category "Arab" ("Palestinians" is a non-existent category in state references to the Arab citizens), reflecting the hegemonic framing of Israeli society as composed of either Jews or Others. However, since the 1990s, following the arrival of hundreds of thousands of non-Jewish immigrants as part of the massive waves of immigration from the former Soviet Union, the euphemizing of Arabs as "non-Jews" has lost its statistical usefulness. This is particularly true for the category single mothers. This specific publication alternates between using "non-Jews" and "Arab," and this is reflected in the table.

Adapted from Toledano and Eliav. 2011

and zero. And while the state is committed to ensure a modest allowance to mothers and their young children, the actual application of the Child Support (Payment Allowance) Law has been inconsistent (Herbst 2012). As one of the interviewees put it, "Here they simply crush the divorcees. If you earn more they cut down your child support, as if I am the one who is supposed to pay child support for myself." The absence of the children's fathers, particularly when they fail to pay child support, often also means irregular visits and related messages of inconsistent emotional commitment to the children. And as I discuss at length elsewhere (Sa'ar 2009b), low-income women tend to take the emotional neglect of their children's fathers much more to heart than their financial neglect.

Then again, divorce does not automatically imply a turn for the worse in a woman's situation. Since in many cases the retreat of the men from their parental and spousal obligations begins long before the actual separation, the latter often signifies a positive turn that allows women to begin to regain control of their lives, redress their emotional state, and attempt new economic initiatives. The survey I conducted as part of the Microentrepreneurship Study revealed that for low-income families, the man's income was not the most important source of a household's revenue. Across the board, social benefits constituted its primary source, with the man's salary coming second in the case of the Arab participants, and third in the case of the Jewish participants, who actually marked their own income as the second most important.

Summary

Drawing a general outline of the situation of low-income women, this chapter focused on their vulnerabilities and on some of the major structural mechanisms that reinforce their marginalization. These women are susceptible to many forms of violence—at home, around the home, and in the work place. Like middle-class women, they are liable to experience a breakdown of the normative "gender contract" that promises lifelong financial and social protection. Yet unlike women of firmer financial standing, the implications of the collapsed contract are much harsher for them. The continuous juggling of domestic and public work is a central factor influencing the women's workforce participation. While this theme too is not unique to low-income women, in their case the loopholes that open at the interface of the two work spheres are particularly wide, and the efforts required to manipulate diminishing resources and manage on inconceivably low sums of money are substantial. And while, in Ayala's words, "they get by somehow," the constant struggle is debilitating, and the odds of failure grow longer with age and with the complications that occur in their relationships and in the lives of their loved ones.

Besides their hard domestic labor, low-income women in the paid workforce are structurally predisposed to nonstandard employment and to becoming trapped in a vicious circle of bad jobs (Motzafi-Haller 2012). Sequences of unstable jobs, frequent redundancies, and ludicrous wages, as well as insidious mistreatment, leave emotional scars, deflate their self-image and self-confidence, and create in many of them a sense of futility. Passing the age of forty and finding that the kind of jobs they can get have gone from bad to worse, women watch in trepidation as their long-nurtured hopes of finding the right job, which they might securely settle into and enjoy, disintegrate.

That said, this chapter also emphasized the diversity of low-income women. Despite their shared class-bound disadvantages, the practical implications of poverty and social exclusion differ significantly among women between and within ethnic, national, linguistic, and religious groups. They vary in the chances of sinking from low-income to poor, in the depth and severity of poverty, in the degree to which it incurs stigma, and in the meanings that women attach to their situation. Palestinian women, for example, have multiple disadvantages. State benefits are less effective in elevating them; they have narrower job opportunities and less access to subsidized childcare. But they too are not uniformly positioned within the gender-class-ethnic complex. I dwelt on the distinctions between women from urban and rural communities, and between women from different religious and ethnic backgrounds, and we will return to them in Chapter 4. On a different level still, the chances of falling behind or slowly moving forward also depend on women's access to intimacy and emotional support, and on their capacity to seek out such support, which is of course true across the spectrum of gender, ethnicity, and class. Such capacities are discussed in greater detail in the following chapters.

Other important intersections that affect the practical meaning of low income are ethnic and other sociodemographic distinctions within the Jewish majority group. Not by chance, many of the women cited in this chapter were of Mizrahi origin. While Mizrahim have long entered the middle class and the different social and political elites, they are still overrepresented on the social periphery. Recent immigrants, by contrast, have many support mechanisms that are designed to push them upward, and which have been particularly effective for the Ashkenazim among them. Yet those left out carry with them the added burden of dislocation and strangeness, and here too immigrants from the Muslim republics of the FSU or from Ethiopia, or non-Jewish women, are doubly vulnerable.

Within these different disadvantaged settings, the breakup of a marriage characteristically makes women particularly exposed to the potential risks that surround them. Divorce and poverty are decidedly not correlated in any simplistic causal sense. The stories of women presented throughout this book show a complex picture whereby economic distress often precedes or co-occurs with the disintegration of marriage. They also underscore the rapidly diminishing returns of the normative gender contract for women on the margins of the gender-ethnic-class order. In fact, the examples that highlight this most powerfully are found in the two communities where divorce is least prevalent: the Palestinians and the ultra-Orthodox Jews.

This chapter also focused on the vulnerabilities of the women, so as to set the background against which we can better grasp the significance of their empowerment. Yet needy and underprivileged as some of them are, the stories have shown how much these women, without exception, are also so very "normal" (see also Motzafi-Haller 2012). Their lives are full and meaningful. Their work-related practices are imbued with cultural scripts of morality, propriety, and the right way of being in the world. And as mentioned, the social distance between them and members of their communities who are economically better off is usually very small. This proximity is important to bear in mind as we listen, in the following chapters, to their hopes and visions as they painstakingly pave the way for their inclusion.

Notes

1. The Mahut Center worked with Jewish and Palestinian women. While the present study includes only Jewish women among the clients of this NGO, its published research reports include women from both national groups.
2. According to Jonatan Farminger (2010: 134), in 2002, the Israeli Central Bureau of Statistics estimated the number of temporary employees at around 58,000 (3%), the Ministry of Labor gave an estimate of 105,000, the State Comptroller's reported 120,000, the National Insurance Institute gave an estimate of 8.5%, and civil society organizations estimated the rate to be about 10%.
3. According to a report released by the Knesset Center for Research and Information, in 2010 the Israel Police opened 241 files on charges of sexual harassment and the labor courts 29 such files; 90 complaints were filed with the Civil Service Commission. The same year, the rape crisis and sexual assault centers throughout the country registered 972 complaints of sexual harassment, 45% of which was harassment at the work place (Levi 2010).
4. This excerpt appears also in Buksbaum et al. 2009: 29.
5. Personal communication with Ayelet Ilani, December 2012.
6. CBS Statistical Abstracts of Israel 2012, Table 2.1 "Population, by population group."
7. In the Negev region, for example, less than 3% of Bedouin women are registered as employed, and their average wage is 55% of the average wage of women employees in Israel. Center for Bedouin Studies and Development, Annual Statistical Review (2004), report accessed September 2013, http://cmsprod.bgu.ac.il/Centers/bedouin/statistic_yearbook/chapter4.htm.
8. The incidence of polygyny among Bedouins in Israel is estimated to be about 30–35% (Cwickel and Barak 2002).
9. A report published by the Knesset Center for Research and Information evaluated this rate as 50% (Almagor-Loten 2008).
10. Israel, Central Bureau of Statistics, Time Series DataBank, retrieved 14 January 2013.

11. Avram Bornstein (2002) reports that in 1998 Palestinian textile workers in the Palestinian Authority earned NIS 36 a day. By comparison, the legal minimum daily wage in Israel that year was NIS 121, which with the mandatory transfers of additional 30% for National Insurance and Health Tax, brought the daily cost of labor to NIS 157. This said, Drori's (2000) study of textile work places in Galilee indicates that employers operating inside Israel apparently evaded paying the full legal wage.
12. In Lavie (2006). See also "Textile Crisis: Kittan Version" in *Globes* Magazine, accessed September 2013, http://www.globes.co.il/news/article.aspx?did=1000614599.
13. Michal Schwartz and Asma Aghbaria-Zahalka, "Arab Women between a Neo-Liberal Work Market and National Discrimination: The Experience of Maan Workers Advice Centre," talk presented at the conference Changing Capitalism/Changing Feminism, Jerusalem: Van Leer Institute, (November 2012)
14. Israel, National Insurance Institute 2012. The Scope of Poverty and Social Inequalities, an Annual Report, Table 9, p. 27, accessed September 2013, http://www.btl.gov.il/Publications/oni_report/Pages/oni2011.aspx.
15. Israel, Central Bureau of Statistics. 2012. "Press release: The Muslim Population in Israel," accessed September 2013, http://www.cbs.gov.il/reader/newhodaot/hodaa_template.html?hodaa=201211289. Press release: The Druze Population in Israel," accessed September 2013 http://www.cbs.gov.il/reader/newhodaot/hodaa_template.html?hodaa=201211102. "Women and Men in Israel (Statisti-lite), accessed September 2013, http://www.cbs.gov.il/www/statistical/mw2011_h.pdf.
16. Calculations presented by the National Insurance Institute show that in stark distinction to non-Orthodox Jews as well as from Palestinian Arabs, among ultra-Orthodox Jews increase in the severity of poverty is positively associated with increasing employment (Endeweld et al. 2012, graph 6d).
17. Israel, Central Bureau of Statistics. 2012. "Press Release: Selected Data for International Women's Day 2012," accessed September 2013, http://www.cbs.gov.il/reader/newhodaot/hodaa_template_eng.html?hodaa=201211055.
18. Israel, National Insurance Institute 2012. The Scope of Poverty and Social Inequalities, an Annual Report, accessed September 2013, http://www.btl.gov.il/Publications/oni_report/Pages/oni2011.aspx. On poverty and marginality of female-headed single-parent households see also Swirski et al. (2002); Herbst (2012); Lavie (2014).

CHAPTER 3

Empowerment

In December 2014 I took my feminist anthropology class on a visit in a Palestinian village forty minutes' drive south of Haifa. The tour was organized by one of the students, a resident of the village, who arranged for us to meet with four impressive women, including her mother and her mother-in-law, a consultant on women's affairs to the head of the local council, and Rawdha al-Haj, director of a small voluntary women's association, which I will call "Out and About." Rawdha, who was about sixty-five, met us just outside her home, wearing a long black rural-style gown and a white headscarf. She ushered us directly into her kitchen and began what proved to be a brilliant performance. Self-consciously dramatizing the contrast between the first impression she gave—that of a middle-aged peasant woman—and her soon-to-be-revealed persona of a longstanding, sophisticated politician-cum-entrepreneur, she spoke to us in perfect Hebrew, interspersed with expressions popular with progressive Jewish intellectuals: "my partner" instead of "my husband," or "I'm so glad that you are all women so I can talk in the feminine." As we gathered in her spacious kitchen, facing a large pile of jars with pickled vegetables ready for sale, Rawdha said, "I've invited you into my kitchen, but actually I don't like women coming in here for I have spent my life trying to get women out of the kitchen … and out of the closet. Alas, I'm going to invite you now to walk into my closet." Here she paused and observed us with an amused smile, "Note that this is not the same meaning that you give to the term *closet*. I mean it quite literally. See this door [pointing at one of the kitchen cabinet doors]? Please open it and walk right through." Much to our amusement, behind what looked exactly like a kitchen cabinet door was a spacious room with a large plastic table in the middle and chairs to accommodate more than thirty people. This was the location of Out and About. Here Rawdha organized workshops and courses for women, entertained visitors, and did the association's office work. On the walls we could see numerous awards and certificates, as well as artwork produced at the workshops. I did not record Rawdha's speech at the time. However, since her association had been included in our Van Leer Survey four years earlier, I went back later that evening to the interview that she had given to Liraz Sapir. The narrative was identical almost to the letter.

Here is an excerpt from Rawdha's interview with Liraz:

> In the beginning we wanted to market women's traditional arts: pickles, honey ... things that a woman can make in the kitchen. We wanted to employ as many women as possible and we wanted to have as many people as possible tasting the wonderful organic taste of our products. So we worked with a food engineer for almost two years but we still weren't making a profit—until I managed to get our jars into the Green Action competition in Tel Aviv. The tasting contest was aired on TV and we won first place. But then we had difficulty marketing our products to supermarkets because they are not kosher. We then tried new products and I took them to Shula Keshet from the Achoti [a Mizrahi feminist group], because I knew that they were into fair trade. Now they have a shop in Tel Aviv. Well, I was among the first women who initiated the opening of that shop. I started taking beaded scarves, embroideries, honey—simple products. But the important thing was that we believed in these products and that Achoti did as well. This was the true partnership between us, it was a win-win ... Most of the women are unemployed, there's no public transportation, not too many things that could make a woman feel that she was capable ... In 2006 we received some help from Shatil [a New Israel Fund organization that consults NGOs] to register the association and started writing grant applications. In 2008 we won the Knesset Speaker's Award for improving women's quality of life ... We've had many projects, including workshops on parenting, leadership, general empowerment, economic empowerment, women's health. We've organized trips for women. Most of our women don't speak Hebrew and don't go alone to Tel Aviv. I usually collect them from their villages and drive them to Tel Aviv. We've had over 900 women participating in our activities so far. These women then act as ambassadors on behalf of Out and About. They invite their neighbors and tell them what they learned.

Rawdha's experience in talking to visitors was obvious not just in the fluency and the specific content of her words, but also in her capacity to tailor the visit to the exact time that had been allotted (half an hour). When the organizer signaled to her that our time was up, she took no more than a few seconds to wrap up. Finally, directing us to leave through a different door from where we entered, she moved to the wall opposite the "kitchen closet" and drew apart the heavy curtain that had covered it, exposing a glass door that opened directly to the street. "I invite women into the closet, but eventually I want them to come out to the light, not return to the kitchen."

A week later, when we discussed the visit in class, the students, who were mostly Jewish, were talking about Rawdha in admiration. Then, insisting to be the last to talk, Aḥlam, a Palestinian student, said, "I wanted to hear you all first before I tell you that my opinion is diametrically opposed to yours." She then launched a harshly critical commentary, claiming that in contrast to the other three women we met during the visit, who spoke to us openly and genuinely, Rawdha's performance was just that—a show for Jews by a woman who knew what they wanted to hear and had no qualms twisting reality to create the right façade. Aḥlam was particularly resentful of Rawdha's depiction of Arab women as simple and of herself as their savior. "To say that she was the first woman in the village to drive a car, and the one who had introduced other women to the idea of driving, is scandalous. I went home that evening and asked my mother and aunts [same generation as Rawdha and residents of a neighboring village] and of course, as I had suspected, they had been driving for years and they'd never heard of her."

For many intellectuals and critical scholars *empowerment* is a contested term. Particular criticism is leveled against its use in development programs that target women in the poorest regions of the world for unwittingly impoverishing their clients even more, by abusing their traditional survival skills and plunging them ever deeper into debt. In the Israeli context too, scholars and activists often point out the limitation of empowerment projects in generating tangible change in women's economic and political status (Helman 2013; Kemp and Berkovitch 2013). As will become evident in this chapter, I also take a critical stand toward empowerment, but my commitment as an ethnographer to the complex reactions of women on the ground does not allow me to dismiss the idea out of hand. While in Israel too economic empowerment is often unable to improve low-income women's standard of living, and the achievements that *are* registered have no bearing on the structure of social inequalities, its implications in this high-GDP country are not as detrimental as those described for much poorer countries. Besides, as we shall see, it seems to yield some secondary gains that make it attractive, if ambiguously so.

The chapter opens with a genealogy of empowerment in social science literatures, which shows that the term has been fraught with contradiction and ambivalence since its inception. The lion's share of the chapter is then dedicated to ethnographic accounts of women's empowerment in the Israeli field of social economy and traces the dissemination of the idea from grassroots radical feminist circles to more conservative circles, following an economic turn in feminist activism in the late 1990s. To close, I review some of the semantic layers that the term has assumed in and around the field of social economy. I argue that the combined quality of being widely popular yet somewhat vague—different people implying different things when they talk about it—imparts to the idea of empowerment the quality of a key symbol, or more specifically a key scenario, which mediates competing definitions of reality. As such, it plays an important role in a broader conversation in social economy about entitlement and economic citizenship. As I show more fully in Chapter 5, ideas of economic citizenship link together notions of rights, self-fulfillment, belonging, and inequalities, and offer odd discursive mixtures of collective responsibility, compassion, and justice on the one hand, and utilitarian, commodifying approaches to people and labor on the other. The language of empowerment, with the importance it assigns to emotional articulations of the self, serves as a good mediator of such seemingly contradictory ideas and worldviews. The chapter therefore concludes with a discussion of empowerment as an emblematic token of "emotional capitalism" (Illouz 2007).

"Emotional talk," or popularized versions of the therapeutic narrative, is a prominent characteristic of empowerment, whatever the context. It runs like a golden thread through the diverse implementations of empowerment, whether in feminist consciousness-raising circles, political enfranchisement initiatives, psychotherapeutic treatments, life-coaching sessions, New Age invitations to connect to the inner I, or any combination of these. Concomitantly, it features in diverse socioeconomic contexts simultaneously, along the full gamut of poor, middle-, or upper-middle-class people, free-spirited intellectuals, high-aspiring executives, or anonymous consumers of talk shows and life-improvement entertainment programs. Far from anecdotal, the popularization of emotional narratives reflects what Dierdra Reber (2012) has identified as the peak of an epistemic shift from reason to affect that characterizes the present moment of late capitalism. In fact, the quest for emotional connection and universal significance has been as inherent to secular modernity as the faith in the objective and liberating truth of instrumental, detached reason. According to Charles Lindholm (2008, 2013), the modern ideal of expressive authenticity—the belief that underneath the "cultured" person there is an inner child who is a bearer of eternal truth—begins with Jean Jacques Rousseau and grows stronger with the gradual triumph of capitalism, as wage work is increasingly seen as alienating and destructive of the soul. As affect replaces cogito and seems to issue from different areas of social life ("artificial intelligence" in science, "emotional intelligence" in labor management, "grounded cognition" in holistic theories of health ...), feelings are advanced as the new basis of subjectivity. The move of emotion to center stage certainly does not indicate an antimaterialistic shift. On the contrary, it attests to a ripening of emotional capitalism whereby, in Illouz's (2007) characterization, narratives of the self are increasingly integrated into the market, weaving together notions of rights, entitlement, and self-realization. As mounting numbers of people learn to master the psychotherapeutic narrative and engage in public performances of self, emotional competence becomes a form of cultural capital, and self-realization a market commodity.

The ethnographic documentation presented in this chapter—of implementations of women's empowerment in the Israeli field of social economy, shows how ideas of inner strength, emotional competence, and self-realization are enlisted in the service of different, sometimes outright contradictory, worldviews. Constantly on the move, the idea of empowerment does not become lodged in any single ideological sphere. Although its incorporation into the domain of mass consumption does seem to have a strong deradicalizing effect, it has not—as yet—been completely cleansed of critical consciousness. Rather, the ethnographic recording of its discursive flow suggests a more complex development: the collaboration of social activists, business people, philanthropists, state agents, and professionals of sorts in empowering low-income women carries some deep ironies. At the same time, it also produces ongoing communication and ideological adjustments in all parties involved.

Empowerment—A Historical Concept Replete with Contradictions

The notion of empowerment has a certain range of meanings, some contradictory, and it appears increasingly in several tangential discourses that still remain separate and sometimes even diametrically opposed. Thematically, empowerment obviously draws on the idea of power, which itself has assumed very diverse meanings in social theory across the full array from destructiveness to productiveness: power against (Marxist and neo-Marxist emphases on domination and oppression) and power as a productive force (Foucault's theory), power over (Weber's idea of power as authority), power for (as in feminist theorizations that stress women's power to nurture), or power with (New Age articulations of power as an energy of mutual growth and collective creativity). Much of this theoretical diversity resonates in the debates on and the critiques of empowerment.

Although the word *empowerment*—in English, Hebrew, and Arabic—became widespread in Israel mainly from the late 1980s and early 1990s, the ideas that it carries are older. They appear at the interface of social research and social action in various periods under different names, and the contrariety built into the term is evident throughout. In the United States, ideas of self-governmentality and autonomy *combined* with an emphasis on structural violence lay at the core of the civil activities of the 1960s, whether in the War on Poverty or in the grassroots activism generally referred to as the New Left, notably the civil rights, black power, antiwar, and environmental movements. This prepared the ground for ideas of empowerment well before the term itself came into use. In the feminist movement specifically, in Israel as elsewhere, evident from the start was a dual perception of power as a source of suppression and capacity. The dual emphasis on political oppression and personal agency is likewise prominent in movements for community rights and for sexual minorities' rights, and in discourses on radical pedagogy.

Besides its importance in critical political discussions, empowerment as an idea has also been present for several decades in more mainstream discourses on labor management, organizational relations, and industrial democracy. Noteworthy among these is the approach developed in the United States by Kurt Levin and his students, who researched group dynamics in workplaces in the 1930s and 1940s. This approach, which focused on human relations as key to organizational development, promoted a perception that efficient work teams were those committed to dialogue and directed especially to interethnic tensions and power relations within the organization. Contemporaneously, British researchers at the Tavistock Institute advanced a discourse of democratization of work places, whose precursor resounded in the movements for industrial democracy in the first half of the twentieth century, and resurfaced in the movement for quality-of-life at work in its latter half (Maurer and Githens 2010). Early platforms of this kind promoted the familiar content of recognizing power relations, cooperation, dialogue, and strengthening agents at the bottom of the pyramid, although the word *empowerment* did not appear at today's frequency. In this context, Boje and Rosile (2001) argue that although the word is relatively new, the debate on empowerment and disempowerment has lain at the heart of attempts to democratize capitalism for 150 years.

Alongside employees, or "productive" members of society, those deemed nonproductive—the poor and the delinquent—have become the object of ideas linking subjective capacities, democracy, and citizenship. Barbara Cruikshank (1999) traces the idea of self-help to the social reformists and philanthropists of nineteenth-century England, who aimed to reorient Christian charity from alms and handouts to teaching the poor to be self-dependent; a teach-them-to-fish rather than give-them-a-fish approach. Governing approaches to the insane and the criminal added "the poor" to those whose isolation the reformists increasingly sought to end through their reintegration into society. With the advent of state welfare, this developed into a governing technique centered on the constitution of poor people's subjectivity by grounding it in the realm of the social. And in recent decades solving the problems of the poor and regulating social affairs have shifted more and more from the purview of the state to that of the market. At the same time, ideas of self-help, self-esteem, and empowerment have spread across class, race, and ethnic divisions, and also ventured out globally to "underdeveloped" countries. Such multilateral dissemination of empowerment and related ideas has created interesting class and cultural hybrids. The convergence of middle-class language of reflexivity with the didactic style commonly practiced in interactions with lower-class clients has created an illusion of blurred socioeconomic boundaries. This illusive effect—for, if anything, global and national inequalities have worsened and empowerment has done nothing to mitigate them—is part of the more general paradox of subjectivation (Butler 1993) where the very processes and conditions that secure a subject's subordination are also the means by which she takes on a self-conscious identity and becomes an agent. In this respect, empowerment is merely a contemporary articulation of the deeply contradictory logic that characterizes democratic governance throughout, where "individuals learn to recognize themselves as subjects of democratic citizenship and so become self-governing" (Cruikshank 1999: 96).

In addition to gathering more and more meanings, empowerment has spread into ever-expanding social territories. For one thing, it now encompasses not only the "nonproductive other" of the official labor force—the poor and unemployed—but also its ultimate reproductive other: women in the domestic sphere. Here again, a paradoxical process ensues, whereby acknowledging the productive contribution of women's domestic labor—a quintessential triumph of feminist struggles—in effect paves the way to its usurpation by the capitalist system. This is most prominent in development interventions in the majority world, where schemes for the economic empowerment of women in very poor countries have latched onto their hidden survival capacities, such as operating voluntary saving groups or selling homemade produce, and made them "bankable" (e.g., Rankin 2001, 2002; Berkovitch and Kemp 2010). All too often, as shown by Karim (2011), Sharma (2008), and others, such schemes draw women into vicious circles of debt and leave them even more destitute than they were, because they are presided over by an economic rationality that ignores the complex social forces that inform poor women's lives. In high-GDP countries, as shown also in this ethnography, the spread of empowerment into the sphere of poor women's domestic labor creates less detrimental effects, yet it has its own paradoxes and ironies. As I discuss in Chapter 4, these include eliminating women's ability to claim the home as an extramarket territory or reinforcing the love-work axis, which invariably weakens women's bargaining position in the official workforce.

In the world development industry, empowerment, particularly with respect to women, has been subject to massive criticism, going even as far as demands to drop it altogether. Scholars, activists, and professionals frequently contend that empowerment is a Eurocentric, paternalist notion that promotes an essentialist perception of "dark" women, and duplicates class, ethnic, and global hierarchies, even if not intentionally. Yet it is striking that much of the criticism leveled against the paradigm of Women in Development (WID), which was dominant in the development approach to women from the 1960s to the mid-1980s, actually echoed the feminist arguments that gave it rise in the first place. WID was a direct achievement of feminist activists who struggled to put women on the agenda of the United Nations as both employees and decision makers, and as recipients of "development." Women in Development, as articulated in the first three world conferences on women held between 1975 and 1985, aimed to integrate into existing development schemes an awareness of women's economic contributions. Critical studies, inspired by the path-breaking work of Ester Boserup (1970), showed that development projects often adversely affected women's lives because they were guided by a mistaken concept of universal modernization and by culturally biased assumptions on the universal effects of economic progress (Kabeer 1994). Concomitantly, misguided models of kinship, which envisioned men as breadwinners and women as economically dependent caretakers, yielded grandiose projects of mechanization that prioritized the purchase of agricultural machinery or livestock for men's use, or the appointment of men to operate newly installed infrastructure systems (for irrigation, sewerage, etc.), dominating spheres that had been women's responsibility. This typically resulted in eroding women's existing economic autonomy and in introducing new forms of dependency. Studies also showed that because economic growth does not trickle down to the poorest segments of the population, it often does not benefit poor women.

Exposing these and similar biases, feminist advocates and scholars sought to reform development models so as to take poor women's real economic interests into account. Yet despite the significant rise in women employees at the United Nations and other global development bodies (Tinker 1990), the amount of change in the industry that might be expected from the integration of the women's perspective remained heavily debated (Bunch and Carrillo 1990), particularly as more and more studies showed the persistent blindness of development projects to poor women's needs and interests. In the mid-1980s the term WID was therefore replaced by Gender and Development (GAD). Its proponents were influenced by a broader paradigm shift in social sciences from modernization to dependency and world system theories, as well as by the vocal criticism of postcolonial feminists; hence they claimed that its good intentions notwithstanding, WID failed to unpack the basic paradigm of modernization, or to challenge the ethnocentric and androcentric assumptions that underlay the dominant models of economic growth (Sharma 2008). By replacing "women's status" with "gender inequalities" these critics sought to focus on the dynamic and relational aspects of social inequalities, develop more nuanced and comprehensive measurements, and move away from the stereotypical view of third-world women as categorically poor, passive, and dependent (Moghadam 1995; Moghadam and Senftova 2005).

Throughout these debates the term *empowerment* has often been equated with development's discontents (Karim 2011; Batliwala and Dhanraj 2004). At the cynical end, as Julia Elyachar (2005) exemplifies in the case of Egypt, some subjects have quickly adapted to using "empowerment" as a side source of income, posing for donors and staging the effects they know developers are looking for. More seriously perhaps, Elyachar (2002, 2005) also points out, in the case of Egypt, the irony of a third-world state becoming the primary beneficiary of international development funds, which are originally intended to empower local communities to engage in free-market activities by bypassing the corrupt and incorrigible state. In a different ironic development, Adriana

Kemp and Nitza Berkovitch (2013) point out, in the case of Israel, the gap between the extensive investments in financial pedagogy and actual access to credit and finance. Yet another paradoxical repercussion, again raised by Kemp and Berkovitch (2013), is the inadvertent complicity of grassroots feminist organizations—despite their self-conscious position *against* neoliberalism—in making the logic of finance appear natural, necessary, and even progressive in gendered struggles against inequality.

Nevertheless, "empowerment" has never been abandoned altogether even by postcolonial subjects. Grassroots feminists used and continue to use empowerment as a positive element in their discourse and vision (see, e.g., Kabeer 1994; Abu-Rabia-Queder 2007; Sharma 2008; Moghadam 2005a, 2008), even when they are acutely aware of the harm caused by its top-down implementation by powerful actors such as the state, development bodies, and large-scale corporate-style NGOs. For grassroots activists in poor and rich countries alike, empowerment connotes an ongoing process of consciousness-raising that is a prerequisite for social action. In the words of black feminist author Patricia Hill Collins:

> Empowerment involves rejecting the dimensions of knowledge, whether personal, cultural or institutional, that perpetuate objectification and dehumanization. African-American women and other individuals in subordinate groups become empowered when we understand and use those dimensions of our individual, group, and disciplinary ways of knowing that foster our humanity as fully human subjects. (Collins 1990: 230)

Moreover, for Collins, a self-defined Afrocentric feminist consciousness "is a fundamental factor in empowering Black women to change the conditions of our lives" (110).

Back with Collins in the United States, a more individualized albeit still distinctly political version of self-knowledge is found in the idea of self-esteem, as articulated by white feminist activist Gloria Steinem. Reviewing her earlier journalistic experiences and nascent feminist consciousness, Steinem writes, "But not until sometime in my thirties did I begin to suspect that there might be an internal center of power I was neglecting. Though the way I'd grown up had encouraged me to locate power almost anywhere but within myself, I began to be increasingly aware of its pinpoint of beginning within—my gender and neighborhood training notwithstanding" (Steinem 1991: 22). With this swift turning of her critical eye inward, Steinem proceeds with a litany of personal stories, her own and others', to underscore the essential importance of self-esteem for becoming reflexive about the causes of one's destructive or self-defeating behaviors, and consequently ending them. In the particular case of Gloria Steinem, self-esteem is connected to a critical feminist consciousness and organized action. Yet critical consciousness is hardly an obvious outcome of self-esteem. In *Will to Empower*, Barbara Cruikshank (1999) places Steinem's book within a larger trend that she calls the self-esteem movement, a liberation-therapy discourse that became popular in the United States in the 1980s and 1990s as a method to discipline social delinquents. In 1983 the state of California established a Task Force to Promote Self-Esteem and Social and Personal Responsibility. It recruited high-profile experts to design programs in which individuals with a criminal background were required to write and tell their personal narratives with an eye to the social good. It likewise commissioned research that procured "scientific evidence ... [that] a lack of self-esteem, negative or criminal self-image and feeling of distrust and personal powerlessness are prevalent among violent offenders and highly recidivistic criminals" (Cruikshank 1999: 94).

Whether voluntarily, as in the case of Steinem, or coercively, as in the Task Force example, cultivating self-esteem entails active subjective participation. It is therefore identified by Cruikshank, together with empowerment, as "but one in a long line of technologies of citizenship." Like empowerment, it applies *across* class lines and other social divides. For example, the former California legislator who established the California Task Force testified that his efforts grew out of his own "personal struggle despite repeated successes and achievements in my life to develop my own self-esteem" (in Cruikshank 1999: 90). Together with empowerment, life-coaching, self-help, and related terms, self-esteem echoes the psychological turn in discourses of citizenship, which reframes "rights" in terms of quality of life and well-being. The focus on emotional balance and well-being (*it's love, not possessions, that will make you happy*) gives "rights" a distinctly apolitical and nonmaterialistic appearance, and effectively detaches them from discourses of collective discrimination and class inequalities. Yet as Eva Illouz (2007) shows in her analysis of emotional capitalism, their packaging as consumer goods immerses them ever deeper in the domain of the market.

The spread of the self-realization narrative, in empowerment among other settings of emotional capitalism, is part of a progressive trend of psychotherapy becoming accessible to a growing number of audiences. In this process self-development becomes an important "right"—in the liberal version of rights, and realizing it is increasingly seen as the path to success. As Illouz puts it, "The therapeutic narrative is located at the tenuous, conflict-ridden and unstable junction between the market and the language of rights which saturates civil society" (Illouz 2007: 56). One marked effect of the rechanneling of rights to the emotional field is the efficient silencing of all discussion of power. However, as this ethnography hopes to show, emotional discourses have multidirectional effects. Therefore, the active engagements of low-income women with the discourse of empowerment has potentially diverse outcomes, from reaffirmation of the status quo, through pragmatic negotiations of personal opportunities, to political radicalization.

In sum, empowerment—which not so incidentally has no agreed-upon definition—carries an inbuilt tension between a political idea of collective resistance and a psychological and distinctly individualistic perspective, which mostly exerts a strong effect of depoliticizing consciousness. The dual focus on subjection and subjectivity—the feminist idea that "the personal is the political"—is the central ideological source of empowerment and the epicenter of its attractiveness. But as many women argue, it is also its Achilles' heel. In Israel in the past twenty years empowerment has spread into all the social sciences, the health professions, education, social work, law, the planning professions, public policy, and different areas of the humanities. While early uses of empowerment were grounded in feminist consciousness-raising circles and carried politically critical overtones, its rapid proliferation to the therapeutic branches of the different disciplines has greatly reinforced the individualist and apolitical emphasis sown in it in the first place. Today, all these meanings in fact exist together. The word encompasses varieties of knowledge and activity, including theoretical writing, case studies, intervention models, and poetry. In its reverse passage from academia to the outside and from civil society organizations to the welfare system, empowerment has come to rest concomitantly in the domains of activism, professional therapy, and public service bureaucracies, as well as in the diffuse space of consumer culture, in the form of self-help, life-coaching, televised journeys of self-improvement, and the like.

Implementation of Empowerment on the Ground

In feminist activism in Israel, feminist empowerment is a key ideological component. At its heart lies the belief that women have capacities, wisdom, and powers that have been systematically disparaged under multiple forms of patriarchal domination and consequently alienated from them. Feminist empowerment aims to resurrect these capacities, help women find their voice, and recover their powers, as a preliminary stage before they can fight for the elimination of their oppression. To be set in motion, the process of resurrection is believed to need the safe haven of women's feminist solidarity groups. Such groups allow their participants to experiment with forbidden emotions, notably anger and erotic attractions, reverse the all-too-common devaluation of their ideas and achievements, explore new visions, and invent new role models and a new language. This process of exploration integrates psychological and ideological elements, and is at once personal and collective. It is regarded as a critical precondition for successful action in any of the institutional fields that affect women's lives—the family, the workforce, the political arena, civil society, etc.—which because of their patriarchal nature reproduce women's symbolic denigration and sociopolitical discrimination. Despite a clear convergence of grassroots activism toward *economic* empowerment, feminist initiatives throughout Israel continue to run dynamic groups and operate elaborate projects that draw on a broader, more integrative concept of empowerment. In the following section I draw a picture of grassroots feminist activism through a (nonexhaustive) list of projects active today in the field.

Radical Feminist Initiatives of General Empowerment

One prominent feature in Israeli grassroots feminism is a strong tendency to separatist, identity-bound activism, particularly of Palestinian, Mizrahi, and lesbian women. The upshot of a lively discourse on identities and power differentials led by Mizrahi and Palestinian feminists from the mid-1980s through the 1990s, these organizations have brought strong counterhegemonic voices into the movement, with direct implications for empowerment (e.g., Herzog 1999b; Dahan-Kalev 2001; Damary-Madar 2002; Lavie 2011). I present here one version of this concept, through the project of the Nazareth-based al-Tufula (Arabic "childhood") Center in the recently recognized villages in Galilee, which I documented as part of the Bedouin Village Study. I complete the description in a more general overview of other grassroots initiatives, both ethnically separatist and inclusive. The next section, on economic empowerment programs more specifically, shows how the ideological elements that characterize radical feminist thinking in Israel continue and evolve as many of these groups shift their focus to the economic domain.

As mentioned in introduction, this study includes two projects of al-Tufula Center: the recently recognized villages in the Galilee (the Bedouin Village Study) and the Atida project. Unlike the latter, which was more narrowly focused on increasing women's workforce participation, the project in the recently recognized villages was defined much more broadly. Its implementation therefore provides a better sense of the way this organization envisions feminist empowerment. Al-Tufula's approach to empowerment, as articulated in that project, included several principles.[1] One was a capacity-centered approach, which aimed to reverse attitudes to minority women and frame them as capable rather than needy. The participants, whom the al-Tufula moderators had encouraged to set the agenda of the project by themselves, chose to focus their efforts on tackling the village's poor social and physical infrastructure. Their first mission was to open and run a library for children, where they also operated regular extracurricular activities and held their own weekly meetings. After they managed to secure an actual room (an achievement in itself considering the dearth of public facilities in the village) and established regular opening hours, they moved on to initiate additional activities, all oriented to improving conditions in the village. Parallel to these community-oriented activities, a core of some thirteen members met weekly to discuss issues that concerned them directly as women. At these meetings a dual course was followed: lectures or the acquisition of new knowledge, and moderated discussions premised on the psychotherapeutic principle of reflexive narrations of self. As shown below for other projects, such discussions are an essential component of group work in the culture of Israeli social activism, particularly in feminist consciousness-raising and Jewish-Arab dialogue groups. Because they rest on some general principles of group therapy (Wilfred Bion being one of the popular sources), which pays particular attention to group dynamics, they are commonly dubbed "dynamic discussions." As for the project of the recently recognized villages, the knowledge-acquisition sessions included lectures on topics directly bearing on the women's lives, such as child rearing, women's health, nutrition and sports, domestic violence, creating a hazard-free domestic environment, and the like. Complementing them, the dynamic meetings were dedicated to sharing and discussing touchy subjects, primarily the resistance of practically all the husbands and some other relatives to the women's participation in the project, which was perceived with much suspicion as alien to local norms, too radical, and likely to get people into political trouble, and to their venturing into new spheres of activities, such as paid employment, learning to drive, or getting vocational training. During these confidential discussions the women shared tips, and comforted, commended, and encouraged each other.

The regular meetings of the women in "a room of their own" represented a second guiding principle in al-Tufula's empowerment approach: cultivating solidarity among women. In this respect, group members took pride in the fact that they were from different lineages, including some whose husbands were not on speaking terms, and had diverse educational backgrounds. While most of the women had ten to twelve years of schooling, two or three were practically illiterate; two had university degrees. One of the latter decided, following the formation of the group, to start a literacy project for women. She used the library to hold weekly meetings with six older illiterate women, some also members in the Sawa Empowerment Project, teaching them to read the Koran.

The project's third principle was a holistic, community-oriented approach, namely, an emphasis on women's embedment in complex gender- and age-mixed settings. Here al-Tufula's self-perceived mission was not just to empower the women as women but to address the longstanding discrimination against their indigenous community. It therefore made the distinct geopolitical situation of the village, which had struggled for decades to gain recognition and was still deprived of basic rights and services even after recognition, a central component of its feminist intervention. In keeping with this holistic approach, several types of activities were promoted in concentric circles of personal, communal, and political empowerment, which went beyond the all-women, closed-door group discussions.

Once the library and the children's activities became a familiar institution in the village, the women started to organize larger public occasions. They organized several festive events, in the month of Ramadan, on Mother's Day, and during summer vacation, with homemade food and children's games. They were held at the village center; men, as well as women and children, attended. Despite the light-entertainment character of these events, their outdoor location and their framing as community as opposed to women-and-children events signaled an expansion in the women's initiatives toward more direct participation in the village leadership. At the encouragement of the facilitator from al-Tufula, the women made a point of inviting the village committee to sponsor the events with them. The head of the village committee spoke at the opening, commending the women and giving them his paternalistic approval. Then the chairperson of the group also rose before the entire community and gave her own public speech. Thus despite the mockery, suspicion, and direct threats to which group members were subjected throughout the process, the public events were one of several milestones that contributed to marking women's empowerment as community-cohesive rather than disorderly. Next, group members started engaging in direct advocacy work with authority figures on the regional council. They approached different officials, demanding better services for the village: from subsidized transportation to the schools through the construction of a community center and a clinic to paving new roads and installing proper electricity and telephone lines. On more than one of these issues they registered resounding success. In these activities too, the women regularly updated the village committee and invited them to be partners, until they actually got a permanent seat in this previously all-men's institution.

Of the various grassroots initiatives operating in Israel, such a distinctly community-oriented approach to women's empowerment is characteristic mostly of programs run by and for minority women, particularly Palestinian women, where women's vulnerability is aggravated by collective discrimination and poor infrastructure and public services. Certainly, feminist bodies are not the only Palestinian organizations to address the latter deficiencies. Over the past three decades quite a dense field has developed of nonprofit organizations (see, e.g., Faier 2005; Payes 2005), secular and religious, and more recently also private-sector initiatives, which offer services in numerous spheres. Yet the unique characteristic of the feminist groups is their dual agenda of tackling patriarchal and national oppression together (see, e.g., Abdu 2008). Since the mid-2000s the Haifa-based feminist group Kayan (Arabic "existence") has initiated women's leadership projects with a distinct community orientation in over twenty villages and towns. The foremost achievements of these projects are the establishment of an all-women's community center and the introduction of public transportation into the Arab villages. Parallel to the local projects, Kayan has facilitated networking and coalition building among groups throughout the country, which engage in a critical feminist dialogue. Members of al-Tufula as well as representatives from the women's group in the village of Hseiniyye have participated in these forums.

Jewish Mizrahi women, as members of the largest Jewish sociological minority, have also directed their feminism against multiple oppressions. Mizrahi feminism has not been community oriented in the way Palestinian feminism has, because as Jews, Mizrahi citizens have more access to public services than Palestinians. Instead, their activism has taken the form of identity politics and consciousness-raising groups, with a strong though not exclusive emphasis on women in low-income neighborhoods and peripheral towns. In the 1980s Mizrahi feminists started a critical discourse within the feminist movement that took to task the domination and alleged racism of Ashkenazi activists (Dahan-Kalev 2001; Motzafi-Haller 2001; Lavie 2014). A decade or so later, this critical discourse yielded "the quarters" policy, which demanded equal self-representation of Mizrahi, Ashkenazi, lesbian, and Palestinian women (Shiran 2002) in all the major feminist activities. This policy is still retained today in some organizations, such as the Haifa-based group Isha le Isha (Hebrew, "woman to woman"), and at the national feminist conferences held every few years. Parallel to this development, in the mid- and late 1990s Mizrahi feminists started to form independent groups and organizations. A prominent feature in Mizrahi feminism is their engagement in cultural empowerment, through organizing reading groups of traditional Jewish scriptures or community theater groups, and supporting and disseminating diverse forms of artistic creation, including film making, poetry, fiction writing, and painting and other plastic arts.

In 2000, Mizrahi feminists established Achoti (Hebrew, "sister"), basing it on the principles of feminists of color, to address the needs of women who are not a part of Israel's hegemonic culture, which, as explained in Chapter 1, is predominantly Jewish and Ashkenazi. Achoti acts to advance social and economic justice within a broad feminist perspective that ties together ethnicity, identity, social class, nationality, and gender. It aims to broaden the political and cultural inclusion of women from peripheral groups, advance their critical consciousness and create socioeconomic alternatives for them. Achoti's discourse, while distinctly Mizrahi, joins other left-wing activists in Israel in exposing the connection between Israel's economic policies and its position on the Israeli-Palestinian conflict, and in the commitment to fight discrimination against gender and sexual minorities. As can be traced from the organization's website, since its establishment, Achoti has worked with women of diverse backgrounds, including Mizrahi, Ethiopian immigrants, migrant workers, Israeli Palestinians, and residents of one town in the Palestinian Authority.[2]

Declarations notwithstanding, it is noteworthy that in practice, this inclusive position is often kept very low key. As Lavie (2014) explains, Mizrahi women in Israel tend to be overwhelmingly right-wing and anti-Arab, and so the leaders of the organization tread a delicate line trying to accommodate their own belief that the oppression of Mizrahim cannot be detached from that of Palestinians, and the popular sentiment among Mizrahi women.

Achoti's leading projects, besides its aforementioned involvement in artistic production, are distinctly oriented at women's economic empowerment. They include a fair-trade shop that sells products of low-income women's collectives and other economic empowerment projects, and a community kitchen, run in collaboration with the Jerusalem-based Kol Ha'isha (Hebrew, "woman's voice"). Its very first project, The Year of the Worker, which operated for a few years in the late 1990s and early 2000s, likewise targeted women on the margins of the workforce, such as textile and agricultural workers. Mizrahi activists, in other words, were important agents in the eventual economic shift in Israeli feminism.

Other important distinct voices in Israeli feminism have been those of lesbian women or, as some groups now prefer to name themselves, GLBTQ (gay, lesbian, bisexual, transsexual, and queer). The old-timer Klaf (Hebrew acronym for lesbian feminist community), a predominantly Jewish and Ashkenazi group, was established in 1987 and still operates mainly in Tel Aviv and other large cities. Since the new millennium, other groups have been formed that attempt to address the needs and concerns of specific ethnic, linguistic, national, and religious groups of lesbians. Some of these groups have also taken explicit stand on the Israeli occupation, thus challenging the common tendency to classify queer politics as "social," in the Israeli sense as explained in Chapter 1. Kvisa Shehora (Hebrew, "black laundry"; also a pun on black sheep) was formed in 2001 as a direct response to the second intifada. This queer antioccupation group, which grew out of the Israeli feminist peace movement, staged provocative protest performances against the Israeli occupation (Baum 2006). In 2002 the Haifa-based Palestinian gay women's group Aswat (Arabic, "voices") was formed to provide a safe and supportive space for gay Palestinian women to find their voice and articulate their identities. This group, which is still active in 2013, holds regular empowerment groups, parties, lectures, and conferences, operates a hotline, and publishes original materials in Arabic. A sister organization is the Jerusalem-based al-Qaws (Arabic, "rainbow"), a Palestinian LGBTQ group that has operated since the early 2000s. This group identifies itself as feminist and aims to instate diverse sexual identities into the forming Palestinian civil society (Hochberg, Maikey, and Saraya 2010; Nidhal 2013). Bat Kol (Hebrew, "divine voice") is a group of religious Jewish lesbian women that has been active since 2005. It provides support for lesbians who want to remain part of the Jewish religious community.

Besides the growing tendency to form groups that are ethnic/national/sexuality specific but don't confine themselves to that agenda, general feminist organizations continue to operate and many of the activists in the separatist groups continue also to belong to these mother organizations. A case in point is the aforementioned Isha le Isha, established in 1983. This organization provides a safe space for women to perform sisterhood and act for women's rights and interests. It is committed to fight all forms of discrimination, violence, and oppression of women, to defend women's rights to their bodies and sexualities, and to promote cross-cultural dialogue among women. Over the years it has launched and operated different projects on matters such as women, peace and security (antimilitarism and conflict transformation initiatives), prostitution and trafficking in women, women and medical technologies, women and physical disabilities, third-age sexuality, women in a democratic society, women against racism, and many more. Some of these projects eventually developed into independent organizations, but the activists who started them remained active also in Isha le Isha. Several organizations, such as the hotline for battered women and an emergency shelter for victims of domestic violence, which now are completely independent, started in Isha le Isha. Other groups, such as Kayan, Aswat, Itach/Ma'aki (Hebrew and Arabic, "with you"), Lawyers for Women's Rights, or the Haifa Rape Crisis Center, share a home with Isha as part of the Haifa Coalition of Women's Organizations. Last but not least, Isha le Isha has been the mother organization of Economic Empowerment for Women (EEW) and of the Mahut Center, which are leading actors in the field of social economy.

To return to the concept of empowerment, this brief outline shows that in Israeli feminism, empowerment stands first and foremost for women coming together to name the inequalities that affect their lives, trace the historical and political roots of their personal disadvantages, and initiate collective action against their discrimination. While the feminist movement has increasingly concentrated and held heated debates on power differences among women, even within the movement itself, it has been able to contain the groups that split off from the general organizations or started out on particularistic ethnic, national, and sexuality lines. The ability to have women from different social peripheries articulate their own agendas, design their own projects, and speak for themselves, and at the same time act as leading members of the general movement, testifies, for me, that in Israeli grassroots feminism, empowerment is directed first and foremost at the activists themselves. At least within the circles of grassroots activism, this interpretation appears sounder than the dodgy altruistic attitude to Other, presumably less liberated, women that empowerment is so often criticized for. Clearly, as I show in the rest of this chapter, the institutionalization and fast ramification of empowerment schemes, within the movement and still more outside it, and particularly the economic shift and the focus on low-income women have challenged and complicated this interpretation of empowerment. Yet despite the ironies that emerge as the idea of empowerment travels to the spheres of privatized welfare and emotional capitalist consumption, the legacy of feminist activism remains an important aspect of it as well.

The Economic Shift in Grassroots Feminist Activism

The economic shift in grassroots feminism began in the late 1990s with initiatives such as the microentrepreneurship program of Isha le Isha activists, who in 2000 registered Economic Empowerment for Women as an independent organization, and the "Year of the Workers" project led by Mizrahi activists and followed by the establishment of Achoti, also in 2000. These early initiatives signaled a growing preoccupation, among feminist activists, with the effects of economic liberalization on groups on the social periphery, and particularly on women. Further into the 2000s, more and more projects appeared on the scene. As described in Chapter 1, these programs were mostly operated by existing organizations that adapted their agendas to tap into the growing tide of economic empowerment.

At the background were some earlier initiatives, notably Adva (Hebrew, "ripple") Center and Kav La'oved (Hebrew, "line for the worker"), both founded in 1991. Adva Center produces and disseminates critical analyses of public policy in the areas of the state budget, taxation, and social services, and monitors the implications of these policies for peripheral groups. Now a major actor in social economy, Adva Center issues highly credible analyses and reports that are extensively used in social policy campaigns and regularly cited in academic studies. Kav La'oved is dedicated to defending the labor rights of the most deprived workers in the Israeli workforce, notably work migrants, Palestinians from the Palestinian Authority (PA), asylum seekers, and people who had been trafficked, but works also with Israeli citizens. During 2012 it reports helping over 35,000 workers retain a total of 16 million shekels of payments that had been withheld. In addition to individual assistance, Kav La'oved acts to change legislation and to raise public awareness about workers' rights.[3]

Similarly, there are three more grassroots organizations that focus on workers' rights, which may be counted as part of the immediate environment of feminist economic activism. In late 1990s, activists from the previously left-wing Hanitsots/Tariq al-Sharara (Hebrew and Arabic, "the spark") founded the Workers' Advice Center (WAC; or Ma'an—Arabic, "together"; Hebrew, "address") as an alternative workers' union. Like Adva and Kav La'oved, this is not a distinctly gender-oriented group. However, because its unionizing efforts are branch-specific, it has been effectively involved in gender aspects of work, for example in organizing all-female agricultural and cleaning workers, or the all-male truck drivers. Another workers' rights organization, Sawt il-'Amel (Arabic, "voice of the worker"), was established in 2000. Distinct from the other groups described here, this organization has an explicitly *national* Palestinian rhetoric. Its activities include lending individual support to Palestinian workers from Israel and the PA (particularly the unemployed who are denied benefits and workers who had been injured), empowerment of women workers, educating workers about their rights, staging demonstrations and related protest actions, unionizing workers, and printing booklets and brochure with workers' rights. Since 2005 Sawt il-'Amel also operates a coalition aiming to advance the cause of working women, more specifically. Lastly, Koach la-'ovdim (Hebrew, "power to the workers"), established in 2007, is a general trade union that aims to strengthen organized labor in Israel through helping unorganized workers to unionize. This organization, again, engages gender through its branch-specific activities, most emblematically the case of the early-childhood home-based caretakers' union, which I shall return to in Chapter 4.

Economic empowerment then, in its Israeli version, began from below with the decision by grassroots activists to acquire professional expertise in issues such as banking for the poor, microlending, microentrepreneurship, or organizing workers' cooperatives, and to become directly involved in the business and financial communities, so as to start addressing women's heightened economic vulnerability. Because of their background, these activists sought Jewish-Arab partnerships from the very beginning, and their most natural circles of reference were other civil society organizations, primarily minority rights groups. This orientation, which has grown and consolidated since the early 2000s, has yielded several organized actions, such as collective kitchens or the aforementioned early-childhood caretakers union. Yet in keeping with the "educational turn" in the discourse of microfinance NGOs (Kemp and Berkovitch 2013), most initiatives, more than all other forms of action, have assumed a didactic form. The remainder of this chapter is dedicated to ethnographic exploration of the different meanings of empowerment, as they are articulated during the courses and workshops offered in the field.

That empowerment means different things to different actors is central to my analysis, as it provides a lens into the emerging discourses on justice and entitlement. Yet before I tend to the questions, "What does empowerment mean and why does it matter?" I should note that for the majority of actors in the field, the foremost interesting question is "Does it work?" As we shall see later, the tempting endeavor to quantify and evaluate empowerment is deeply contentious even in the field itself, yet all the organizations try to do it nevertheless. Many of the programs that operate in the field provide impact evaluations, focusing on indicators such as rise in household/personal income, number of operative and profitable businesses, number of loans taken and returned, and employment rates among program graduates. Many of these evaluation reports show tangible achievements: over 30 percent of businesses are operative and profitable five years after entrance to the EEW microentrepreneurship program and a steady increase in employment rates among its graduates; about 50 percent placements in the Atida project and similar figures among the Mahut Center and Kol Ha'isha graduates. Often, reports also include quantitative components that emphasize experiences of personal growth, encouragement, and hope. These undertones reverberate very strongly also in my own material below, albeit with some important complications.

Bringing Empowerment to Bear on Business Entrepreneurship

The first economic empowerment courses that were offered always included, besides information and skills, a group-dynamics component designed to facilitate emotional processing of whatever "hang-ups" women had concerning money, authority, self-sufficiency, and other aspects of income generation. The belief was that to turn the new knowledge acquired in the courses into actionable knowledge (Chaskin and Rosenfeld 2008), women needed to develop a sense of entitlement to rewards for their work. Course facilitators therefore worked in pairs. One of the two, typically called a "business lecturer," would have a background in business, economics, or finance, and the other, "the empowerment moderator," specialized in facilitating dynamic group discussions. The importance accorded to the group-dynamics component, or dynamic facilitating as it is commonly called in the field, clearly resonates with feminist empowerment, as explained earlier. Many of the older moderators working in the field came of age in the feminist circles of the 1970s and 1980s, and acquired their skills working in women's and girls' consciousness-raising projects, facilitating Jewish-Arab dialogue groups, and doing identity work with Mizrahi, Palestinian, or lesbian women. In direct continuation of this, their new work on economic empowerment focused on cultivating women's sense of entitlement and self-worth, and addressed issues such as assertiveness; conflict management; negotiations with superiors, suppliers, and customers; and overcoming their guilt when they charge for their labor.

In March 2004 I participated in a study day organized by EEW for its employees, supporters, and volunteers. It included a lecture on legal aspects of the Income Supplement Law and then an open discussion on challenges that arise in the courses. Of the thirty women who stayed for the second part of the day, twenty-two were freelancers who worked concurrently in several economic empowerment projects. Twelve of them were "business lecturers" and ten were "empowerment moderators." The rest were permanent staff members, steering committee members, myself in the capacity of project evaluator, and a student doing her MA research on EEW workshops. Eight participants were Arabs, the rest Jews. The average age of the moderators and lecturers was in the mid-forties, with some already in their fifties. The first excerpt from that discussion gives a taste of the common conviction among actors in the field of the cardinal importance of emotional processing.

During a discussion of how to balance the dynamic and the business components of the course, Sima Itshaki, a business lecturer, said that the women in her group were not very attentive during her classes, and surmised that the reason was that they would get very tense because she expected them to talk about money. Lital Mo'alem, an empowerment moderator and Sima's partner in that course, confirmed that impression. She said, "In my sessions they allow themselves to rest. In Sima's classes they have to report what they did or didn't do in their business, and it stresses them a great deal. With me they relax and talk about their feelings." She described an assignment that she had given, which was designed to combine cognitive and emotional components. In the part that she had classified (to herself) as cognitive, she asked the women to first talk about money. In the second emotional part she asked them to talk about fear. The result was that in the first part they all talked about fear and in the second part they did not talk at all. Some of the other moderators present in the room agreed with Lital and Sima. Nily Dov, for example, said that when she asked the women in her group to talk about something personal they did not respond, but when they moved to talk about their businesses they all started talking about their families. And Dalit Salman retorted, "To me it's clear that it's all about empowerment. If a woman doesn't accept herself she won't be able to open a business."

As the meeting proceeded, the participants moved from a psychological analysis of women's inhibitions to questions of power and their own agency in directing the content of the discussion. In the tradition of co-moderating, one of the participants, Nurit Keinan, led a discussion on the content of empowerment, using her own approach to the subject as an opener. For Nurit, empowerment meant first and foremost keeping an optimistic outlook. Although she did not deny the difficulties, she said, she explicitly avoided dwelling on them. Instead, she would try to let the difficulties gradually sink and move to the rear, while focusing her efforts on giving women tools that would push them forward. Here she mentioned positive thinking, female solidarity, the strength that can be derived from a group, as well as diversity and equality within the group. I record here parts of the discussion that followed, which started with a question that Tsipy Katz, a sixty-year-old volunteer member of the steering committee and one of the founders of the organization, directed at Nurit:

> Tsipy: [Nurit,] how come you don't have gender in your program or in your definition of empowerment? When do they get to discuss their growing up as women in a chauvinistic society? All the available business models, the problem-solving models, and the business-thinking models are male. What do you do with that?

Nurit: I don't [feel that I] have the mandate to deal with gender although, of course, it's built into the program. Fact is, this is not MATI [an agency of the Ministry of Labor, Trade, and Industry that gives consultancy services for small businesses]. We have lots of laughter and crying over women's issues, talking about men and children. I don't go into the deficient social order. This is a given which we're not going to change in the foreseeable future. Instead of being angry we ought to think how to improve our standing within the given conditions. For me, the right way is to understand the structure of the swamp and find the best ways to move within it. I'm constantly [maintaining] the experience of having a choice, of knowing where I come from and what I choose. This to me is a process of focusing control.

Lital Mo'alem: I actually feel that I do have a mandate to talk about gender. How can I not? Not out of anger or rebellion, but out of consciousness. Consciousness is liberating. We know that as women we're facing so many internalized blocks and our tendency is always to blame ourselves, so analyzing external reality helps us understand why the world is as it seems ... Many of the stories that the women bring up illustrate the trap of the motherly role. In the description that Nurit gave earlier we saw that women have difficulty putting themselves at the center. Why is that? It's internalized oppression [and it is still so] even when there are no men around. That's why consciousness is such an essential component of liberation. On the other hand, I often feel that it's above their heads. All those models that Tsipy mentioned, it's above their heads and that's a problem.

Su'ād Abd-al-Hadi: If we don't give a name to things, that's a message too. It's a kind of collaboration. To come all the way here and not touch that, not conceptualize it and present it as arguments that can be discussed, that's a huge miss. At the same time, it's important to be sensitive to the place that the women are coming from—after the workshop they go back home [read: it would be irresponsible to just tarnish the institution that is the anchor of their identity without giving them tools to continue living in it]. The challenge is to dare to conceptualize it as something that the women can talk about. We need to bring in the context ... I'm missing here the experience of working with Arab women, which is incredible. These are women who on the one hand have outstanding personal powers but on the other have internalized their oppression, [meaning] going along with whatever I'm told and walking the path that has been marked for me. They need conceptualizing and they need to see that what their mothers and grandmothers did can be put in words and acknowledged.

Ziva Eilon: What I'm missing is gender as a source of power, not oppression. We as women have skills that are different from men's and can be translated into the business world.

Nurit: I agree, I don't connect with what Su'ād and Lital have said. In one of the exercises that I give in my sessions, we make a list of housewives' chores and price them, to show the real strengths that women have. It's more effective than getting all worked up about being oppressed. That's a waste of time.

Anat Tsadok: I agree with Tsipy's question. I'm very feminist. I admit that during the course I don't really have time for this, but it comes in anyway through the way I talk—when I say, for example, "We as women earn less ..."

Perla Guterman: I totally connect to what Tsipy has said. My connection to gender comes from what I call my own private laboratory. I use the negotiations that I do with my partner and children as a training session to negotiate with suppliers.

Adva Goren: This reminds me of discussions at the rape crisis center. Do we or don't we have the right to sell them something that is different from their worldview? When we give women an opening to a feminist worldview it's a kind of a present. [We allow them] to see the obvious in a different light. It's not obvious that women have to factor cleaning and cooking into their time budget, or that they should be the primary caretakers.

This discussion touches on a basic tension that runs all through the projects. At one end we find an approach to empowerment as a tool for politicizing women by making them aware of the effects on their own lives of larger mechanisms of structural and historical oppression. At the other end there is an attempt to redirect women's focus away from such formidable barriers as those set by the gender/class/ethnonational order, which can be paralyzing, and to concentrate instead on nurturing their self-esteem and cultivating their personal agency. Among other things, this basic tension touches on whether women's anger is perceived as productive or destructive and whether it is legitimate. The discussion reveals that while the ideological position of feminists on such matters may be unambiguous—feminists have long argued for women's entitlement to anger and self-assertion and have long seen gender as power-bound—its implementation is equivocal. And if this was the case for this group of mature and experienced lecturers and moderators, the task of retaining a political perspective in the process of economic empowerment proved much more complicated with younger moderators, who came of age in a different political and institutional climate, and who tend to regard organized feminism as an establishment in itself.

From Empowerment to Coaching

From about the mid-2000s, as grassroots economic empowerment initiatives became more visible, their discourse started to resonate also with professionals and officials in the social services and state ministries. Considering that these agencies themselves were already well on the way to privatizing their programs and constantly on the lookout for partners to pool resources with, their initial dismissal of the grassroots programs began to give way to a more thoughtful and inclusive attitude. The rapid dissemination of the discourse and associated practices of economic empowerment, together with growing opportunities for fundraising and fund matching, provided the necessary impetus for the emergence of ever more programs, with the engagement of actors across the full range of social change organizations, private philanthropies, public services, and private business initiatives, often in mutual collaboration. Typically, the new programs have tended to adopt the basic format of courses that combine informative and therapeutic (or *dynamic* as they are referred to in the local vernacular) components. Yet because by this stage the projects were not unique to feminist or social change organizations, the guidelines of the dynamic workshops, or in fact the understanding of empowerment, took a subtle but significant turn. In growing numbers of programs the politicizing component took a back seat or vanished entirely (e.g., Helman 2013). Instead, the focus of the courses shifted to workforce-related skills that are readily acquirable: from demeanor, looks, and speech style through basic literacy in Information and Communication Technology to Hebrew language skills, the whole, as shown shortly, accompanied by ample pop-psychology.

As participants in "the progressive fusion of the market repertoires and languages of the self" under emotional capitalism (Illouz 2007: 108), moderators in economic empowerment workshops in Israel now show a growing attraction to "life coaching," or as it is locally referred to, *coaching* (the English word has been absorbed into spoken Hebrew and Arabic). It has become an enormously popular practice in Israel in the past decade or so, far beyond the field of social economy. In her ethnography of coaching and the making of Israeli selfhood, Tamar Kaneh-Shalit (2015) notes that this concept, which is borrowed from the field of competitive sports, appeared in the Israeli business world in the 1990s, as senior executives began to hire the services of professional trainers to help them develop their leadership skills and management agendas. Next, a more comprehensive notion of "life coaching" appeared as a popular and tenable tool for solving problems in any number of spheres, including romantic relationships, parenthood, health, substance abuse, eating disorders, consumption habits, spirituality, and more. The implementation of coaching, which draws on popular therapeutic practices and philosophies of the self, commonly entails dyadic relationships in which a coach offers a trainee (or a group of trainees in the case of families) a conceptual toolkit to self-explore, articulate goals, and work toward fulfilling them. Emphatically, in the passage of the term from the business world to private lives, the business metaphor has prevailed. Like good businesses, private lives need to have clearly defined goals, and individuals need to be able to use rational planning and to allocate their resources in a calculated way in order to achieve them. Operating within the neoliberal dogma that will, or rather planned ambition, can achieve practically anything, coaches lead trainees to see their living circumstances as resulting from their own choices, and to believe that a clear vision of their desirable lives, careful planning, and disciplined adherence to their own plan will allow them to change their lives for the better.

In the second half of the 2000s moderators in the field of social economy, clearly influenced by the growing popularity and wide propagation in Israeli culture of coaching, started gradually to use this term and empowerment interchangeably, seemingly without paying much attention to their fine distinctions. But several distinctions *can* be discerned between the two. Contrary to empowerment, coaching is distinctly target-oriented, individualistic, and utilitarian. Also, while empowerment is commonly conducted in low-cost or fully subsidized courses run by nonprofit institutions, coaching is an entirely private business. In contrast to empowerment, which targets almost exclusively women and thrives mostly among low-income women, coaching attracts high-aspiring professional women *and* men, and those who get the highest media exposure and the highest pay are mostly men. Coaching, like empowerment, is a rapidly growing industry in Israel, with various schools and at least two professional associations attempting to standardize, license, and delineate the boundaries of this new expertise (Kaneh-Shalit 2015). But unlike empowerment, coaching is a profession, and a very alluring one at that. It resonates with the older and lucrative vocation of psychologist, except that the track to qualification, at least for the time being, is faster, cheaper, and more flexible; As Kaneh-Shalit explains, the process of standardizing the profession is still underway. Hence many moderators in the social economy field have taken to regarding their work in empowerment programs as training for coaching. In increasing numbers they elect to enroll in coaching courses parallel to their work in the projects; moreover, some of the projects have started offering such courses as complementary professional training for their staff.

The increasing encroachment of the goal-oriented, positive-psychology frame of mind associated with coaching on economic empowerment workshops, and those workshops serving as training grounds for would-be coaches, is linked to the changing sociological features of the industry. For one thing, it is connected to the expanding involvement of mainstream bodies, such as state agencies, philanthropists, or businesses, with their preference for professionals with university education and bureaucratic experience. For another, it reflects a generational shift at the level of project employees. The emergence, within a very short time span, of numerous economic empowerment programs throughout Israel created a plethora of new positions for moderators, lecturers, program managers, and economic consultants. These jobs have been filled mostly by women, many of them young Mizrahis or Palestinians with university degrees in social work, psychology, sociology, law, organizational consultancy, and management.

For many of the younger employees, working in economic empowerment programs is above all a job. Quite differently from the older generation, now in their fifties or older, who created these organizations as yet another tool in their time-honored struggle for women's rights and social justice, the younger employees see the organizations for what they have become: an industry, and for them personally a career path. While many of them identify as feminists and feel good to be working in such an ideological environment, they do not necessarily look up to the older actors in the field as foremothers. Fresh out of the university, these Y-generation women are tech-savvy, confident, ambitious, and achievement oriented. They want a better work/life balance and are not in any hurry to "lose themselves" in any cause other than their own happiness. Many of them have very slight knowledge of the feminist struggles of the 1970s and 1980s and, as I found in separate research on generational relations within Israeli feminism (Sa'ar and Gooldin 2009), many of them are quick to judge the older generation for their alleged "victim feminism" and eager to instate themselves as different. They have a strong sense of personal agency; they claim more space within the movement for self-expression; and tend to regard feminism, first and foremost, as yet another arena of identity work.

These generational attributes, together with the general improvement of professionalism in the field, leave their mark on the content of empowerment as implemented in the field of social economy. Unlike older moderators, whose skill in dynamic group processes was acquired in the setting of political opposition, the younger moderators see themselves as professionals primarily. They draw less on the legacy of feminist consciousness-raising circles or the peace movement, although many of them still identify with the peace camp, and more on theories of organizational management. These theories, at least in their popularized version as I have encountered it in my observations, also put high value on discovering people's inner strength, cultivating their vision and creativity, and promoting individual autonomy within the work environment. Yet unlike the narrative of empowerment as presented earlier, they replace the old emphasis on power, oppression, and collective action by a positive-psychology mindset that emphasizes individual happiness. Consequently, they promote a distinctly apolitical perspective.

The following description is based on my observation, in summer 2010, of an Arabic-speaking economic empowerment course. Aḥlam Fahúm, an unmarried Muslim woman in her early thirties, has a masters' degree in organizational consulting and has worked in several NGOs as a group moderator, policy paper writer, and administrator in human and women's rights projects. In the project at hand she was the course's chief coordinator and moderator of the empowerment sessions. At the meeting described here, which was one of a series on "My growth in the work place," Aḥlam worked with a group of twelve participants in their early twenties on the specific issue of "how to develop an entrepreneurial or proactive personality." She used the Arabic translation of Stephen Covey's best-selling book *The Seven Habits of Highly Effective People* as a basis for a PowerPoint presentation on "How to transform passive attitudes into proactive ones."

The first slide presented directives such as "Take initiative," "Start with the most important before the important," or "Think of the benefit for everyone — win/win." For each statement, Aḥlam asked the women to elaborate. She then used a regular board that was placed on the side of the screened wall to draw a circle with lines sticking out in a shape of a sun. Inside the circle she wrote the directive and at the end of each line she wrote a specific quality that the women suggested, such as "courage," "giving," "enthusiasm," "volunteering," and "help." The next slide, titled "A proactive attitude includes," spelled out the following sayings: "Taking responsibility for our lives," "Our behavior reflects our decisions, not our circumstances," "It is our initiative and responsibility to create events," "We have the ability to choose and respond," "Our behavior is the result of a conscious choice that depends on our values, not of objective conditions," and "What matters is not what happens to us but how we respond to it."

The following slide contained a series of short statements that the women were invited to classify as proactive or passive. To the statement "I can't do anything about it" for example, which to Aḥlam's approving nod the participants classified as passive, they offered counterstatements such as "I'm responsible for myself" or "I can bring my skills up to date." To another statement, "This is exactly my way," the women were encouraged to say "I shall try to change my ways," which Aḥlam completed by pointing out the relevant words on the board, "initiative, responsibility, control, choice." Except for one woman, Ikhlāṣ, who occasionally argued back, most of the participants responded positively to Aḥlam's instructions and tended to offer answers that she approved. The few disagreements voiced by Ikhlāṣ were handled with firm authority. For example, to Ikhlāṣ's suggestion that "This is exactly my way" actually represented a proactive attitude, Aḥlam retorted, "In what way does this imply taking responsibility? How does this imply choice? What changeability do you see in this?"

During the discussion Aḥlam recurrently reminded the women to talk in "a language of I" (*lughat il-ana*), by which she meant to veer away from the common tendency to use third person, plural, or passive forms but to use the first person singular instead. This, she stressed, would help them realize their agency and responsibility. Along the same lines, she encouraged the women to stop wasting energy trying to change their objective circumstances and instead adopt a practical approach by thinking how to work around them. In one example, the common complaint, "If only my husband were more patient," was used to represent passivity, since there is no point in dwelling on an objective fact (husband's character) that is beyond a woman's control. A proactive approach in that particular example was to use ingenuity and plan in advance, in order to foresee and avoid the hurdle.

One of the underlying dicta throughout the session was "We have no control over the teaser, but we can choose how to react." So regarding a slide titled "The sphere of worries and the sphere of influence," the women were asked to think together how they might limit the effect of the former and expand that of the latter, so that they would be moving away from victimhood and increasing their agency. People who always blame their circumstances, Aḥlam stressed, are sentimental (*infi'alyyin*), not proactive (*fa'alyyin*). They have no choice, no initiative, no ability to influence their own lives. They have a victim's mentality. "To say, for example, that I can't find a job because the job market discriminates against Arab women, doesn't get us very far," she stated.

Strikingly, the written text that Aḥlam presented, as well as her spoken language, used masculine nouns, verbs, and inflections throughout. Such were all the imperatives (take initiative♂ [kun mubadir] ... make a start♂ [ibda' walmanal fi dhihnak] ... start♂ with the most important [ibda' bil'ahamm] ...), all the pronouns (this is who♂ I am [ana huwi heik] ...) and all the verbs (I am committed♂ to [ana mulzam] ... I am forced♂ to [ana majbur] ...) that she used.[4] Arguably, this should not be regarded as problematic since, as I show elsewhere (Sa'ar 2007a), masculine talk among female Arabic and Hebrew speakers in Israel is very common and predominantly subconscious. Such a speech style, moreover, was recorded throughout the workshops that I observed in the field. In this particular case, though, the disagreement, as it were, between the grammatical gender and the speakers' stood in stark contrast to Aḥlam's persistent urgings that the women should shift to "a language of I." Some fifteen minutes into the discussion one of the participants spontaneously shifted to talk in the feminine, and a few others followed suit. Aḥlam, in a subconscious response, thereupon summarized their interpretations on the board using a gender-neutral form. Thus, women's suggestions that "[a woman] needs♀ to take initiatives means that [she] can help♀ herself (an takun mubādira y'ani mumkin an tusā'id nafsha)," or "[she'll] discover♀ herself and will encourage♀ others (tiktshif ḥalha, itshaje' ilāk̲arīn)," were summarized on the board as "the discovery of the self" and "the encouragement of others." Otherwise, Aḥlam kept to the masculine form.

When I observed Aḥlam give that session, its coaching-style neoliberal elements were quite obvious to me. But two years later, when I was writing this chapter, I sent Aḥlam an email, inquiring about her source for her presentation and asking whether the Arabic translation was hers. I did not disclose to her in that email that the reason for my inquiry was my interest in her heavy use of masculine language. In her reply, Aḥlam voluntarily sent me, besides the full name of the book, a copy of the presentation. To my great surprise, when I reread it I discovered that she had modified the language: she had made all the phrases gender-inclusive and replaced some of the pictures of men with pictures of women. So clearly, Aḥlam, like all her colleagues, is a reflexive person and alongside the apolitical, high-efficiency, sky's-the-limit ethos that seemed to dominate her narrative, the influences that the field exerts on her are in fact multidirectional.

Irrespective of the soaring popularity of neoliberal messages throughout the field, feminist—even radical feminist— voices are not disappearing. As a founder of one of the active NGOs testified early in our acquaintance, "I'm a new-born fifty-year-old feminist." Having worked for twenty-odd years as a well-paid private consultant in human resources before she started running a nonprofit organization for low-income women, this woman underwent a powerful process of politicization in her new employment phase. Similar radicalization occurs throughout the field, although admittedly the neoliberal outlook commonly appears to have a mesmerizing effect.

Empowerment in the Eyes of the Women Who Enroll in the Projects

> I think that the course was very important because before [I enrolled in] it I didn't have a direction. I did the software course and got the Microsoft certificate, but didn't know how to proceed from there. I went to Mati [the agency of the Ministry of Industry, Trade, and Labor that provides consultancy services for small businesses] and they referred me to the EEW course. It was very cheap, only NIS 400 [approximately US$100] so I figured there was nothing to lose. An hour with a business consultant costs more. I was very pleased with the course. I got plenty of important information, and it also helped me to do a mental transition from someone who doesn't know what to do with herself to someone who's trying to start up a business. Today I'm mentally better prepared to build a business, to be self-employed. I know what it takes and I accept myself. I also liked being part of a group of women who are all deliberating and doubting and have similar concerns. It's more pleasant to go through it together. The sharing, the learning from each other …

Rivka Lalum, about fifty years old at the time of the interview, is an ultra-Orthodox mother of eleven from Bnei Brak. When Adi Romano interviewed her in 2004 Rivka was trying to start a business to market a computer program that she had developed for school managers.

A large majority of the women who enrolled in the projects reported high levels of satisfaction. This finding is intriguing if we take into account that while some women indeed found new (nonstandard) jobs and registered moderate increases in their income, for many others, the projects did not yield a higher income or economic independence. The finding, moreover, is even disturbing if we consider that during their participation in the projects many of these women became engrossed in the notion of the self-made woman, and adopted a discourse of success, individual responsibility, and self-governmentality that unintentionally rendered perfect justification to their stereotyping as embodiments of the exact opposite of this ideal. But before I dwell on the deep ironies of using empowerment as a strategy for poverty reduction and civil inclusion, I draw on the materials of the Microentrepreneurship Study to describe the women's positive responses to the workshops, and to try to understand what precisely they experienced as rewarding.

The follow-up questionnaires were completed by 195 women. To the question "What did you gain from the course?" the most popular answer among them was "General empowerment" (57 percent of the Jewish respondents, 88 percent of the Arab respondents). When asked to elaborate in the open questions, the in-depth interviews, and the focus groups, women talked about the opportunity to get valuable education; to do something "for their own sake"; to share their vulnerability and painful experiences in a safe, nonjudgmental environment; to make new friends; and just to go out and have a good time. For many, the very experience of being taken seriously was remarkable.

For many people the opportunity to reflect on painful experiences in their past and present relationships, in a protected setting directed by an experienced moderator, is potentially valuable and rewarding. This may apply all the more to low-income women, considering the high cost and stigmatized image of professional therapy. In the workshops that I observed, though, "talking about things" often meant not just airing and reflecting but also an opportunity to acquire a new emotional linguistic register. The workshops gave women a new toolkit, as it were, to engage in a speech style that lies at the center of what Eva Illouz (2007) calls emotional capitalism, or the progressive fusion of market repertoires and languages of the self. In Illouz's characterization, emotional capitalism draws simultaneously on the languages of psychotherapy, economic accountability, and feminism. Among other things, it enhances a quintessentially middle-class cultural model of communication that frames emotions as objects to be thought of, expressed, talked about, negotiated, and justified. Part of what makes low-income women feel confident that they indeed *can* appropriate this speech style is the fact that in their work-life histories, as I discuss in Chapter 4, the entwining of intimacy, labor, and contractual relationships has always been quite close to the surface. Following their participation in empowerment sessions, more and more women, Jewish and Arab, began to use expressions such as "I'm more connected to myself" or "I take responsibility for [the way I talk to my children/the things that I do ...]," which are distinctly foreign to the speech style of lower-class people in Israel. Some participants even went so far as to match their newly acquired vernacular with a slight alteration in the way they dressed.[5] They consciously endorsed such an upgraded style as a form of cultural capital, and hoped that it would yield rewards in job interviews or when associating with people outside their regular social network. Most of them, alas, still lacked other forms of social and human capital—from credentials to connections to more deep-seated cultural repertoires. Such forms of capital would be critical in allowing them to cash in on the promise embedded in the emotional linguistic register, namely, talking middle class could actually make them middle class; I return to this point, with some more ethnographic detail, in the next chapter.

Getting an education was another important benefit noted by many participants. Almost a third (31 percent) of the women who answered the follow-up questionnaire in the Microentrepreneurship Study were enrolled in some educational program by the time they graduated the course, and more than half of them said that their studies ensued from their participation. The in-depth interviews show a strong thirst for education among the women; they are intensely aware that education, and professional certificates, are essential for their upward mobility. Yet far beyond the functional value of credentials, their yearning for knowledge is related to a sense of belonging and to their wish for social participation. For many of the women who were interviewed the lack of formal education was a very sore point that emerged repeatedly in their life-history narratives. Against this background, many women noted with appreciation the high professional level and the studiousness of the EEW courses. Treating the opportunity to learn as a privilege is not unique to the women in this study. Similar reactions are reported, for example, in a study of religious enrichment programs for women in an East Jerusalem Palestinian village, documented by Afnan Masarwah-Srour (2013), where women are subject to severe restrictions on their freedom of movement and are rigorously deprived of access to knowledge and learning. According to Masarwah-Srour, when religious enrichment programs were offered in the mosque, women were eager to attend even if they were critical of the actual content, because they provided them with a rare legitimate opportunity to go out of the house, socialize, and engage in intellectual activity. Such reactions underscore the degree to which the acquisition of knowledge—the very act of learning—is rewarding (See also El-Or 1994).

To fully appreciate the significance of education, we need to look beyond its immediate, pragmatic value. In professional discourses on quality of work-life, the idea that people should retain an ongoing component of learning is regarded as at once a necessity for the employer and a basic benefit for the employees. Besides pay, good jobs are measured by the level of autonomy and authority that employees can exercise, and the room that they allow them to grow and develop. Medium- and higher-paying jobs offer employees various opportunities to study and expand their horizons. Large employers may subsidize the fee of their employees' continuing education, allow them to use some of their work time for school work, organize study days and retreats for them, give them sabbaticals, reimburse them for professional literature and field trips, and so on. Such benefits, which are almost taken for granted among middle- and upper-middle-income employees, are beyond the reach of low-paid and unpaid workers. Economic empowerment projects now offer women the opportunity to attend such events. So in a sense this is yet another venue for participation in a middle-class lifestyle and cashing in on some of the benefits presumably included in the liberal bargain (Sa'ar 2005), which they generally do not get to enjoy.

A third notable benefit of participation in the program, which again was seemingly not directly related to the women's capacity to increase their earnings, was what they defined as an opportunity to focus on *their own* needs, wants, and ideas. Initially, this shift in focus, including the very step of taking time off from their continuous care-and-cash work, actually worried many women. Some were concerned that attending the course, and later getting busy with their enterprise, would be at the expense of their children or their households. Some anticipated hostile reactions from their families. But because the process was framed in a coherent language of rights and entitlements that linked the women's efforts to earn money to their motherly and care responsibilities, many participants found, to their delight, that they actually succeeded in transforming their spouses' and children's attitudes from resentment and scorn to respect and active support. Directly related to this, a fourth motif stated by several interviewees was that their participation in the empowerment workshops fostered their allowing themselves to receive—a reversal of their habitual compulsion to give. Breaking away from that lifelong habit and seeking fulfillment through it, women reported that they started to expect a return for their effort, which they now felt that they deserved. They also said that they had become less eager to "save" others. For many of the interviewees, the sense that they were entitled to get a reward for their work, including their emotional work, was a new and revolutionary feeling.

To understand the sense of revolution that accompanied the idea that they were doing something for themselves and allowing themselves to receive, we need to consider the centrality of altruism in women's work. As I discuss in Chapter 4, interlacing love and women's labor through the normative gender contract has had a powerful effect on women's workforce participation. Among other things, it has created a habitus that ties normative femininity to altruistic giving and selflessness. The sense of awe that some participants in the Microentrepreneurship Study felt when "putting themselves first" was related to a general, and deeply gendered, reorientation connected to their attempt to become business entrepreneurs.

A fifth motif in the women's feedbacks, albeit less prominent, was that the empowerment projects gave them an opportunity to expand and elaborate their networks. A select group of graduates of the microbusiness courses who could show entrepreneurial activity did receive extensive escorting. It included hooking them up with adoptive businesses in the community; providing subsidized services of accounting, marketing, and product finishing; and creating support groups for entrepreneurs. Women also received some online publicity, were included in business directories, and—quite popular, this one—were invited to market their merchandise or services at occasional fairs in shopping malls and other public places. A handful of women also got press coverage if they were included in stories on the projects.

Other networking, not strictly speaking business related, was perhaps more meaningful. EEW graduates, like those of other empowerment projects, would be invited to a variety of subsidized conferences, one-day workshops, recreational outings, seminars, and the like. For some women such continuous involvement, although mostly sporadic, yielded new connections and experiences. For example, some low-income graduates became active in other women's organizations, this time as members rather than as "empowerment clients"; or many women went on to participate in additional empowerment courses, not necessarily economically oriented. In the words of a woman I interviewed for a different study, "We got many empowerments" (Sa'ar 2009a). Through these varying degrees of involvement, low-income women stand a good chance of meeting and forging relationships with a range of people, primarily women, of socioeconomic and ethnic backgrounds usually beyond their reach. As another angle of the same phenomenon, the common activities in the field create recurring opportunities for extended interactions between low-income Jewish and Palestinian women, seemingly very odd allies in the Israeli political culture.

Being part of a group, lastly, was another feature of empowerment that emerged as important for women, although it also involved some ambivalence. The group as a setting was central to all the empowerment projects that I encountered in the field. Generally speaking, groups were designed so that participants would go through the process of empowerment with other women who were "like themselves." Within a certain range, project organizers showed a consistent tendency to cluster the women along lines of linguistic, ethnic, and religious similarity. There would be separate groups for Arabic speakers and Hebrew speakers, and when the majority of the participants were Russian speakers the organizers would make an effort to hire a Russian-speaking moderator. Ultra-Orthodox women, likewise, tended to have groups of their own, as did Bedouin women, a circumstance reinforced by the fact that most of the groups were location-bound. Yet within this general unifying setting, there were actually some interesting distinguishing lines among the participants of each group, particularly in education levels, but also in age, marital status, and histories of disadvantage. So central was the group that it became the default formation for other types of activities too. "Access-to-markets," "greenhouse for project graduates," "study days" and similar activities arranged for graduates of various programs again showed a clear preference for group discussions, and attempts were made to create ongoing support groups for women in similar situations. True, group dynamics were never devoid of interpersonal frictions, and some women experienced them as hostile, gossipy, and excluding; but many more said that they experienced the group as friendly and safe enough to test their business ideas or dreams without being ridiculed or automatically alerted to their improbability. Many also appreciated the opportunity to make new friends through the groups.

Before rounding off the participants' perspective on empowerment, I want to complicate the picture by presenting less-celebratory responses that emerged in the encounters of the women with the organization. In May 2008 I attended an EEW study day for graduates of their economic empowerment courses. The venue this time was the Arab town of Sakheneen and women were bussed from different locations in Haifa and Galilee to participate in the long day, which included workshops, lectures, and lunch. The several dozen participants were Jewish and Arab, as were the moderators and lecturers who were invited to facilitate the discussions and give presentations. As in most such EEW activities, the binational character of the event and the (extremely uncommon) arrangement whereby Jews are bussed to an Arab locale for a study day that is not about Arabs or Jewish-Arab relations, were not an issue. Instead, the women were invited to talk about their businesses. They could choose to attend lectures on accounting or marketing, or join in dynamic discussions to share their experiences, impressions, and dilemmas, and reflect on what they had derived from the courses.

At one of the workshops that I attended women talked about the serpentine road they trod, trying to get a business going, juggling several business ideas, and consuming "empowerments," like a pile of cookies, where they could get them for free. As I had heard so often before, several women praised the EEW course they had done, and expressed deep gratitude and affection for the moderators. Yet somewhat exceptionally, I also heard voices of anger and frustration. Admittedly, the two participants who imparted the critical tone, Ronit Sela and Lea Amir, were not angry with EEW alone. One of them intimated multiple disadvantages—her debts, her health, and some vague problem related to her husband—that prevented her from fulfilling the potential she believed she had. The other talked about the limited job selection in her little home town and the difficulty getting a business going in that environment. Still, most of their anger was directed at EEW, for disappointing them, discouraging them, and not being there for them as they thought it should have been. Ronit said sharply, "I wanted to start a management business and EEW wanted me to string beads." She was alluding here to the popularity of arts and crafts among women who attended the courses and who believed they could turn their hobbies into profitable businesses, and to what appeared to her as EEW's failing to problematize such enterprises. Ronit's ambitions were clearly much bigger than that. But her narrative was full of contradictions. She angrily retorted that she was not "a woman in distress" and hinted that she had education, resources, and connections. But then she also revealed that "at present" she was actually experiencing very acute distress. And while she refused to give any details, she let slip statements ("I couldn't attend the classes regularly because I didn't have a babysitter") suggesting a burdensome combination of economic and marital problems. The gap between Ronit's self-assurance and daringly critical words, and the evident signs of her vulnerability, generated very strong tension in and around her. Some women at once dismissed her criticism and avowed how wonderful EEW was. But her anger and bitterness also clearly struck a chord with other participants. Thus Ronit and Lea gave an opening in this follow-up session to emotions very different from those I usually encountered at the workshops, when the dominant collective sentiments oscillated between defenselessness and euphoria.

Outside the workshops, though, EEW employees, like those of all the other grassroots organizations for economic empowerment, were actually quite familiar with women's negative sentiments. Dwindling resources and partial privatization of public social services cause state and municipal agencies increasingly to refer their clients to civil society organizations. As a result the latter have inadvertently found themselves pushed into the position of service providers, despite their persistent attempts to distance themselves from that role. As described in Chapter 1, the broadening collaboration and small social distance between social service officials and many of the NGO employees have significantly intensified the entanglement of these two types of institutions. Consequently, some women who enroll in the projects treat the NGOs as merely one more actor in a web of organizations they turn to for relief. In my long conversations with several NGO managers, who became key informants in this research, they talked about the attrition caused by their continuous encounters with some of the projects' clients. These were women in deep and longstanding poverty, unemployed and often unemployable, who were coping with multiple traumas. Very often their life histories, as confirmed in many of the in-depth interviews, included painful experiences of domestic and sexual violence, which invariably also entailed desertion and helplessness. Some had lost children or husbands to gang violence. These were women full of deep, enduring sorrow, anger, and frustration. Such women would typically be regular clients of the welfare services, who were unable to improve their situation in any substantial sense. Ironically, the inability of the social workers (or of the NGOs workers) to help these women, and the inevitable rotation through their appointed caseworkers, merely re-enacted, in a vicious circle of repetition compulsion, the original, formative sense of desertion that most of them carried within them.

Empowerment as Lingua Franca

In Israeli social economy the term *empowerment* is used concurrently in radical, liberal, and conservative circles, and appears simultaneously in the political, activist, professional, and consumerist domains. Alongside its salience *within* the field of social economy, empowerment features also in several interfacing discursive fields, notably in the therapeutic professions, where it originates, business discourses, marketing, and expanding consumerist spheres, through talk shows, reality TV, and leisure activities. A random online search for the Hebrew word *ha'atsama* ("empowerment") yields an avalanche of consumer products, mostly workshops, courses, books, videos, and coaching packages that promise improved physical, mental, spiritual, social, and financial well-being. A more specific search of *women's* empowerment somewhat alters the strictly individualistic and market connotations. It yields more mixed results that echo both gender equality and social justice, and products more readily identified as consumer goods par excellence, such as guided sessions for artistic or spiritual development. A parallel search of the Arabic word *tamkeen* yields results that resonate with the language of "development," education, and to a lesser degree individual growth—personal, business, and spiritual. The more specific term *tamkeen il-mar'a* ("woman's empowerment"), in turn, brings up women's political participation, social equality, and economic advancement. Lastly, the term *tamkeen al-mar'a* qualified with the word Palestine, to narrow the search to that particular region within the Arab world, immediately focuses the results on political, economic, and social empowerment, with much fewer results of the "consumer product" type. To return to the Israeli context, "empowerment" changes its emphases, terminology, and meanings as it flows within and between these tangential fields, yet it retains a familiar sound that makes sense across them all. Empowerment, in other words, is a key symbol, or more finely a key scenario, in Sherry Ortner's (1973) typology of key symbols, which provides a mode of action appropriate to correct and successful living in the culture. As such, it operates as a mediating term between rival definitions of reality.

Multiple Meanings of Empowerment

At least three semantic layers can be discerned in the use of "empowerment" in and around the field of social economy, which may accidentally overlap rival sets of meanings. In the first, as presented earlier, empowerment is perceived as a psychological process that is at the same time distinctly feminist. It indicates emotional healing from offenses that the women suffered *as women*, combined with a discovery of their internal sources of power and raising consciousness of gender-power. Well aware that many low-income women do not actually improve their economic situation after being in the programs, activists and project managers often underscore the importance of general empowerment, as a profound experience that is not quantifiable. A typical argument holds that even when a considerable proportion of participants did not significantly raise their income level, and did not manage to open a business or get a new job, the process that they underwent in the workshops was significant in and of itself: they acquired a sense of entitlement to a better life, they joined up with women like themselves and discovered that they were not alone in the struggle; they learned a language in which to speak about what was happening to them. General empowerment, in other words, is perceived as a necessary condition for economic empowerment. The following quote, from an interview with Fatima Ziad, manager of a project for Bedouin women, is characteristic of the perception that prevails in the field. The interview was conducted in 2010 by Liraz Sapir as part of the Van Leer Research Group Survey.

> The special thing about the program—it's that we reach the women, reach them at home. The beginning is really door to door, house to house. Telling them, interesting them. I started out with an assumption, and these four years have proved to me [that I was right], that a situation has come about where the Bedouin women have lost all faith in their capacities. It's like a self-fulfilling prophecy: she's at home and can't do anything—the women have adopted this attitude. [Against this background], the very act of our field worker approaching a woman to tell her, "You can, just begin to think" [is cardinal]. We were the little push that gave her the first impulse, and if she progresses and flourishes it's due to her abilities, which existed but were covered in dust. It dusts her off in this struggle, and she can spread her wings.

The underlying assumption wrapped in this quote, that *overall personal empowerment* will lead naturally to *economic* empowerment, forcefully reflects the interface between an activist orientation, which challenges traditional family gender roles (women can and should engage in independent income-generating activities) and a professional therapeutic orientation that underscores the importance of personal emotional healing (regaining faith in her capacities). A second, if less obvious, discursive interface is that between a feminist and a business orientation. In emphasizing the achievement of getting women to trust their own capacities, the speaker was alluding to the pressure on her, as a project manager, to show "hard" proof of economic success. Reference to donors' preoccupation with the projects' cost-effectiveness is more explicit in the next quote, from an interview with Galit Hod, manager of a women's organization in the Jerusalem area that operates several projects for women's empowerment. She too was interviewed by Liraz Sapir in 2010.

> L. S.: What has been the main success of your projects?
> G. H.: ... The women who come here—you could really scrape them off the sidewalk. And with a great deal of support and dedication ... they feel wanted, and we're concerned about what happens to them. And the renewed gathering of strength in the process they undergo here makes this possible. This is the most meaningful thing.
> Q.: And what were the main difficulties?
> G.H.: It is very difficult for our organization to survive economically. As a manager I worry every single month. It has become hard for medium-sized organizations to mobilize funds and to succeed, and to show that they succeed, because very many foundations prefer to give to quantity. So if we hold a course for twenty

women it's harder to convince them even if these are women whose lives we have really saved … A disempowered population demands action that is expensive. It's not enough to give a course of ten meetings … This is a population that's not easy to work with … Sometimes it really [means] getting them to get out of bed. It's very much hands-on and grinding work.

Following from this last point, measurement, in the dual sense of general empowerment as a measure of the success of the projects and as a target that is measurable, comprises a second semantic layer. In the first sense, several reports by external evaluators (among others Sa'ar 2007c), have repeated the assertion voiced by these two project managers: participation in the workshops gives women a sense of entitlement to a better life, makes them aware that they are not alone in their struggle, and provides them with a language in which to speak about what is happening to them, all of which will presumably pave the way later for their engagement in more focused economic actions. This approach of general-empowerment-as-measurement-of-economic-empowerment is emphatically antiquantitative. Admittedly, the argument that general empowerment should be regarded as success even if no economic improvement is registered is somewhat circular, as the premise asserts its own conclusion regarding the profitability of the financial investment in the projects. Interestingly, however, besides being ideologically convincing to many feminists, this argument is also attractive to donors, who look for a persuasive narrative in order to continue sending money to enterprises whose economic outcomes are uncertain.

Ambivalence as to whether empowerment can or should be measured is not unique to the Israeli case. Scholars of gender and development have debated the problem of using standardized scales to measure change that is primarily qualitative and culturally particular. Following the understanding that women's well-being does not improve automatically when they generate more income, because resource distribution is mediated through domestic power relations and communal notions of entitlement, Amartya Sen (1999) advocated a shift in development policies from a focus on income per person to a more comprehensive idea of capabilities, insisting, moreover, that capabilities as freedom are not amenable to quantification. Endorsing this paradigmatic shift, other critical scholars (e.g., Kabeer 1999; Nussbaum 2003; Moghadam and Senftova 2005; or Walby 2005) have nevertheless maintained that empowerment, development, and the well-being of women should be monitored and compared across cultures, social classes, regions, and continents. These scholars have put forth complex, multidimensional, mixed-methodology frameworks that integrate variables as diverse as "resources," "capacities," "rights," "agency," "achievements," or "participation," and determine collective progress, beyond the level of individual growth.

Back to Israel, despite the strong belief of field activists that empowerment cannot be quantified, there is a pressing need to measure success in the social economy field. Projects are permanently subject to evaluation, to the extent that a subindustry of evaluation studies has become an integral part of the social economy field. This rapidly developing activity involves scholars, as well as independent researchers and private firms, that compete for stature and budgets. Mixing notions deriving from management, economics, psychology, and ethics, this industry is driven, among other things, by the moral turn in neoliberal economics that impels conglomerates to adopt a position of social responsibility (Shamir 2008), and therefore taps well into the discourse of emotional capitalism that saturates the field. One of the thriving companies in the field in Israel during the last three years of this research, the Midot Corporation, is a good example. With a reported 2011 budget of NIS 2.5 million and five "social analysts" in a team of eight employees, Midot sells its services to large philanthropic bodies. The close to eighty public-good organizations that it examined between 2008 and 2011 included several NGOs covered by my research. Midot, which styles itself as a body active in a global environment of similar organizations in the world, developed a methodology for measuring "efficiency" and "social influence" or "impact"—terms that it wishes to promote in the array of calculations of funding bodies and NGOs alike.[6] Not coincidentally, this and other companies that operate in Israel work in close collaboration and consider themselves part of a global industry of social impact assessment that thrives on the collaboration of philanthropists, social and environmental activists, nonprofit organizations, financial and business sectors, and policy makers.[7]

A similar vocabulary is coming increasingly to the fore in the discussions of the organizations themselves. I recorded the following quotes in my field diary at a meeting of several organizations in September 2009 in Jerusalem to plan a joint project. At some point in the discussion the representative of the funding body said: "Our entry into the project involves a built-in strategy of *exit* ... The aim is to depart, and leave organizations strengthened." Later this representative declared: "Our purpose is to think how to create an *impact*, [considering that] in the world of organizations there is more noise than in other arenas"—a comment that sparked a response that "the feminist organizations have been the most *effective*." During this and similar discussions, all in Hebrew, the words "impact," "effective," and "exit" were used in their original English version. A further illustration is taken from an interview with Sasha Babayoff, a project manager in a philanthropic organization classified by a Bank of Israel report as one of the largest in Israel (Nagar and Zussman 2006). This organization, which among other things engages in food distribution, runs a course on business enterprises for women and men on the poverty line, and lists "empowerment" as one of its major aims (as stated in the interview). This manager's narrative, in her 2010 interview with Liraz Sapir, again displays a perception of efficacy as a property that can be measured objectively, in contrast to the perception presented above of personal empowerment as a hazy measure of economic empowerment.

> A year and a half before the beginning of our project a large international organization that we worked with [names a well-known international microfinance organization] conducted a large-scale feasibility study [*mehkar hitachnut*] for us. We didn't just dive in at the deep end—if there's no added value there's no point. It all starts off as a pilot, first of all … [And later:] We don't admit all and sundry—absolutely not. So if at the moment she's in the middle of very fractious divorce proceedings maybe this is not the right time for her [to start up a business]. There has to be high motivation, commitment to the process, basic qualifications or ability. We assign the candidates homework: when someone comes with an idea we check how flexible her thinking is: Can she modify the idea? Can she take criticism? If at that moment she's fighting for survival it's reasonable to suppose that she won't be available for it … If you take a look at [names another NGO], a small percentage of the women [who graduate from their project] actually open a business. Maybe one of the reasons is that they take in whoever wants to join. We don't want that.

Emphatically, the challenges and potential paradoxes in attempting to quantify and measure empowerment do not go unnoticed by the actors themselves. Eitan Shani, a social analyst I interviewed in 2013, gave me the following explanation:

> E. S.: Everyone understands that it is very difficult to measure social value. Monetary value is much easier to measure … In the mid- or late 1990s new models appeared, courageous models I should say, that attempted to do qualitative measuring of social projects. I'm talking about ten or so organizations that started to operate in the US, in South Africa, in Britain … and also in Israel. Around that time corporations started to understand that there was a connection between being green, efficient, marketable, and supporting social causes. So at first they would give inconsistently, following their hearts. X [names an organization in Israel] set out to change this attitude and help corporations plan their charity better … What distinguishes the new models is that they measure nontangible outcomes and are judgmental; they rely on the analysts' interpretations. However, although it seemed attractive at first, the trend of qualitative measuring might have been short lived. All these measuring companies are at risk now and I don't know how long they will last. Donors soon lost interest in these measurements because the process is too long and not cost effective. They want quantities and unequivocal recommendations. So now, for example, you find new companies [mentions two names], who have these ridiculous scales. One uses surfers' ratings, you know how, when you go online and they ask you to rate something? That's what they are using. It's totally unreliable but people like it because it uses peer evaluation. The other has a group of experts and they

periodically ask them to grade projects. Again, it's not reliable. It's not that these experts actually go and interview people in those projects. But it's popular ...

A. S.: What you are saying resonates with the position of some actors in the field, who claim that you can't really measure empowerment ...

E.S.: How do you mean? I'm a great believer in measuring. I belong to those people who are not ashamed to say that you *can* measure social value. The point is that I believe in in-depth measuring, one that takes time and produces long, wordy reports. Investors—by the way, I like to call them investors rather than donors—they don't want to read long reports ... The original staff in [the impact-evaluation company where he works], we were motivated by an ideological passion for measuring. We did think that everything was measurable and we used to get into arguments with the NGOs over that. But then our own board of directors changed tune and started demanding that we adopt a lighter tool that would enable us to cover more projects. They pressured us to cut down the time that it took us to produce a report to about a fifth. Eventually we had to abandon our original tool. But I still believe that it is so much better.

A third semantic layer is empowerment as a consumer good. Here, the familiar idea of empowerment as a psychological process reappears, but without the complementary political consciousness-raising. If the first interpretation indicated that general empowerment sets in motion a process of healing from the effects of structural violence, the third semantic layer swiftly glosses over oppression and deprivation. Instead, the key to economic success is self-realization, which is indicated, among other things, by emotionally sophisticated speech and manners. Rather than focusing on socioeconomic inequalities, empowerment as a consumer good implies that opportunities for economic success are open to all, and what women need to realize them are clear vision, a positive attitude, and a work plan. This mindset, which we met earlier in relation to coaching, is shared by many of the actors in the field, including a fair number of the projects' clients. Here too, hard economic measures of success are pushed to the back, and the focus is shifted instead to the very opportunity to *consume* personal development.

As mentioned, the workshops impart to the great majority of participants the feeling that they can acquire a bit more self-knowledge, a bit more assertiveness, a bit more connection to the inner I—and all this without a university degree or expensive—and stigmatizing—psychotherapy. While in Israel this type of emotion talk is traditionally identified as middle rather than lower class, low-income women tend to feel confident that they can appropriate the emotional language when they encounter it in the workshops, and use it successfully outside that setting as well. After all, emotion work is what they have been doing all along, so it seems familiar—except, of course, that they lack the habitus (which is class-bound) necessary to make this newly adopted speech style profitable. On several occasions, women I met in subsidized economic empowerment workshops decided to go on consuming pseudotherapeutic experiences in other settings as well. I escorted women that I met in the courses to numerous such settings, from free Twelve Steps programs that address a large variety of addictions, including emotional addiction, through pyramid schemes that demanded investment of several hundred shekels (and promised very high returns), to more lucrative forums, such as the Landmark Education Forum, that cost thousands of shekels. In all these, heavy use of empowerment lingo was closely linked to the promise of a better, more affluent life.

At this end of the continuum "women's empowerment" becomes a product of leisure culture, offered for sale alongside yoga classes, personal coaching, silence-in-nature workshops, or extreme sports, as in the example of the lucrative and costly Desert Queen women-only tours. As the latter is presented on the official website of the Jewish Agency, the organizer of the Israeli version of the international Desert Queen, "this journey, which takes place in some of the most exotic and challenging places in the world ... combines competitive outdoor adventure and four-wheel driving expedition with personal empowerment."[8] Complementary to "empowerment" being a product that women love to consume, it sometimes is also featured as a business venue for women, alongside holistic treatments, cosmetics, or private tutoring. I came across such a case on a course of business training in which I did participant observation, where the "empowerment moderator" was herself a graduate of an earlier course of the same organization, who had chosen "empowerment" as her trade. We shall hear more about this woman's framing of empowerment in the next chapter.

A Mediating Term between Competing Definitions of Reality

Low-income women in Israel encounter expanding opportunities to "do" empowerment. Diverse in type and effect, these opportunities reassert them, alternatively, as social, political, or consumerist subjects (in the locally specific meanings of "social" and "political," as presented in Chapter 1). In a spiral "paradox of subjectivation" (Butler 1993), participation in multiple empowerments simultaneously disciplines women and allows them room to assert their agency and creativity. The discursive flow (Comaroff and Comaroff 2003a) of the term *empowerment* reveals that it has acquired several semantic layers that differ and even contradict each other, while retaining an overlap wide enough to allow comfortable passage from one discursive field to another. For example, we saw that empowerment as measurement involves contradictory types of representation: it solicits thick, moving textual accounts of women's growth and self-discovery that at once accentuate their exoticization and clothe them in universal humanity by presenting them as self-actualizing individuals, like everyone else. At the same time, a growing appetite for objective, quantifiable accounts creates strong pressures on the organizations to produce slim, numerical representations, which again yields a dual effect of stuffing empowerment subjects ever more tightly into placard-like categories of needy members of society—Bedouin women, single moms, Arab women, ultra-Orthodox women, Ethiopians, etc.—and giving them agency. For through their figuring in reports that assess their purchasing power, their repayment capacities, or their income-generating potential, low-income women are effectively treated as customers (of banks, of life coaches, of reality TV, and, for that matter, also of social services bureaus and civil society organizations), like any others. Similar contradictory effects are evident also in the other semantic layers, whereby personal growth and well-being are either accompanied by or devoid of critical political discourse, and emotional processes are increasingly interlaced with market repertoires of action and logic or, again, with critical political consciousness. Here too, the field of social economy features the full range of meanings, notwithstanding obvious preferences of many of the old-time activists for narratives of social change and minority rights.

The three semantic layers I have depicted in this section, then, suggest that "empowerment" serves as a concept mediating between business and professional ethics, and an ethics of social change. The multiplicity of meanings associated with the term facilitates a seemingly uninterrupted flow of empowerment lingo across tangential institutional fields. As such, it plays an important role in a broader process of cultural production that occurs in the ongoing interactions between civil society initiatives for social justice and social responsibility, and business and state efforts to enhance individual self-sufficiency. As I discuss in the concluding chapter, these interactions entail interesting and somewhat unexpected discursive articulations, of which "empowerment" is at once a reflection and a catalyst.

Conclusion

This chapter reviewed the multiple meanings of empowerment in and around the Israeli field of social economy. I traced the discursive flow of the term as it travels from grassroots feminist activism to more mainstream domains, engaging state, business, and philanthropic officials, and as it becomes a popular token of cultural consumption. In Israel today *empowerment* is a term in constant flux, serving radical, liberal, and conservative circles, and appearing at once in the political, activist, professional, and consumerist domains. The different players in the field invest it with a variety of meanings, at times contradictory, when groups and individuals seem to speak the same language but actually imply different sets of values. Part of what makes this bridging effect possible, at least in the case of the empowerment of low-income women, is the construction of empowerment as a form of emotional competence that people like to imagine would be easily transformed into economic profit. The dual connotation of empowerment as market-bound and nonmaterialistic, likewise, makes it appear tenable across class and ethnic differences. It also makes it a particularly emblematic instance of emotional capitalism.

In *Cold Intimacies,* Eva Illouz (2007) notes that emotional competence, or proficiency in the psychological model of communication, is increasingly used as a social currency. As shown in this chapter, low-income women use economic empowerment workshops as opportunities to experiment with a sophisticated emotional speech style that is generally the prerogative of a professional class and beyond the boundaries of their own habitus. Such cultural venturing is facilitated by the fact that the professionals they meet at the workshops, the moderators and lecturers, often have a similar ethnic or national background and are commonly very encouraging. This renders the workshops important opportunities to consume empowerment as an emotional commodity; important, but not unique. Many of the ideas that the women encounter in the workshops reverberate in books, talk shows, and videos. Such materials are available in abundance on TV or through social media, free of charge and translated into Hebrew or Arabic.

In its ongoing flow between domains of cultural production, empowerment acquires and sheds semantic connotations, and the women performing it navigate among various subject positions. The prominence of emotional language in the different semantic layers, whether paired with efficiency and feasibility, well-being, or political radicalization, implies complex effects of expanding the women's cultural comfort zone and reinforcing their marginalization. Low-income women, although relative newcomers to the linguistic performances of rationalizing emotions and dissecting the self in a spiraling process of reflexivity, are generally all too familiar with the intertwining of economic activities and intimate relationships. As I discuss in the next chapter, their concentration in the unpaid domestic workforce lifts the mutual spillover of intimate relationships and economic bargaining much closer to the surface than these two appear in middle-class imagination. So on encountering emotional lingo in the workshops, many women feel that they are treading familiar ground, and that they actually have a good vantage point to improving their earning capacities. Most of them, though, lack the credentials, the connections, and mostly the habitus, which are necessary to make their newly acquired emotional competence effective.

But the effect of empowerment on women's lives is paradoxical also beyond the temptation to invest in a type of cultural capital whose economic rewards are doubtful. I mentioned that many women experience their participation in the workshops as highly gratifying, and emphasized that despite the pressing need to increase their income, women value the opportunity for self-growth, intellectual engagement, social networking, and leisure activity. These and related gains, interestingly, fit well with both feminist ideas of women's liberation and neoliberal quality-of-life measures. Yet regardless of the enormous investment of grassroots feminists in women's empowerment, in practice participants tend to endorse the latter interpretation much more readily than the former.

A third contradictory effect results from the central role that the social services and philanthropists, the traditional disciplinarians of the poor, play in the workshops. Although many of these actors are very keen on ideas of social responsibility and often have much sympathy for the social-change organizations that operate the projects, their professional outlook conditions them to classify the participants of the workshops as welfare clients, primarily. As indicated in Chapter 2, the vulnerability of many of these women is quite overwhelming, and participation in the programs mostly does not eradicate their dependence on welfare. Hence the economic empowerment of low-income women acquires, alongside the apolitical, individualistic orientation and the feminist-political one, a strong disciplinary undertone. In this respect, the performance of empowerment by welfare recipients or the unmistakable "poor" highlights especially the paradoxes of democratic subjectivity where, following De Tocqueville, Cruikshank (1999: 96) comments that self-government entails more than the exercise of subjectivity; it entails also the subjection of the self.

Notes

1. See Sa'ar 2012 for a detailed description of the project and the philosophy behind it.
2. "Sister, for women in Israel," website accessed September 2013, http://www.achoti.org.il/?page_id=414.
3. Workers' Hotline, website accessed September 2013, http://www.kavlaoved.org.il/.
4. The symbols ♀ and ♂ are used to designate feminine and masculine grammatical gender, respectively. For more see Sa'ar (2007a).
5. For an ethnographic example of such elaborate adaptation of style see Sa'ar 2007b.
6. http://midot.org.il.
7. Salient examples are the British New Philanthropy Capital or the US-based Root Cause.
8. The Jewish Agency for Israel, "Desert queen Israel jeep expedition for women 2010," accessed 28 March 2013, http://www.jewishagency.org/JewishAgency/English/Israel/Partnerships/DesertQueen.

CHAPTER 4

Entitlement

Shlomit Avraham was a divorced mother of two in her late thirties when Tamar Kaneh interviewed her in Haifa in 2006. When Tamar and I met her on the economic empowerment project, Shlomit, daughter of ultra-Orthodox parents and one of eleven siblings, had already ceased being observant for more than twenty years. She was one of very few participants in the business entrepreneurship course who already had an operating and officially registered business when she enrolled. However, she was barely breaking even and not making enough profit. To make ends meet she would take on odd jobs, cleaning, babysitting, or caring for an elderly neighbor, which she kept unreported in order not to lose the already very low (because of her business) child support she received from the National Insurance. Shlomit was very satisfied with the EEW course, which she had joined almost by chance, simply because it was more affordable than the one offered by MATI (the subsidiary of the Ministry of Industry, Trade, and Labor that supports small businesses). She learned important skills ("My management before was all wrong. I've become much more organized and accurate in my calculations"), but mostly, she felt that she received much-needed support:

> How shall I put it, Woman-to-Woman is something else entirely. It's like ... if I have a problem I can always contact them. They always respond. It's a very nonbusinesslike place ... And the course was really serious and high quality. I can appreciate it now, because I'm taking another course and it's not at all ...

Since her divorce some four years earlier, Shlomit has been the sole provider for her family. Her ex-husband paid no child support, yet he remained a high-maintenance factor. "What makes it difficult for me is the father of my kids, who takes up a lot of energy ... an extreme person who doesn't let go."

After her successful completion of the course, Shlomit was invited to enroll in EEW's business hothouse, where I met her again in 2007. The hothouse provided women who had profitable businesses with hands-on financial and business support, with the aim of helping them double their profits and become self-sustainable. Participants met periodically for a guided peer discussion of different aspects of their business operation, and were entitled to individual coaching and professional counseling on matters pertaining to each particular business. In one of the "business club" meetings that I observed, one of the participants, Neomy, also divorced, who had developed an educational tool that she was marketing to schools, shared her anxieties that people might steal her idea, which was original but easy enough to copy. Although she had received legal assistance in drafting a contract, she still felt very insecure and tried to convince the lawyer, who was present at that meeting, to conduct the negotiations on her behalf. During Neomy's passionate explanation about how badly she needed that support, Shlomit commented that it would have been much easier if she were married. An argument ensued. Two other participants, Nava, a divorced mother now living in cohabitation with a new partner, and Basma, who was married, insisted that their lot was not easier in the least. They too needed to make a living. Basma also reminded us that she was working primarily to pay off her husband's debts. Even Neomy herself admitted that her economic situation as a divorcee was better than when she was married, but she still agreed with Shlomit, saying that she felt very vulnerable and alone. Shlomit identified: "I feel exactly the same." Nava was not convinced. "I was here and there [read: I was married and now I'm divorced], and I can't see any significant difference." But Shlomit persisted: "I would give up my business any day if only I could find someone to support me."

Admittedly, I was flabbergasted when I heard Shlomit talk. After all, she was EEW's face of success. Coming from a lower-class Mizrahi Orthodox background, she now had word-perfect command of middle-class, New Age jargon. She also looked the part—slim and beautiful in her long, all-cotton fashionable gowns, which also made her a perfect fit for media coverage. Indeed, not only I but also some of her peers were uncomfortable with her declaration that she would give up her business any day if she could only find a man to support her. However, her statement, and Neomy's agreement, encapsulates a deep ambivalence that I later came to identify as central to women's approach to wage work: they consider it an important form of social participation and cherish the opportunity to have direct access to money, yet resent the idea of becoming primary breadwinners, and are quite content to continue leaving this burden to the men.

Following our scrutiny of the vulnerabilities of low-income women and the efforts to empower them, this chapter explores how the women themselves approach the idea of earning a living. A key component in the analysis is the cultural schema of the "gender contract," which underlies women's (and men's) understanding of the significance of paid work for their overall responsibilities, and deeper still for their identities. I delineate two versions of this general schema, which I term *family-centered* and *market-centered,* according to the dominant type of services used by households to care for their members and the respective repercussions of each type for women's labor. These two versions of the gender contract informed the ambitions and guided the strategic behaviors of the women who participated in this study. With some important variations, which largely also apply to the distinctions between Jews and Palestinians, in both versions the ideal modern woman is one who participates in paid employment but declines the role of main breadwinner or even equal wage earner. Instead, both versions of the gender contract, again with important distinctions as detailed below, direct women to channel their main efforts to domestic care work, and keep a paying job only as long as they feel that they can "balance" it with that. Implicit here is an expectation that their economic needs will be met by their male partners, and perhaps also by the state. However, the job insecurity and low income levels of the men with whom these women share their lives, the high rates of divorce particularly among Jews, and the rapid shrinking of the welfare state place these ideals of femininity beyond most of these women's reach. Keeping in mind these gaps between real and ideal, in this chapter we shall trace the ways in which women verbalize and act on these mental designs as they make concrete efforts to increase their earnings.

The ethnography is organized around three main aspects of the centrality of caregiving in the work of low-income women. I begin with women's initiatives to capitalize on their domestic care skills, either by trying to blend care or service jobs in their own homes with their unpaid domestic chores, or through partial, strategic venturing out while maintaining the domestic arena as the center of their labor. Next I look at some of the implications of the gender contract for women in the official workforce, as either employees or business owners. Here my focus is not on how the cultural schema affects their opportunities, wages, or status (topics well documented in the literature) but on how it affects their own subjective experiences, specifically their sense of entitlement, their determination, and their will to succeed. Lastly, the third section of the ethnography concentrates on the ways in which women talk about work. This section, which unlike the first two is primarily about Jewish women, documents a discourse saturated with emotional linguistic references.

Running like a thread throughout these practical and verbal approaches of women to income-generating work is a deep-seated sense of ambivalence. Clearly, Jewish and Palestinian women in Israel alike are keen to earn a wage. Most of them regard this as a must for a normative woman, who is ideally semi-independent and semisupported. At the same time, their past and present experiences as wage earners teach them that the image of the labor force as a place for personal growth and self-fulfillment is largely irrelevant for people in their class. This experience becomes embodied knowledge, which guides their constant strategizing along the domestic-public work continuum. As they navigate the tensions inherent in the schema of the gender contract—aggravated by the rapidly changing division of power between state, family, and the economy, they continuously fine-tune it.

Conceptualizing Gender Division of Labor: Contracts, Bargains, Scripts

Feminist approaches to the gender analysis of labor are commonly based on the following premises.[1]

A. Gender is a mechanism broader than the identities of the individuals who embody it. As a basic classificatory system, it is woven into the very fabric of institutional structures, from family through the state apparatus to the religious, educational, legal, and other social institutions, where it is inscribed in positions, roles, and relationships. Thus it acquires the cumulative effect of a regime—a system or ordered way of doing things. People move through social reality as gendered beings, and this marker is reflected back to them through the distribution of power, resources, prestige, and influence.

B. "Work," as a practice that has economic consequences, is neither limited to the official workforce nor measured solely by fiscal reward. It includes both monetary and nonmonetary activities, and occurs in diverse settings along a continuum of public, semipublic, and domestic spaces.

C. Work is gendered in several related respects: cultures the world over assign to women and men particular roles, which eventually become identified as feminine or masculine (such identification is contingent and may change over time). The gender identification of roles has an important, though not exclusive, bearing on their value, status, and prestige. And work is gendered also because the institutional settings in which it takes place are invariably gendered.

D. The split organization of work-life in late-modern capitalist economies creates value hierarchies between activities that are monetarily rewarded, and therefore deemed "productive work," and other activities, primarily care and maintenance conducted in the domestic sphere, which are viewed as "nonwork." In this respect, there are important variations on both the state and the world-system levels. In societies on the periphery of the world system, where subsistence economy still plays an important role, the framing of domestic labor as "nonwork" is largely immaterial. In industrial and postindustrial countries, by contrast, it has acute implications for ethnic minorities, work migrants, and lower classes.

E. Families are central to the organization of work. In their capacity as a main anchor of identity and bureaucratic governance, and as main resource-pooling and consumption units, they impact the full spectrum of work forms. Most family forms in the contemporary world capitalist system are patriarchal, important variations and exceptions notwithstanding. At the same time, they are not unilaterally oppressive to women and young people, but tend to have a dual supportive/oppressive character.

F. States are another central actor in the interaction of gender and work. Through their provision (or nonprovision) of care services, welfare benefits, and employment regulations, and through their regulation of the institution of the family, states play a critical role in the particular classification of economic activities along the work continuum.

G. Capitalist states are patriarchal. While scholars debate whether the term *patriarchy* remains adequate, considering the significant variety among modern states in the economic, legal, and symbolic position of women, they tend to agree that the institutional—and concomitantly the economic—domination of men remains universal and that states play an active role in this.

H. At the same time, gender relations are historically dynamic, marked by crisis tendencies and structural change. On the personal level, their distinctly embodied and performative qualities allow their ongoing interpretations, hence provide ample space for agency.

Within this basic conceptual framework, feminist scholars have offered several analytical terms for a grasp of the family/state regulated arrangements that reproduce men's economic prerogatives—"the patriarchal dividend" (Connell 1996)—and women's corresponding disadvantages. Researchers commonly take as their vantage point institutionalized heterosexuality, or the idea that women and men complement each other and therefore need to collaborate in accomplishing the tasks of procuring cash ("production"), caring ("reproduction"), and maintaining social status; and they grapple with the challenge of capturing the underlying structural forces that perpetuate gender hierarchies without oversimplifying the variations between and within class, ethnic, cultural, and political contexts. The task of generalizing without losing sight of the particular, and of delineating formidable structural forces without dismissing internal disharmonies, agentive capacities, and ultimately also change, has given rise to some debates concerning terminology, which I will not go into here except to mention that common terms include the male breadwinner/female caregiver *model* (Lewis 2001; Gottfried and O'Reilly 2002; Warren et al. 2009; Broomhill and Sharp 2005; Budig, Misra, and Boeckmann 2012), the gender/patriarchal *contract* (Moghadam 1998; Gottfried 2000, 2013; Olmsted 2005; Sa'ar 2009b; Goldstein-Gidoni 2012), gender or reproductive *bargains* (Kandiyoti 1988; Sen 1990; Blumberg 1991; Sa'ar 2005; Gottfried 2013), or kin-scripts, scenarios, and strategies (Stack and Burton 1993; Singerman and Hoodfar 1996).

For the purpose of this chapter, I have chosen to talk about gender contracts, by which I refer to the cultural schemas that frame women's and men's expectations regarding gender and work, and the institutionalized valuations of their respective contributions. Gender contracts are influenced by institutional arrangements—notably families, religious courts, and state policies—market forces, and long-standing cultural norms that combine to form an overall social system that, following Sylvia Walby (2004), may be called a "gender regime."[2] Such regimes are plural and dynamic, and so are the cultural schemas that translate them into meaningful and actionable knowledge (the gender contracts). By identifying those that operate in Israel, my aim is to trace the underlying blueprint with which the women who participated in this study approach the task of generating income through their work.

Israeli Gender Regimes and Gender Contracts

Inspired by the works of Connell and Walby, I define "gender regime" as an overall system in which gender is a central, though never isolated, principle of social and symbolic organization of production, reproduction, identities, relationships, and entitlements. Complex societies commonly have multiple gender regimes, which are in an ongoing state of transformation from domestic-centered to public-centered. Walby (2004) outlines three main types of gender regimes for industrial and postindustrial countries, all public-centered: market-led, welfare state-led, and regulatory polity-led. These generic titles yield particular variations, which are corollaries of social policies, economic restructuring, legislative efforts, and the position of particular groups in the overall structure of inequalities.

In Israel, the dominant form of gender regime among the majority Jewish population is currently in a state of transformation from a welfare state-led to a market-led form. From very early on Jewish women enjoyed a bundle of important civil, labor, and social rights. These were reflected in high levels of workforce participation, albeit not matched by economic and political equality. With the transformation to a market-led gender regime, Jewish women gained new opportunities for employment and political participation, but also experienced growing vulnerabilities. Notably, a regulatory polity-led gender regime has operated alongside the market-led one, taking the form of gender-specific legislation and court rulings on issues of personal status, taxation, employment contracts, and the like. Over the past two decades or so, the legislative policy-making apparatus has been utilized extensively by local civil society organizations, often working in collaboration with individual Knesset members, as well as by supranational bodies such as the European Union or the United Nations, which exert outside pressure on the state to conform to international platforms of human and women's rights.

Among the Palestinian citizens, who as detailed in Chapter 1 were largely excluded from the state welfare system during the first decades of Israeli statehood, the gender regime remained predominantly domestic-centered with very low levels of female workforce and political participation, and a much smaller-scale public-centered version among the better-educated groups that did manage to integrate into the public sector. Over the past twenty-odd years, with galloping privatization of the economy, Israeli Palestinians have experienced strong pressures to shift directly to a market-led gender regime. In contrast to the Jewish-Israelis, for the Palestinians this process was not facilitated by a period of a welfare state-led public-centered regime. Also, the overall weakness of the enclave economy means a much more volatile and potentially more aggressive process of transition. Among other things, the forming market-led gender regime has entailed growing pressures—and desires—for fast integration of women into the official workforce, a process that alas holds out rather poor economic prospects for them. As we learn from comparative ethnographic case studies (e.g., Guyer 1988; Mencher 1988; Hoodfar 1988), a passage from subsistence to a cash economy not mediated by state-led protection mechanisms tends to have an adverse effect on women's economic well-being: as they lose their traditional access to production, they have very little hope of compensation through the market; this in turn makes them much more dependent on men, and in all likelihood impoverishes them. One important mitigating factor in this gloomy prospect is the regulatory polity-led gender regime mentioned above. Palestinian feminist groups have worked quite skillfully, utilizing coalition work, lobbying, and soliciting international bodies to promote affirmative action and other protective mechanisms (e.g., WGSPWCI 2005).

Within this institutional and political setting, my focus in this chapter is the process by which low-income women interpret their opportunities and act on these understandings. My working assumption is that such an interpretation, as a mental process, is meditated by the cultural schema of gender contract, which articulates the practical meanings—the claims and responsibilities—of being a normative woman. Two main versions of the gender contract emerged as central to the women in this study. I call them family-centered and market-centered, to represent the level of dependency of households on market-based care services. Both are class-specific (they do not represent the more affluent sections of the society), but are distributed differently among Jewish and Palestinian women. The family-centered gender contract is based on heterosexual domestic units with stable and complementary gender roles. These units are often embedded in extended families, which play an important role in their economy and social lives. Men are the primary breadwinners and are categorically exempt from domestic care labor; women are the primary caretakers and occasional wage earners when their domestic responsibilities allow. In the market-centered gender contract, the norm remains one of heterosexual domestic units but allows more diversity in household types (including single-sex dual-parent, single-parent, or shared parenthood with two separate households). Extended families play a much smaller role in the economy of nuclear households, although they do not stop being relevant altogether. Men and women alike are wage earners, and both incomes are important to the household economy. Women remain the primary managers, but not the sole performers of care work, which is instead delegated to the semiformal, low-paid work of other women. Men perform domestic labor partially and inconsistently. The market-centered gender contract enhances the chances of women in the official workforce, as it loosens their bond to domesticity. However, in times of crisis, or if they fail to find substitutes, they are expected to prioritize the domestic over the public work roles.

These are (two of several) ideal types that are culturally relevant among Jews and Palestinians in Israel. As we shall see in the ethnography, the actual, lived arrangements are more diverse and represent stopping points along a continuum between them. To an important degree, these and the remaining gender contracts feed on each other, because when women enroll in the official workforce they rely primarily on the work of other women, the low cost of which is maintained by the image that it is temporary and semivoluntary, because they are essentially *not* working (Mohanty 1999). As Gottfried (2013: 125) put it, "The intervention of the market weakens the male breadwinner model while at the same time reinforcing class differences between families." This last point, then, underscores the relevance of gender contracts not only for men's and women's expectations and strategies, but also for their respective opportunities—their earning levels, their bargaining power, the penalties they will pay for being mothers but not for being fathers, and their overall susceptibility or privilege.

The Economic Value of Domestic Work and Women's Attempts to Turn Care into Cash

> At first they thought that the woman eats at their expense. They didn't know how tired she gets during the day. By the way, I sometimes say, when a Jewish woman asks me what I do for a living, I say I'm a housewife. But in reality, if you bring in someone to clean, and someone to cook, and someone to raise your daughter, it adds up to more than 5,000 shekels. I did want to work at some point. My sister-in-law said to me, "Come and join me in the [packing] factory. You'll earn," she said. But my husband didn't want me to. He said to me, "You're raising our children is as if you have brought me a wage of 5,000 shekels and put it right here on the table. I don't want you to bring in money." He knows that if I'm not at home ... One day I had to go to the hospital and when I got back the house was a total mess ...
>
> They think that only she who brings in money works. No. She who sits at home also brings in money. You can manage your home so that ... you could bring in money and then spend it all, but if you sit at home you spend less, right? You don't

> go to the market every day. You don't buy things that you don't need. The money that you save is a wage that you bring in to your husband while you sit at home. It's called management. (Kawthar Sawa'id, married mother of three in her thirties; interviewed by Nisreen Mazzawi in 2010 as part of the Bedouin Village Study.)

Feminists' demand to acknowledge the economic value of domestic labor is longstanding (Oakley 1974; Folbre 1991). It dates back to the mid-nineteenth century (Berkovitch 1997), in fact very soon after the initial invention of the "housewife" as an ostensibly nonworking person. This has been an uphill battle, albeit with some significant victories, as popular and scholarly opinions alike continue to consider women who are not in the workforce as "not working." In this respect Kawthar's lucid self-awareness is striking. Yet despite similar glimpses among a few other Palestinian and Jewish women, for most of the participants in this study this would be only a half-convincing argument. The fact that Kawthar's opinion was not shared by everyone in her surroundings may be deduced from her argumentative tone (they think that the woman eats at their expense, they don't know how hard she works) and from her own use of the phrase "sits at home" for women who are not in the official workforce. Also, despite these assertions, many of the interviewees had a dire need for cash, as Kawthar herself admits in other parts of her interview, as well as a strong desire to earn their own money.

The economic contribution of women's domestic work takes several forms. It saves expenditure, as we have seen in some of the examples in Chapter 3 when women related their calculated decision to drop out of the workforce and take care of their children. Besides this, women use their domestic skills as their default strategy for generating income. Almost all the women who participated in this research did that at one point or another, some taking on sporadic cleaning, caretaking, and cooking jobs when they really needed cash, others using these skills, particularly caretaking, as a more permanent occupation. In some cases women literally bring their paid work into the home, preparing produce for sale, taking in mending jobs, or using some of the space to receive customers or children for care. Often, such choices, which seem perfect at first, because they allow the women to be home for their children and to economize at the same time, prove quite problematic. They almost invariably intensify the women's labor, since their children and spouses (sometimes also their extended families) expect them to be available as if caring for them were their only responsibility. Another common adverse effect is devaluation of their work in the customers' eyes. As one home-based hairdresser put it, "They expect me to give them coffee and sweets, they sit there for a long time, and on top of that they want to pay less than in a proper hair salon."

The ambiguity that occurs in such situations brings to the fore a more general problematic of the dual domestic-public nature of women's labor. I cite here two ethnographic cases to represent some of this complexity. The first illustrates a strategy of limited and selective engagement in income-generating activities inside and outside the home. By this strategy women seize and even actively seek out opportunities to earn money, but consciously refrain from becoming full-time wage earners. In the second case women use their homes to provide daycare services as a form of long-lasting, sustainable occupation. These cases offer a glimpse into the delicate maneuverings that are needed at the interface between care and cash, the rewards, the costs, the risks, and the built-in contradictions.

Convenient and Partial Engagements in Income-Generating Activities

Jeanette Haddad, a Christian Palestinian married mother of four, was forty-six when I met her in an economic empowerment course in Haifa in 2003. One of the more outgoing and successful participants of that project, Jeanette opened a small confectionery shop shortly after the beginning of the course. She rented a vacant space in a busy commercial district and the impression she gave in her weekly reports to the group was that she had hit a good niche. Sales were good. She had many Jewish customers who liked her merchandise, and benefitted from the fact that no other business in the neighborhood sold these products. After a few months she even asked for, and received, a small loan to buy a cash register. Then suddenly, just a week after her loan came through, she announced at the group's meeting that she had closed the shop down. She sold the merchandise to one of the other women and used the loan to cover her overdraft. To the dismayed queries of her colleagues and the business instructor, who had been her personal coach throughout this enterprise, she explained passionately that for the last two months there had been a slowdown and she was getting overdrawn and using her own money to keep the business afloat. April in particular had been bad: her products were non-Passover kosher, so the Jewish customers suddenly stopped coming. She concluded that the business was not tenable and decided to pull out before she got into worse financial trouble. To the business instructor's irate exclamations that she should have at least consulted her, and that it was a breach of confidence as the organization had given her a loan to develop the business, Jeanette insisted that she had not deceived them, since she herself did not know that she would close down. "One evening I simply told everyone that tomorrow I'd close the shop, and that's how it was. No one could talk me out of it." When asked what she planned to do next, Jeanette said, "Stay home and not go out again."

In a personal interview with Jeanette a few months earlier, she told me that she had been trained as a hairdresser and that she had a small hair salon at home for nearly twenty years. Her main clientele was a group of families from a nearby high rise, who would come to her regularly, mothers and their daughters together. These women eventually moved out and she was not getting new clients. At that time a relative told her about the vacant store at the market, and this seemed like a perfect opportunity to move on to something new. In the interview, as well as during the group meetings, Jeanette repeatedly emphasized how empowering it was for her to be out of the house, and how this alone was worth the low turnover. "Now that I've gotten out of the house," she said, "I feel that my work has value, and so do others."

In her presentation of self, Jeanette was a highly resourceful woman. Throughout her married life it was she who led the way in all the major economic decisions. She orchestrated the purchase of her and her husband's apartment, and she planned, financed, and oversaw its renovation, which took several years. Her way of managing exceptional expenses was through short-term loans and exchange transactions with neighbors and relatives. She used this method continuously, never remaining in debt for more than a few weeks, and as far as possible not taking loans from the bank. Also, she had been very creative in ideas on how to make a living, for herself and her relatives. She always kept an eye on the market, following trends to forecast future business directions. While her husband was the main and steady breadwinner of the family, her income provided the additional sums that allowed them to move forward—to purchase and renovate the apartment, pay for the children's tuition, and even take a trip to the United States. Two repeated motifs in Jeanette's narrative were her centrality in her household's economic functioning and the sharp and decisive fashion of her decision making. "My husband is afraid to make decisions about big expenses. I've always been the one taking those decisions, even when it wasn't clear that we would be able to finance them. And I always managed. I've always paid my debts." After she closed down the market stall Jeanette said, "I never expected to become a millionaire. I told my husband that my goal was to earn a woman's salary, something in the neighborhood of 2,800 shekels [US$750]."

Jeanette is a *qawiyyi* (Arabic, "strong woman"), a common female type in Palestinian-Israeli culture. As I show in my previous work on this discourse of gender propriety (Sa'ar 2006b), a woman likely to earn the title *qawiyyi* is a savvy, strategizing actor with an assertive personality and strong will, who knows how to stand on her own, to maximize her resources, and to survive harsh circumstances with honor. She never flags in resisting attempts of other people, especially her male relatives, to control her and put her down. Yet she is not what local people would call in dismay a "feminist." A *qawiyyi* derives her prestige first and foremost from her excellent performance in a wide range of feminine roles, and from her ability to maneuver optimally domestic and public responsibilities. As a woman who is *qawiyyi,* Jeanette derives her prestige from her capacity to keep her resourcefulness within the limits of good taste and not to upset the balance of her gender relations. So while her statement that she now wanted to stay home and not go out again may have indicated discouragement, it could also be interpreted as the proud statement of a woman pleased that she can afford to stay away from the job market.

Like all ethnographic illustrations, this particular example is both representative and nonrepresentative of low-income women's approach to the idea of earning a living. For one thing, Jeanette was not a woman in acute financial distress. More accurately described as lower-middle income, she was contentedly married to an employed man; they owned their apartment, they managed to send all their children to private schools and, as of the time of the interview, her eldest son was attending law school. As a Palestinian she benefitted from living close to her extended family and from the close-knit exchange network that it operated. At the same time, the employment and schooling opportunities available to her and her family were limited from the outset. For example, the reason she and her husband sent their children to private schools was the notoriously poor quality of the Arabic-language public schools. But in other respects her story resonates with topics recurrent in the experience of many of the women who participated in this study, Palestinian and Jewish. They include combining formal and informal economic activities, shifting their efforts back and forth between the domestic and the public work spheres, pooling resources, exercising economic creativity, and, notably, cherishing (or yearning for) the option of a home in which, if necessary, they could "stay ... and not go out again."

The Union of Home-Based Early Childhood Caregivers

Probably the most emblematic incidence of "cashing in" on domestic care work is when women turn their own homes into daycare facilities for other women's children. The following case, the unionization of home-based caregivers, offers a striking example of the multiple contradictions inherent at the interface of "work" and "care." In Israel, compulsory public education for children begins at the age of three. Institutional arrangements for younger babies and toddlers are therefore predominantly market-based. In 2004, 63 percent of Jewish mothers used such services. The rest either dedicated themselves full time to the unpaid care of their children (27 percent) or assigned this task to unpaid female relatives so that they themselves might engage in part-time employment. The figures are very different for Palestinian women who, as explained in previous chapters, are much more limited in their financial means and have much less access to quality daycare services. In that year, the vast majority (70 percent) of Palestinian mothers of infants and toddlers were full-time caretakers of their children and not otherwise employed. About 13 percent were employed, relying on unpaid female relatives to look after their children, and only 16 percent used market solutions (Ron and Ronen 2005).

Private institutions are not systematically regulated. Some carry an approval tag from the Ministry of Industry, Trade, and Labor (MITL), indicating that they have been inspected and meet its standards. Others, catering to about 19 percent of babies and toddlers nationwide, are actively supervised and partially subsidized by the MITL. These institutions are of two types. The *ma'on yom* (day crèche—plural *me'onot yom*) operates in public facilities and employs several caretakers, each with up to a few dozen babies and toddlers. There were about 1,700 such institutions in 2008. The *mishpahton* (plural *mishpahtonim*), a Hebrew neologism combining the words for family and crèche, are much smaller, home-based daycare services, each catering to up to five babies. In 2008 they numbered approximately 3,000 (Fried, Harris, and Fichtelberg-Barmats 2009). The women who run the *mishpahtonim* are the protagonists of the story related here. Before I tell it, I should mention that the children who enroll in *mishpahtonim* are divided into "work children" (the majority), whose mothers are employed, and "welfare children" (the MITL term), whose mothers are registered with the welfare bureau. The lion's share of tuition for the latter category is covered by the MITL: the ministry remits the money to the welfare bureaus in the local municipalities. These pass it on to the caretakers after ascertaining that their homes meet the required standards and that the regulated menu and the safety rules are followed.

In 2003 the Israeli government decided to move the "Woman's Status Section, *Me'onot* and *Mishpahtonim*" from the Welfare and Labor Ministry to the new Ministry of Industry, Trade, and Labor, which undertook to increase the number of institutions as a way of encouraging more women to join the labor force. As a secondary gain, this policy also encouraged more women to turn their homes into *mishpahtonim* and realize what seemed like a low-cost, convenient venue for business entrepreneurship. But a few years into the implementation of this initiative, the operators of the services, usually residents of low-income neighborhoods, found themselves caught between a rock and a hard place: they discovered that they were not making any profit and sometimes were actually losing money. They had invested considerable sums in preparing their houses to meet the strict regulations and were constantly required by inspectors from the municipal welfare bureaus to update their menus and equipment. Yet the fees, which were determined according to the parents' income level and over which the caregivers had no control, were never updated; so with the rising cost of living the caregivers' income declined to a level below the minimum wage (Schwartz 2009). To make matters worse, the local municipalities regularly withheld remittance of the fees, so caregivers would go for months on end with no income while working full time and paying for food, electricity, and insurance. This situation turned their profit—low to begin with, and reduced still lower because the fees were not updated—into an actual deficit. In 2009 a group of caregivers decided to unionize. The following description is based the work of Yael Shostak-Pascal (2011), an anthropology student and social activist, who followed and documented this struggle.

The first attempt by caregivers to address their predicament had been in 1996, when a group of them sued the Jerusalem municipality for withholding their money. That appeal was rejected on the grounds that they were not bound to the municipality by an employer-employee relationship. Six years later the feminist organization Kayan (Arabic: existence) began an empowerment project with Palestinian *mishpahtonim* owners who found themselves in a double bind, as the pernicious withholding of their money by the municipalities was augmented by the endemic nonpayment of that part of the fees due directly from the parents. In 2008 a group of caregivers, led by two ultra-Orthodox Jewish women from Bnei Brak, applied to the Histadrut to help them unionize, but they were turned down on the grounds that their occupational status was not clear. At last, in 2009 they managed to unionize with the assistance of Koach La'ovdim (Hebrew, "power to the workers," mentioned in Chapter 3). Three years later the union had 2,000 members, amounting to about two thirds of *mishpahtonim* owners. They included Jews and Arabs, secular and ultra-Orthodox, and they came from diverse localities around the country. They demonstrated, held conferences, launched media campaigns, and got themselves invited to attend deliberations of several Knesset committees. In late 2011 they registered a raise of 8.5 percent in their fees. By 2012 they had succeeded in obtaining official exemption from VAT; their union continues to struggle to secure their pension rights.

Despite the innovative nature of the home-based caregivers' struggle and its important implications for social economy—this group was among Koach La'ovdim's first clients and is one of the buds of the 2011 social protest—their situation is a salient example of the vulnerability of low-income women's work. The liminal character of the *mishpahton*—a business that is also a home, and whose owner is also an exploited worker—directs the spotlight at the very heart of its volatile and contradictory nature: the *mishpahton* allows women to do work they feel that they are good at with very little—and affordable—official training. Many women find this rewarding, but also exhausting. Working with "welfare children" gives some of the women a sense of moral calling, and reassures them of the value of their own knowledge and experience. But it also disempowers them since welfare parents are usually nonpaying clients. The location of the daycare right inside their homes allows the women to "be there" for their families, which presumably eases the tension and the guilt of so many who work outside their homes. Yet it greatly intensifies their work, as it does not allow them to take a break from their domestic chores. Home-based *mishpahtonim* allow women to be their own boss, and do the job with very little investments and financial risk. But they cannot set their own prices, collect their fees, change suppliers, or even pick and choose their customers. Last but not least, turning their care work into an economic pursuit may yield contradictory effects, bringing its economic value to the fore but also reinforcing its taken-for-granted image.

In the following first four excerpts from Yael Shostak-Pascal's interviews with the leaders of the struggle, caregivers highlight the benefits of having a *mishpahton*.

> Maysa, a Muslim from a town in Galilee: Our financial situation was really bad. My husband works for the municipality and he didn't get his wages for six months. We have a mortgage to pay and expenses. Today it's not enough to have one breadwinner. I too had to start working. I looked for something immediate ... I didn't have a high school certificate. I signed up for a caregivers' course with the MITL. There was no tuition. I just had to commit to work for a minimum of two years. Then all the problems started [withholding tuition transfers].
>
> Pnina, an ultra-Orthodox Jew from Bnei-Brak: I opened twelve years ago. I had worked for nine years as an accountant in a big company with more than 100 employees. I left temporarily after I had my fourth child but returned when he was two. I put him in daycare until 4 pm. One day he told me, "Mummy, all the kids have a mom except me." My heart sank. I went to my boss and asked if I could work less and go home earlier, but he wouldn't agree to that. There are plenty of moms here and they manage, he said. I told him that my case was special. He was my baby and he was sad. I could see it on his face that he needed me ... So I quit and the child was happy. I told a friend of mine that I had quit my job and she suggested that I take a caregivers' course. So I did, and eight months later I opened my mishpahton.
>
> Rose, a Christian from Haifa: My problem is that I love my work. This is what's keeping me. I'm actually a cosmetician and a hairdresser. I worked at that for two years. I still do private visits on Fridays when the mishpahton isn't open. We have to. I've got three kids, my husband is self-employed. It's true that we own this house and don't have a mortgage, but each with their lot. And as far as I'm concerned, working with children is best.
>
> Rima, a Druze from Daliat al-Karmel: I'm lucky that my kids like children. Every year we get enthusiastic with the new babies. Even my big boy, and I thought that him being a teenager ... But they are really fine with it. Sometimes I feel as if the babies' biological parents are taking them away from me after two–three years. I'm with them eight hours a day. They become part of the family. My husband is off on Sundays, so once a week he follows their development. He says to me, "This one has new words ... that one does that ..." Also my daughter, when she comes home I tell her "go play with your friends," but she says, "I want to put on his shoes, I want to comb her hair." My kids grow up knowing that there are children in the house. It's not like guests who come for two hours, make a mess and go. My kid can't go past them and not pay attention. He goes in, plays with them ... You know, we decided that we'd only have two kids, but they're growing up in a larger group. Today, with Internet and the computer ... The good thing about the *mishpahton* is that your kids get to know other kids. And we work with welfare

kids. Our children see things that they've never seen. Kids with no clothes, torn shoes. I can tell them that these things exist, but they see it in their own home. They develop compassion.

Other parts of the women's narratives, however, complicate the picture, as women point out the tiresome exercise of drawing and redrawing of boundaries between the *mishpahton* and the home, and between their own "work" and "rest," and the encroachment on the family's privacy.

> Lea, an ultra-Orthodox Jewish caregiver: I've been doing this for nearly eleven years. I was a teacher for four–five years but because I had many kids one after the next—I have eleven children, now aged thirteen to thirty-two—this arrangement was better for me, to take care of babies and also keep one of mine with me. Even though in our sector working women are an ideal, for me it was hard.
> Yael: How did your own children react?
> Lea: My oldest daughter was eleven at the time, so [she reacted] according to her understanding at that age ... At first it was fun, mom who had been out, suddenly returned. But the house turns into a workplace. The advantage is that mom can welcome them when they come home. This is so good, to serve them lunch. We tried to focus on the good part. It was a decision that we made. Not all of them liked it. There was one boy who reacted badly. He was with me along with the other babies but he wanted me all for himself. So we thought about it, my husband and I, and got him out [placed him in another daycare]. The inspector was also involved. She came and observed. The first year with your own baby it's possible, but after that I don't believe that it doesn't disrupt things.
>
> Hiba, a Muslim, from a village in Wadi 'Ara (near the coastal plain): This is not an easy job. I rise at 5 am to cook, tidy up, and clean, then around 7–7:30 I start receiving the children. I give them breakfast, then some games, a nap and then lunch, fruit, vegetables, smoothies, the lot. Like that until around 2 or 2:30 pm. The stuff that I use for the *mishpahton*, I needed to buy everything ... I usually go without payment for periods of two to five months, because it takes time until they transfer our money. And when the local municipalities are having financial difficulties it takes even longer.
> Yael: So why do you continue operating the *mishpahton* and not choose another line of work?
> Hiba (smiling but sharp and decisive): It's like, I can't stop. I love my work. I fill up my time so as to feel that I'm doing something; that I'm alive, not waiting for handouts from my husband. I feel that I'm helping people and doing for my own soul.
> Yael: Till when do you plan to keep going?
> Hiba: I'll go on till I'm old. I'm not thinking of stopping anytime soon. I also don't have any other place that I can work in. There are no jobs in the village.
>
> Rose: This was my kids' room. Now I've moved all three of them to one room. Two girls and a boy, [although] they already want their privacy. They're big, adolescents. In the summer vacation there's a lot of noise and mess here. And

they want their privacy when they bring friends home. But they [the babies] are already part of the family. My husband takes five-minute breaks in the middle of the day and comes in to play with them. The girls [aged fourteen and sixteen] help me change their diapers. In the summer vacation they're with me all the time. It's *keif* [Arabic and Hebrew, "fun"].

Although the arrangement with the MITL is convenient in that it guarantees customers, and possibly a steady income as well, "welfare children" are usually bad-paying and high-maintenance clients, which creates yet another contradictory effect: caregiving stimulates caregivers' generosity, even altruism, but it also makes them vulnerable. It likewise blurs the boundaries between a business enterprise and a charity.

Hiba described a discussion about the payments problem that she and her partners held with the head of the *me'onot* and *mishpahtonim* section in the MITL; the latter told them not to admit children whose parents did not pay their part of the fee:

I explained the situation to her. Some parents need to pay 211 shekels [about US$55 per month], but most of them pay nothing because they don't have it. In the Arab sector this is the biggest problem. Parents don't pay and we end up paying out of our own pocket—ours and our husbands'. I explained to her that if I don't admit these kids they'll be roaming the streets. They won't be at home with their parents, and they'll end up drug addicts and thieves. We do a lot for these kids. We have birthday parties for them. We bake a cake and have a party, bring a present. A kid has a right to live, even if his parents are like that.

And Rose:

The welfare parents are the most difficult. Some kids need clinical treatment. This girl, for example, has a sideways view and the parents still have not taken care of it. That one over there [pointing at a baby who wanted to play with me, touch me, and sit on me from the moment I entered the room—Y.S.-P.], she's already gotten attached [said in a sad voice] ... She has a great lack in love and warmth, so she searches for it from others. She was born out of wedlock. Her mom is from Tel Aviv and she brought her here so that she wouldn't be killed. You know our mentality ... There were days when others came to fetch her. I had days when she stayed here overnight. Now the mom too has moved to Haifa. I also had a boy who used to choke in his sleep. The mother asked me, "Is this unusual?" So I went with her to do medical tests. In this neighborhood, Heaven help us, there are lots of single moms, drug addicts, that kind of thing; mothers as young as fifteen or sixteen. With them I also do home visits. They have no family. They get pulled into prostitution. They don't know how to dress the babies. I go to their homes and teach them basic things ... But all in all, I have a good relationship with the parents. Really strong. There's one girl whose mom calls me mamma to this day. Or that woman that you saw on your way up, she has tears in her eyes when she talks about the relationship that her daughter had with me ...

Spillover Effects of Women-as-Caregivers in the Official Work Sphere

The implications of the gender contract in the official work sphere are discussed in the literature at length.[3] Men have enjoyed a masculine dividend (Connell 1996) that affords them better jobs, better wages, and better and faster mobility. Their sweeping exemption from domestic labor allows them to stay at the workplace for long hours and arrive there regularly, all year round and for years on end, without letting the awkward sides of family life—sick or needy children, school vacations, short school days, homework tutorials, ailing elderly parents, etc.—interfere with their job performance. Women in the work force, by contrast, continue to juggle the double shift. Their participation remains conditioned on "their" ability to find and afford substitutes for care and home maintenance, and their job performance is subject to irregularities due to unexpected—but inevitable—loopholes in the system of care substitutes. The cumbersome passages and the mismatching timelines between the nonpaid and paid work spheres (the missing two months in the summer, the missing two hours in the morning and the afternoon) impose sanctions on women at both ends of the work continuum. At home they face complaints that they are neglectful, not nice, bad homemakers, and worst of all bad mothers. In the paid workplace they are framed as unreliable or hopelessly constrained, which affects conventional ideas about their appropriate rewards and hurts their chances of promotion. They are penalized, that is, for both being mothers and for not being good enough at it. This catch-22, moreover, is much more acute in the case of women on the social peripheries, who have far fewer means to compensate for their gender disadvantage. I presented some of the implications of this multilayered marginality in Chapter 2 (Vulnerability). Here I focus on its more subtle and *internalized* aspects.

Women Want to Work "for Their Own Sake": Dreams, Reality, and Self-Doubt

One intriguing finding, which ran like a golden thread throughout my interviews and observations, was that nearly all the women who participated in this research were keen to become employed, structural barriers and low salaries notwithstanding. More than they wanted money, which they did, they wanted to have a job "for themselves," as many would put it. No matter how destitute, women felt strongly that proper participation in the workforce was important for reasons beyond wages. They regarded it as critical for their self-fulfillment, sense of worth, growth, and well-being. Somewhat surprisingly, the cumulative experiences of low pay, frequent redundancies, maltreatment, exhaustion, and a deluge of criticism did not seem to weaken these expectations.

Ayala: Personally I say [that I want to get a job] so that I can feel that I'm worth something. To feel that yes, something could come out of me. Because I've never felt that. And I received ... I sustained much humiliation because of that ... People spit words at me ... I don't want to repeat them. There's someone from my family that snarls at me every so often, "What, you aren't working? Go get a job ..." You know? And it has made me angry. I feel like, "What, my working in my own household doesn't count? The fact that I'm bringing up three children, that doesn't count?" You see, this is something that I've decided with myself that yes, I want to feel something. And [I'm doing it] for myself, not for anyone else. Just for myself, to prove to myself, not to other people. For my own sake. (Ayala Cohen, forty, separated mother of three, was interviewed by Ya'ara Buksbaum in 2006 as part of the Mahut Center study. Cited also in Chapter 2.)

Latife: I want to work ... well first of all for my own sake and also because of our economic situation, which has become really difficult. But I really want to work for my own sake.
Noor: What do you mean by that?
Latife: I want to change my mood, and my personality will change from within. I want to get out. Don't want to stay sitting all day within four walls with the door closed. I'm not going to work primarily for the money. I want it because I want to change the atmosphere. [Then] the way I interact will also change. A woman [who works]—her mind opens up. She learns to think better. When you stay sitting behind closed doors, what do you have to think about? Your mind closes too.
Noor: You mean to say that you want to see the world [see people, be in society]?
Latife: Not like that. You interact with people, you interact with children [Latife wanted to be a kindergarten assistant]. You have something to get up for in the morning. You get dressed and put on makeup so as to get out of the house. (Latife Khouri, forty-two. Palestinian Christian from Nazareth, married and mother of four, was interviewed by Noor Fallah in 2010 as part of the Atida project.)

In reality, the dream of full-time, steady, and rewarding employment was beyond the reach of most of the women. This engendered an array of negative emotions, including anger, frustration, weariness, despair, depression ... and self-doubt. In contrast to anger and frustration, which may actually lead women to observe the injustice of their situation and the structural nature of their marginalization, self-doubt has the opposite effect. It reinforces the initial schema—the idea of the gender contract, which frames their paid employment as secondary if not wholly out of place. Ironically, this self-perpetuating mechanism is integral to the dynamic nature of the gender contract. In Israel today, Jewish and Palestinian women alike are not just allowed into the official workforce, they are explicitly expected to join it; and when they stay out of it "too long" they risk being stigmatized. With some variations, the ideal woman in both national groups is a happily married, caring mother, who also holds down a paying job and preferably an autonomous occupational identity. For a small group of educated, upper-middle-class women, who participate in the workforce *as if* it were not gendered, this is a viable possibility. However, the chain of social inequalities that supports this new ideal of femininity automatically places it beyond the reach of women on the social peripheries, on whose work its sustainability is founded. Unlike higher-income women, who are allowed to shed their domesticity when they step into the workforce—almost if not exactly like men—low-income women in the paid workforce are walking embodiments of domesticity. As such, their work is immediately devalued: it appears natural to expect them to work for very little or no pay, and it is more permissible to impinge on their bodily and moral integrity.

For many low-income women, the message that the workforce is not their rightful place therefore hits a sensitive spot. Not only do they appear to be fighting a losing battle, considering their unrealistic prospects of steady, gainful employment, but by insisting on staying in they risk losing femininity on the home turf as well. And this is just a shade too close and personal. So despite their true yearning to participate and realize the new ideal of self-supportive femininity, the old-fashioned patriarchal messages that they are better off at home resonate with their subtle but persistent sense of self-doubt.

Wage-Earners but Not Breadwinners: Fine-Tuning the Feminine Ideal

Low-income women evince a strong yearning to participate in paid employment combined with a powerful desire to remain exempt from the responsibility of breadwinning. Ideally, they would like to enjoy the benefits of independent earnings, of socializing with people outside their family, of concentrating their work in the marketplace, and of having a professional identity independent of and therefore more prestigious than their relational one. Most of them, however, dislike the idea of being the main breadwinners for their family. Beyond the fact that their prospects of actually earning "a family wage" (Schultz 2000), or as one of the women put it "a man's salary," are objectively very slight, being the primary, or worse yet the sole, breadwinner is experienced as a daunting and lonely position.

Women of course vary in the degree to which they lament the lost patriarchal promise of economic and social support. Age and ethnonationality are two major factors in such variations. Young women in their twenties and even early thirties commonly have high hopes of attaining the feminine ideal of being secondary breadwinners, who work for a salary but also have the privilege of retreating back home when things go wrong on the job-market front. These women usually expect to return to paid employment when conditions improve for them (their children become more independent; they find a better job), not taking into account that their temporary retreat is almost guaranteed to work against their better interests, that they are at high risk of divorce, or that their husbands are unlikely ever to make the desired "family wage." By their mid- or late thirties many are less romantic about the position of secondary providers, quite worn out by the endless financial struggle, and less preoccupied with dreams of ideal femininity. By then their quest for paid employment tends to be less sentimental and more reality-bound. As I show in a separate analysis (Sa'ar 2009b), those who divorce after having children and being married for several years usually continue to long for a steady heterosexual relationship, but their yearning shifts from economic security to an emotional partnership.

As for the ethnonational factor, reactions of Jewish and Palestinian women reflect different variations of the gender contract, on a continuum from family-centered to market-centered. Jewish low-income women are generally guided by a market-centered schema of a gender division of labor, whereby they expect to be wage earners, but not the main breadwinners. Most of the Jewish women who participated in this study had held a paying job since their late teens, continued to have one several years into their marriage, and even if they left work to stay home with their children, tended to take odd jobs to supplement the family income even before they tried to make a formal comeback. From about their mid- or late thirties, they commonly began to recognize the elusive nature of this feminine ideal. This was when marriages started to fall apart, and/or when the effects of both husbands' and wives' low and inconsistent earnings became more palpable. As this was happening in their lives, many lamented the lost ideal of a semi-independent, semisupported woman and continued to have secret hopes of relief through a new heterosexual partnership. On a separate level, however, they also made practical efforts to improve their own direct earnings.

Palestinian women too, generally seemed to prefer the market-centered gender contract (namely, to seek partial economic independence). Yet they were keener than the Jewish women to keep the path open to withdraw to the family-centered one. This meant that although they tried to secure paying jobs, they were more likely to desert them when they appeared to conflict with their domestic responsibilities. As mentioned, these women live under a gender regime that is in transition from domestic-centered to market-led public-centered. Under the domestic-centered gender regime, a predominantly family-based gender contract dictates a rather rigid division of labor. Men are the main providers of cash, yet women have relatively wide economic autonomy, since the household economy is not entirely cash-driven. This schema changes, however, with the transition to a market-led gender regime. Women are now expected to earn cash both as a direct economic necessity of their families and as a way to fulfill the new ideal of semi-independent modern femininity.[4] We met such women in Chapter 1 among the operators of the empowerment projects. Yet ironically, the conditions of the job market and the overall poverty of the Palestinian enclave economy are such that most women actually stand to lose rather than gain from this transition. Unless they are highly educated and married to middle-income men, their prospective independent earnings are very low; at the same time, reducing the scope of their domestic labor is likely to create adverse economic repercussions on their households, which will now have to purchase those goods and services in the market. While women may not be highly articulate about the pros and cons of the different strategies, their practical choices vividly reflect the ambiguity that accompanies this uncertain transition.

The Ethics of Love and Its Inherent Ironies

Like any effective power mechanism, the gender/ethnic/class/national complex that sustains the official work arena is sophisticatedly disguised through personalized scripts of participation. In the script that has emerged in the ethnography thus far women aspire to be semi-independent wage earners, who continue to enjoy the support of their male partners. I should note in passing, although this component was not documented here directly, that women—particularly the Jewish women and to a lesser degree also the Palestinian—also expect to enjoy the support of the state, through welfare benefits and child support. This section focuses on the ways in which women talk about their work in the empowerment workshops. When the participants in the study talked about paid work, in the workshops or in the personal interviews, they frequently used emotional language, chiefly the terms "love" and "giving." As I started to argue in the last chapter, the appeal to concepts such as love, emotional intelligence, or emotional energy in workforce narratives of mobility acts to depict the work sphere as inclusive. Low-income women respond positively to the language of care, which resonates with their domestic labor practices, and feel confident in their capacity to use it successfully in the public work sphere as well.

Fortuitously or not, the tendency to use an emotional discourse when talking about work was more prevalent among the Jewish than the Palestinian women, even though the Arabic-speaking workshops used a style generally similar to the Hebrew-speaking ones. Accordingly, this section focuses only on Jewish women, as opposed to the first two parts of this chapter, which presented Jewish and Palestinian women together. I postulate that this difference is related to the fact that the two groups are guided by different versions of the gender contract. In the case of the Palestinians, the family-centered gender contract represents a domestic sphere in which female labor is diverse and largely productive, as opposed to the market-centered gender contract, where "care" is already much more commodified, and concomitantly packaged as antithetic to "interest." I expect, though, that the rapid transformations in the

Palestinian-Israeli gender regime, and the pressures on Palestinian women to increase their labor force participation, will ultimately moderate the ways in which they too articulate their visions of work. Traces of such transformations are already discernible in the workshops. However, further ethnographic exploration will be necessary for more conclusive remarks.

A Discourse Saturated in Emotional Linguistic References

In the workshops, women tended to use affective terms generously, in reference to a broad range of topics: to define their business or financial targets, to describe their skills, to articulate their professional identity, to portray their vision of economic success, and more. While this style seemed to blend well with the general "emotional talk" popular in the empowerment scene, it also had some distinct features. The exceptional frequency with which the women used emotional terms was matched by consistent *avoidance* of explicit emotional references to money: they avoided expressing an overt desire to make money, and skirted the practicalities of pricing, calculating profits, or setting operative earning goals. When pressed to do so, they often evinced extreme discomfort and even intimidation. Of course, not all participants matched this characterization. Typical exceptions were traders, who tended to be practical and unapologetic in their evaluation of profits and financial interests; a handful of nontraders also showed no hesitation in talking about money. But these were a distinct minority.

The following excerpts, all representing characteristic episodes, were recorded during my six-month participant observation in a Hebrew-speaking business entrepreneurship course in Haifa in 2007–2008. They show the women's tendency to frame their discussions of earning, wage work, and entrepreneurship in a linguistic style replete with references to love, giving, and care.

Wrapping (Discussions of) Money in Love

The first two examples show the prevalent tendency, during this and similar courses that I observed up close, to open sessions with mental exercises that stimulated emotional and relational language, even about matters that were presumably strictly "business."

In one of a series of sessions on marketing, held in January 2008, lecturer Clara Yogev wrote on the board "The Product" as the topic for the day. Clara, who had migrated from the former Soviet Union in the late 1990s, was very fond of using her own entrepreneurship stories as lecture material. Shortly after she arrived in Israel, divorced and with two small children, she once told the group, she spent all the little she had on a load of cosmetic products for marketing. She recalled sitting at a bus stop with the suitcase full of products, anxiously asking herself, "Where do I start?" Then, about ten years later, there she was, a popular and accomplished business lecturer.... On that particular evening, as an opening for the discussion of their products, Clara asked the participants to think of something that they were proud of. In response, women came up with a list of personal qualities such as "love, softness, giving, and listening" (these terms recurred several times), or "my motherhood, trustworthiness, decisiveness, coping with stressful situations, coping with change, and wisdom." An hour or so later, during a game called "Thinking like a Zebra," Clara pulled out a bundle of cards with animal photos, and instructed the women to choose one randomly and then talk about their businesses through the image of the animal that they came up with. So a photo of a hamster evoked notions of storing and concentrating, a photo of a lizard "the ability to relinquish my tail, my existing knowledge, in order to grow and change." Then, when Rina Cohen, a divorced welfare recipient in her fifties, who worked as a caretaker of old people (a minimum-wage job sponsored by the National Insurance Institute), picked up a photo of a tick, she pondered, read the explanation on the card ("*Kartsiya* [Hebrew, "tick"], feeds on someone else's resources by way of receiving or giving without reward"), then concluded, "The tick represents my work through the quality of giving without asking for any reward."

The next example was recorded a few months earlier, during one of the opening sessions of that same course, which was dedicated to participants' expectations of the course.

The moderator, Sigal Ravid, was somewhat unusual in the scene of project operators. With no previous background in the NGO industry, she was a graduate of a previous business entrepreneurship course, who had chosen "empowerment," that is, working as a freelance moderator, as her line of business. True to its commitment to hire the services of low-income entrepreneurs, the NGO that ran that course decided to take her on to moderate its dynamic component, a job she held for three sessions before she was fired for incompatibility. At this session, Sigal asked each of the thirty participants to write down what she wanted to give and what she wanted to receive from the course, and then asked them to read aloud what they had written while she summarized the main points on the board. The final list on the board read as follows:

> To give: love, warmth, encouragement, consolation, honesty, a smile, friendly attitude, listening, complex insights, collaboration, mutual feedback, optimism, trust, openness, help, hugs, reinforcement, care, spontaneity, experience, thought, light, brainstorming, support, knowledge.
> To receive: a smile, business feedback, brainstorming, proportion, creativity, tools, support, a backrest, collaboration, light, happiness, direction, communication, trust, security, strength, help, knowledge, love, listening, safety net, reinforcement,

a hug, diversity, consolation, experience, business networking, a framework, the key to success.

As was clear from Sigal's comments, the women's answers fitted very well with what she had expected them to say. For example, when a participant said that she expected to give or receive "listening" or "support" Sigal would elaborate, saying "Let's think how we can say things without offending [the listener]. It's important to never say to someone, 'You're talking nonsense. . . .' We should always check with ourselves what it is that we're trying to achieve when we make a comment."

Certainly, other moderators I encountered in the field tended to be less one-dimensional than Sigal in their use of love-and-giving narratives during their sessions. Yet considering her background, her attempt to "talk the talk," awkwardly and ultimately failing, was quite characteristic of the projects' participants more generally (at least three participants said to Sigal at the end of that session, "Thank you for allowing me to dream!"). As I will try to show in the following pages, although their generous use of affective terms echoed the "life coaching" communication style that has become so prevalent in more affluent business environments, the participants' emotional talk had distinct characteristics, which reflected both their structural disempowerment and their potential agency.

Avoiding the Practicalities of Money

In December 2007, business lecturer Nira Bergman dedicated one of her sessions to analyzing the profitability of the women's businesses. She divided the class into groups of three or four, and instructed each business owner in every group to give a detailed account of her activities: income, expenses, investments, profits, losses, her pricing compared with the market, etc. Her partners in the group then had to calculate her net hourly profit, based on a formula that Nira had taught a week earlier. At the end of the exercise, each group shared its conclusions with the rest of the class. Of the six businesses that were analyzed, only one was found profitable: Mira Levy, a divorced cosmetician working out of her parents' apartment, reportedly made an hourly profit that was more than double the minimum wage. All others were earning much below the minimum wage, and none of them had been aware of how little profit she was making. In the most extreme case, a divorced retired practical nurse, who lived off a very low pension but had her own apartment, made 2.5 shekels per hour (the minimum hourly wage at the time was 20 shekels). Yet even Mira, it later turned out, was less market savvy than she depicted herself in class. A casual conversation I had a few weeks later with the director of one of the NGOs that co-sponsored the course revealed that Mira actually had serious difficulty setting a realistic price and charging for her services. That director had sent her daughter to Mira for an acne treatment that lasted ten appointments. Despite her repeated appeals, Mira refused to charge for her work, so the director made an independent calculation and gave her a check for 500 shekels. I found myself in a similar situation that same year, when I signed up my own daughter, then in first grade, for a weekly after-school nature activity. The teacher of that extracurricular activity, a married mother of four who worked part-time as a guide on school trips, was unable to state a price and give us a bill. A month or two after the beginning of the course, when she had not presented us with a bill, I started calling, texting, and approaching her directly, only to be met with an embarrassed smile and a "Sure, I know, I'll get round to it," which continued until the very end of the school year. She never did manage to present me or any of the other parents I asked with a bill, and it was left entirely to our discretion to decide how much to pay, if at all.

Women's unease with "thinking money" was consistent throughout my observations. When asked to present their business vision (a practice that recurred ritualistically in the two business-entrepreneurship courses that I observed in full), women typically dwelt on their wish to realize their productive potential and achieve self-fulfillment, and avoided stipulating an actual sum that they hoped to earn. This was not rare even among participants in the hothouse for active business owners, some of whom were visibly discomfited when requested to quantify their investments and measure them against their earnings. For example, Galit David, who ran a care service for dogs, said when pressed to admit that the expensive food she fed the dogs was making her lose money, "I really can't make such calculations. Everything I give these animals is out of love. I can't translate this into material measurements." For her and many others, the only indication of feasibility was if their businesses provided them with cash for their daily household needs. Galit, for example, knew that she was overdrawn but had no idea how much and admitted that she had not been to the bank for months. All she knew was "I have enough to go to the supermarket." Mira, the cosmetician, told me, "For years I was like an ATM machine. I'd step out of the treatments room and my children would ask me for money to buy this or that. I never kept a proper record of expenses against income, and I was never able to save or invest in the business." And Sagit Paz, an aspiring doula, said, "I came to this course to learn how to charge for something that's related to emotions."

Importantly, the jargon of love and uncalculating generosity also abounds in more affluent capitalist settings. Yet by a fine distinction that many workshop participants seem to miss, the declared preference in such settings to "talk about love, not money" really means *disguising* financial interests, not denying them. The following example was recorded in June 2008 at an open meeting of a company named Avel that does multilevel marketing of nutrition supplements. As mentioned in the previous chapter, several of the women who participated in the empowerment courses were drawn to invest in such programs (popularly referred to as pyramid schemes, although mostly denied as such). By the nature of the enterprise, they would try to convince anyone who listened to join in, so I too was invited to get a first-hand impression.

The moderator of the evening, who presented himself as "a coach and senior member of Avel," gave a brief and energetic talk to an audience of fifty-odd women and men on the affluence that awaited them if they decided to join in. He then invited several individuals to go up onto the stage and tell their success stories. Each of these men was presented as a dear personal friend; each opened by saying how happy he was to set aside everything and travel all the way to Haifa, for the sheer joy of responding to his friend's request and sharing his incredible experience. A typical speech went: "Hi, I'm Ruby, I'm Avel, and I love you all. I really love you … The incredible thing about this business is that money is just a byproduct. What we are doing here is creating a world that is better for us and for the coming generations." As they spoke, a video at the background showed romantic scenes of people gathering in a park, hugging or standing in circles, closing their eyes, and dancing to flute music.

A final related characteristic of women's mental approach to income-generating work, besides setting it in terms of affective exchange and their evident unease at translating this emotional investment into money, was their readiness to volunteer, inside and outside their official workplace. Typical on-the-job volunteering included staying overtime, performing chores that were beyond the official job description, or running personal errands for the employers. Such conduct, which was common among Jewish and Palestinian women alike, occurred mostly among employees of small businesses such as law or accountancy firms, small stores, private kindergartens, and the like. When they talked about it, women usually emphasized the trust and verbal appreciation that their willingness to give without asking for any material reward has earned them, their words echoing the generalized exchange that occurs in intimate but hierarchical settings such as families. Implicit in their accounts was the expectation that their effort would win them paternal protection, if not actual promotion and a salary raise. This, sadly, hardly ever happened. In one story after another, women who had assumed such an approach ended up receiving the standard treatment of nonstandard jobs: a narrow range for self-expression, no raise or promotion, arbitrary dismissal, and no protection whatsoever in times of crisis. The second kind of volunteering, not bound to an official job, was giving goods or services at no charge. One stark example is an ultra-Orthodox mother of ten who reported volunteering at instructing brides in the Halachic rules of family purity. Despite her pressing economic hardship, she did not charge for this service, which she was fully qualified to perform and for which other women reportedly took $200 per session. "It is such a beautiful *mitzva* (good deed) that I can't charge ... I might have been able to make a living by it, but I want to have merit in Heaven."

Learning Reflexivity

Amidst this general talk about love, and the anxiety-laden (or ostensibly greed-free) approach to money, a significant number of the workshops did try to guide women to a more market-shrewd use of emotional talk.

December 2007, an "empowerment session" with twenty-two participants moderated by Hila Ne'eman. Holder of a master's degree in organizational consultancy and a key figure in both the feminist and the social economy scenes, Hila had stepped into the role of empowerment moderator for the course after the dismissal of Sigal. That particular meeting was titled "Communication that Aims to Solve Problems," and the board presented a list of operative goals:

a. To be able to regard myself and the other positively. "I must remember at all times that I have a place and a value in this world," Hila explained as she read out the line.
b. To be aware of my negative emotions (anger, offense ...) in a situation that begs a solution. "To achieve that," Hila elaborated, "we need to learn to channel the energy of the interaction toward a solution without denying our negative emotions, but also without letting them take us over entirely."
c. Boundary maintenance. Problem-solving communication should be oriented to draw boundaries. "Some things, like a client being late for our appointment, can only be allowed to happen so many times."
d. To improve, to understand conflicts (advanced level).

"When negative emotions are involved," Hila said in her introduction, "it is crucially important to admit them but also to understand that their volume is not necessarily proportional to that particular incident, because our negative emotions feed on our history. We need to isolate the powerful roots of these emotions and not project onto the client who shows up late anger and insults that exceed the situation. We need to be able to identify the negative emotion, name it, and decide not to let it dominate our actions. If, for example, we are trying to draw boundaries, we aim to be able to do so firmly, but without letting all our historical humiliations interfere. I, as a business owner, need to keep in mind the best interest of my business."

I looked around the room as Hila presented the topic and noticed that the women seemed to be hypnotized by her authority. She appeared to touch them directly where it mattered. I too was immediately drawn in, thinking about my own turbulent emotions throughout the long and taxing process of my tenure review. Hila then described a situation (I'm waiting for a client and she's running very late) and invited the participants to come up with negative and positive emotions that such a situation stirred in them. Each woman was then asked to locate herself on a continuum from anger to abnegation. "If we seek to please at any price, ready to tolerate anything in order not to lose the client, this is counterproductive. Beneath this kind of communication there is paralysis, self-denial, and avoidance; we are passive and reactive, not proactive. Instead, we need to be able to communicate assertively, with a clear focus on solutions." Hila then wrote on the board a list of principles that comprise an assertive mode of communication:

- Focus on the style more than the content.
- Talk about yourself in a positive way. Do not abnegate, as most women would. Prepare a few ready-to-use key sentences that describe you and your professional capacity.
- Do not display overenthusiasm when others are talking.
- Do not go out of your way to convince.
- Do not give away your assets cheaply. They are valuable. Give 80–90% and never more than 100%."

From that point the session included a series of exercises and simulations intended to draw attention to the differences between dismissive and assertive communication. One of the exercises focused on stressful situations related to running a business: a seamstress who accepts a client who already owes her a large sum and needs to be assertive in collecting her debt; a hairdresser who gets a call from a client in the late evening hours, insisting on being taken at once.... Two women randomly chosen for each scenario had to play client and business owner. When Ricky Schwartz, an unmarried graphic designer in her forties, was called to play the hairdresser she said, as she walked toward the empty chair in the middle of the room, "This immediately makes me angry." Yet a few minutes later, when she had to answer the client's call, she giggled nervously and agreed to take her. In another exercise, which focused on body language, women were invited to stand in front of the class and talk about their business for three minutes while maintaining direct eye contact with the listeners. As the women presented, Hila drew attention to different aspects of their body language: "Note if you have a tendency to wear a compulsive smile—and avoid it; do not stray from your natural voice, don't let your pleasing or angry voice take over...." At one point it was Ilana Alon's turn to talk to the class. This 45-year-old divorced mother of two, a cosmetician who ran a nonprofitable home-based business and a longstanding client of the welfare bureau, was clearly unable to get into the exercise.

For one thing, she would not make eye contact, even with a single woman in the audience. At Hila's insistence Ilana said, "I can't make eye contact. It's too overwhelming for me, because when I look at someone I see straight into their *neshama* [Hebrew "soul"]."

Paradoxes of Low-Income Women's Emotional Discourse

These ethnographic excerpts open a window onto the ways low-income women respond to and appropriate the emotional discourse that has become highly popular in capitalist workforce environments. "Emotional discourse," write Lila Abu-Lughod and Catherine Lutz (1990: 12), "is a form of action that creates effects in the world, effects that are read in a culturally informed way by the audience for emotion talk." Taking this perspective, in the following analysis I focus on the complex interactions between the women's love-work talk and the work environments in which they operate; I look at the ways their talk "establishes, asserts, challenges, or reinforces power or status differences" (Abu-Lughod and Lutz 1990: 14). To start with the latter effects, in several respects the emotional talk of the women in the workshops appears to entrench their subordinate position. For one thing, although they clearly feel comfortable using the language of love-work, which echoes the type of labor they believe they do best, many of them do not manage very well the semantic transitions that occur in the passage from the domestic to the public work sphere. Despite a clear resonance with the neoliberal lingo of "work" as a domain that allows personal growth and self-realization, their emotional talk typically fails to project the air of success and sophistication found in more affluent settings. In real-life business or workforce environments, their tendency to avoid practical matters concerning money mostly weakens their bargaining power. Similarly, their apparent difficulty in handling confrontational relations or outright offensive emotions often works against their interests. If anything, their enthusiastic repetitions of expressions such as "care" and "giving" appear to underscore the stigmatic image of "the emotional female" (Lutz 1990).

Considering the structural position of the women in question in stratified reproduction (Colen 1995)—their location on the lowest-paying strata of the care and reproduction system—their emphatic self-presentation as unilateral givers, who resist quantifying their labor or making explicit the terms for its reward, appears self-defeating. They seem to mishandle, as it were, the transposition of the generosity code from the domestic, unpaid work environment to the paid, public work one, where the dominant code is one of negative exchange, the love jargon notwithstanding. This linguistic performance strengthens their cultural construction as "naturally domestic" and out of place in more formalized settings of economic exchange; therefore it appears self-deprecating. As William M. Reddy asserts (1999: 271), "A normative style of emotional management is a fundamental element of every political regime, of every cultural hegemony. Those who fail to conform may be marginalized or severely sanctioned."

However, emotional discourses have multidirectional effects. Recall, for example, the session in which Hila Ne'eman trained the women to improve their reflexive skills and refine their emotional expressions. On the one hand, this session may be read as a typical instance of "a rhetoric of emotional control" (Lutz 1990). In her study of white Americans' ways of talking about emotions, Lutz notes a deep-seated cultural belief that women are naturally more emotional than men and that their emotionality, much like their sexuality, is a dangerous energy that needs to be kept under control. Yet Hila's session—her direct style, and her reassurances of the women's value and capacities—may also be easily interpreted as a quintessential instance of feminist empowerment. Similarly, Lutz's study reveals that although their discourse was replete with metaphors of control, handling, and management, her interviewees regarded emotions as at once weakening and energizing. In this respect, I find useful Reddy's (1999) distinction between management and navigation of emotions. According to him, emotional claims ("It's too overwhelming," "I give out of love," "This makes me angry") are not really amenable to simple management because they are self-exploring and self-altering, and it is never certain what effect they will have. Reddy therefore suggests replacing the term "management" with "navigation," to communicate the possibility of emotional claims both radically changing course and making constant corrections in order to stay on a chosen course.

We may take the cases of Sigal Ravid and Ilana Alon as examples of the multidirectionality of emotional discourse and the uncertain effects of emotional claims. When Sigal chose "empowerment" as her line of work, she attempted to move onto what Hila Ne'eman called an "advanced level," since a moderator is clearly expected to be a professional "emotion talker." But to succeed as a professional moderator—for her emotional talk to have had the right ring—she would have needed additional cultural capital, including a more intimate familiarity with narratives of the self. In fact, she would have needed a different habitus, that "subjective but not individual system of internalized structures, schemes of perception, conception, and action common to all members of the same group or class and constituting the precondition for all objectification and apperception" (Bourdieu 1977: 86). Still, it is not clear whether the "effect in the world" of Sigal's emotional discourse was categorically different from that of, say, Hila, who had better cultural capital, connections, and education, as well as the right habitus. Similarly, statements such as "All I give to these animals I give out of love, I can't translate this into material measurements" and "The incredible thing about this business is that money is just a byproduct" again are somewhat difficult to set apart, even given the different contexts in which they were spoken. In either context, they each had potentially complex effects of reinforcing and challenging power and status differences.

Unlike Sigal, who tried to break the barrier of class and education, and to make it as a professional in the world of the NGOs, Ilana Alon refused to play the game altogether. On the numerous occasions throughout the course when participants were asked to talk about themselves, I learned that she had been a self-employed cosmetician for more than twenty years and that she did not have too many expectations that the course would change her economic situation. As she put it to me during one of the breaks, "I'm a survivor. I float. I've been doing it for twenty years already … Recently I've taken my father to live with me, and I'm really happy that I'm able to take care of him." Ilana, I learned from people of the NGO who enrolled her in the project, was accepted for the course despite their conviction there that she was hopelessly incapable of orderly workforce participation. As far as she was concerned, the course was worth her while for other reasons. "I came for myself, so that I would have a reason to get out of the house every Monday evening," she said unapologetically during one of the class presentations. "[I came here] for the company, to give and receive love, to learn, and to listen." In contrast to Sigal, Ilana was lucidly aware of the actual market value that emotional talk had for her, and she was not going to pretend otherwise. Her explanation that "when I look at someone, I see straight into their soul" echoed the popular Mizrahi discourse much more than it did the semantic field of emotional capitalism. In all probability it was not voiced as conscious resistance. It was a spontaneous emotional claim that did not quite suit the emotional discourse that was unfolding in the class (but nor was it entirely out of context), and it was largely left to wither away. However, as Reddy (1999: 279) asserts, although emotional claims do not necessarily express "real" or "genuine" feelings, they play a part in the navigation of difficult seas. They may serve to assure mastery, but they may as easily intensify nonconformist sentiment.

Lastly, probably one of the most striking paradoxical aspects of the women's emotional discourse lies in its capacity to enchant. In the expanding literature on the affective turn in social sciences, several scholars have recently challenged the thesis that the modern world is disenchanted. The assumption that the rising rationalities of science, law, policy, and bureaucracy inevitably lead to a loss of belief in mysterious forces is most famously attributed to Max Weber, although in fact it has been a deep-seated idea across a wide range of Western intellectuals (Saler 2006; Woodyer and Geoghegan 2012). Against this common theme, a growing number of scholars now explore the diverse facets of re-enchantment in modernity and late modernity. Some (e.g., Lee 2010) show that the writings of Weber himself, notably the importance he ascribed to charisma and to forces of irrationality, reveal that his understanding of the modern condition was more complex than commonly depicted in popular discourse. These and other scholars dwell on the generation of charm and delight at the very heart of bureaucratic rationality. Such occurrences exist in abundance in both the pompous moments of political and national rituals (Jenkins 2012) and the banality of everyday life: in the aesthetic effects of technological hybrids (Bennett 1997), in the shopping mall (Bennett 2001), in sports (Numerato 2009), or in the ways people relate to their material environment (Navaro-Yashin 2012; Woodyer and Geoghegan 2012).

For the purpose of the present analysis, enchantment can be defined as an "affective tuning in to the charge of the modern world" (Navaro-Yashin 2012: 450), or as "a mixed bodily state of joy and disturbance, a transitory sensuous condition dense and intense enough to stop you in your tracks and toss you onto new terrain, to move you from the actual world to its virtual possibilities" (Bennett 2001: 1). The first definition here is taken from the work of Yael Navaro-Yashin on attachments to space in the postwar Turkish Republic of Northern Cyprus. The second, by Jane Bennett, was formulated with respect to the tension between commodity fetishism and people's fascination with commercial goods. Despite some distinctions in the perspectives of the two authors (Navaro-Yashin 2012: 449), their definitions share an understanding of affect as evolving within relations of power, yet without being entirely determined by them. Both also share an understanding of enchantment as including complex positive and negative sensations. Bringing these interpretations to bear on the women represented in this study, it is possible to understand their overwhelming response to the discourse of emotional capitalism as a case of enchantment. The high levels of satisfaction that women reported regarding the workshops, and the obvious gratification they derived from articulating their capacities to love, give, and care, suggest that this emotional discourse might have been a sort of energetic recharging. More specifically, it may be interpreted as internally generated charisma.

Charisma, notes Charles Lindholm (1990), can take very diverse guises, from world-rejecting cults that center on a volatile leader with extraordinary qualities, through romantic infatuation, which provides an experience of self-loss that makes existence seem worthwhile, to benign forms such as shopping, which provide opportunities for identification and self-transformation. In line with other contemporary thinkers who dispute the compulsory link between modernity and disenchantment, Lindholm believes that people in the modern Western world do in fact have experiences of self-loss that are analogues to, but usually weaker than, those given by grand charismatic involvement. Much like charismatic involvement in small, shamanistic societies and very differently from the charisma of magnificent leaders, these experiences mostly act as maintainers of social order and supporters of the status quo, not as a radicalizing force. They offer their participants an institutionalized, less intense, more easily controlled, but nonetheless satisfying sense of commitment and emotional gratification through inner transformation. Along similar lines, Raymond Lee (2010) suggests thinking about charisma as a mysterious and transformative force with an inspirational quality that resurfaces continuously in the interstices of grandiose events. Besides the predictable cycle of mesmerizing and then ultimately routinizing of Charisma with a capital C, charismatic energy continues to flow in small, intimate channels.

Following such complex, multifaceted understandings of affective engagements, I venture to view the empowerment workshops in which women were talking love instead of money as spaces on the margins where, despite efforts to discipline them in the correct ethics of self-governmentality, charisma still remained as its own power. For the women, the enthusiastic engagement in emotional discourse comprised "an exercise in community" and the workshops, "an arena in which to congregate with others and enjoy a pleasurable disjunction of ordinary awareness within a group" (Lindholm 1990: 176). The workshops, moreover, also had the added benefit of association with the culture of "work," in the coveted, respected sense of the term. For besides their explicit imparting of work skills, the workshops bore a symbolic resemblance to recreational packages offered to employees in organized workplaces, which wrap together commitment to the firm, group spirit, and personal development. For the women in this study, who can only dream about such jobs and such perks, the empowerment workshops therefore offered a comparable opportunity to participate in workforce-like recreational activities, and effectively in that aspect of workforce culture that they have no access to in their common places of employment.

Conclusion

This chapter presented ethnographic documentations of women's approaches to the task of improving their earning capacities, proceeding from practices of home-based income-generating activities, through temporary and permanent enrollment in paid labor, to the ways that women talk about these efforts. In all the different facets of their work, women are guided by a cultural schema—an ideal gender contract, stipulating normative women as semi-independent and semisupported. The Jewish women generally follow a market-centered version of this schema, which means that ideally they expect to spend their adult lives in nuclear, heterosexual domestic units, in which their male partner will be the main breadwinner. While they expect, matter-of-factly, to be wage earners themselves, the main pillar of their identity will remain their ability to care for, nurture, and manage their families. To grasp the stick at both ends they will typically delegate many of their domestic responsibilities to the market. However, in a perceived conflict between the two spheres, the former will be their default priority. Among the Palestinian women, the dominant version is a family-centered gender contract, particularly in communities in which the domestic economy is only partly cash driven, and domestic produce still carries important weight in households' economies. While they too aspire to be wage earners, the pressures on them to prioritize unpaid domestic over paid public labor are greater than among the Jewish women.

The ethnography focused on the ways in which the cultural schema guides women's strategies as they navigate the domestic-public work continuum and try to make the most of their options. It revealed the importance of care as a skill relatively amenable to "cashing in on," and the central role it plays in women's self-identity and in the ways they are perceived in the different work spheres. These different aspects of care impart to women's approach to wage work an element of ambivalence, at once making them vulnerable to exploitation and giving them a sense of competence and worth.

Ambivalence was evident in the women's attempts to transform their home-based care into cash, as they discovered that this seemingly low-risk, low-cost, win-win strategy was intensifying their labor and potentially devaluing it precisely at the point where it was being made marketable. For women who were enrolled more permanently in the official workforce, the gender contract again brought to the fore some acute tensions. In a seemingly contradictory vein, women related cumulative negative experiences of very low salaries, frequent redundancies, ingratitude, etc., but at the same time voiced a strong desire to continue being wage earners. They likewise conveyed a mixed perception of the workforce as concomitantly a sphere of personal growth and self-fulfillment, and an intimidating battleground from which they would like to have the privilege to retreat at will. This tension, I contended, is a corollary of a deep contradiction in the gender contract itself, envisaged as universal whereas in reality it can only work for higher income families. It likewise reveals the irony of centering the project of contemporary femininity on striking a balance (between "home" and "work") in a neoliberal labor market that is growing progressively imbalanced.

Lastly, this chapter continued the exploration, which I began in Chapter 3, of the women's immersion in emotional capitalism, this time through a closer reading of their discourse during the empowerment workshops. Within the general discourse of emotional capitalism, the women's discourse has distinct characteristics, notably extensive linguistic references to love, care, and giving, alongside consistent refraining from talking about the practicalities of making money. Analysis of this discourse brought up yet again the deep ambivalence that accompanies the workforce participation of low-income women. I argued that the women's strong linguistic commitment to an ethics of care bears a dual potential to aggravate their stigmatization as emotional, impractical, and therefore not suitable for "work," and to empower them. While the mental position of "working for love, not money" that this discourse communicates is clearly self-defeating for women who are already framed as natural caregivers, the excessive reiterations of "love-work" in the women's discourse also have a potentially enchanting effect. True, indulging in their capacity to give love brings no "sacks of money falling on them from the sky," as in the parodic story that opens the book. But then, linguistic style is hardly *the* solution to their economic problems in any case. At least, immersing themselves in the discourse of emotional capitalism might have the side benefits of recharging them with affective energy and giving them an opportunity to partake in the grand cultural performance of emotional consumption, at no extra cost.

Notes

1. In sketching this generalized summary I draw on a rich feminist literature, including Anthias (1998), Connell (1996, 2000), Gottfried (2013), Mohanty (1999), and Walby (1990). However, the integration of ideas expressed by these and many other authors, who are cited more specifically later on, is entirely mine.
2. Using similar terminology in a somewhat different way, Connell (1996, 2000) employs the term "gender regime" to describe the regulation of roles, relations, identities, and norms at the level of social institutions. For the higher level of the overall social system in which these institutions exist she offers the term "gender order," which stands for the combined patterning of gender regimes, culture, and personal lives within a society. So, with minor distinctions, Connell's "gender order" is a parallel term to Walby's "gender regime." My choice here to use the latter is guided mainly by Walby's elaborate implementation of the term to state policies regarding welfare and women's workforce participation.
3. See Gottfried (2013) for an updated review.
4. On Palestinian-Israeli ideals of modern femininity see Kanaaneh (2002).

PART III

Economic Citizenship—Between the Right to Work and the Obligation to Be Productive

CHAPTER 5

Discussion—The Emergence of a Hybrid Local Discourse on Inclusion, Productivity, and Care

This ethnography has documented the field of social economy in Israel, where actors from diverse social positions engage in organized efforts to lift people out of poverty, and in the process restore social solidarity and endorse a more moderate version of economic liberalization. I presented the field: the organizations and agencies that initiate economic empowerment projects, the people who operate the projects hands-on, and the discourse that evolves through these activities. The next three chapters were dedicated to the women who are the addressees of this undertaking; I outlined their vulnerabilities, their experiences of empowerment, and their ambivalent approach to earning money. Drawing all these strings together, in this discussion chapter I set out the different meanings of social inclusion and civil entitlement that emerge through the elaborate cultural production that takes place in the field.

Economic citizenship is an analytical, not an emic concept. Unlike "social economy" or "empowerment" it is not often used as a local term. Yet the ideas connected with it, namely, that economic independence is a key to social and civil participation, are directly relevant to the discourses in the field. As shown shortly, in the scholarly literature this concept appears in distinct and sometimes contradictory discourses, conveying diverse understandings of the articulation of economic independence, social justice, and citizenship. Many of these different meanings meet "on the ground" in the Israeli field of social economy, which therefore offers us an empirical, context-bound opportunity to explore the complexity and potential paradoxes of the concept.

Ultimately, the contribution of this chapter is its showing how an idea that appears increasingly in the scholarly literature assumes practical meanings that are more complicated than, sometimes even counterintuitive to, its theoretical meanings. Feminist scholars and activists using the concept of economic citizenship to indicate minority women's right to inclusion rarely take into account the fact that the same concept is used simultaneously, with different implications, by neoconservatives or, in the case of Israel, by bearers of Zionist hegemony. Similarly, business philanthropists and development agents are rarely aware either of the more politicized significance of the concept as used at the grassroots level, or of its narrow utilitarian understandings by politicians and mainstream economists. The latter, lastly, are again using the idea in discursive combinations that would sound quite awful in the ears of activists and even in those of some well-meaning advocates of corporate social responsibility.

It is my contention that this quality of the idea of economic citizenship, which makes parallel sense in very different social and ideological milieus, echoes the deeply paradoxical nature of the evolving neoliberal project. It represents its capacity to coopt critical perspectives and practices, while allowing space for meaningful engagements by the very victims of economic liberalization, and while compelling the sovereign—in this case the Zionist state and the dominant Ashkenazi class—to allocate economic and symbolic resources to the marginalized and the excluded. As such, the idea of economic citizenship captures neoliberalism's paradoxical effect of sowing significant commotion in the ethnonational-cum-patriarchal order, while allowing it to continue to prosper.

Citizenship as Multilayered, Dynamic, and Embedded

The concept of citizenship that I use in this book draws on rich anthropological and feminist traditions that highlight its multilayered, dynamic, and embedded nature. At its minimum, citizenship designates a formal status, hence is a necessary condition for a range of basic rights, such as the right to live and work in a place or the right to travel across national borders. Yet for large categories of people, nominal citizenship does not automatically imply full, secure belonging to a polity. Without exception, social, political, and civil rights in contemporary states are differentially distributed among different ethnic, race, and class groups, with the practical result that members of marked categories (the poor, the "dark," the Others) are systematically less secure, and significantly less privileged (Kandiyoti1991; Yuval-Davis and Werbner 1999a; Mohanty 1999; Joseph 2000). Conversely, for increasing numbers of privileged populations, who hold multiple passports, citizenship is not singular, but plural (Ong 1999).

In contrast to the liberal ideal of civil society as an aggregate of individuals who are rationally motivated to maximize economic gain, who want minimal state intervention in their personal affairs, and who keep their emotional and cultural attachments private, citizenship "on the ground" is shown to operate first and foremost as a moral construct. Collective belongings and deep-seated beliefs about cultural difference inform its very core (Comaroff and Comaroff 2001, 2003b; Shafir and Peled 2002; Yuval-Davis 2011). And although they do not necessarily replace individuality and self-interest, they trap them in local modes of social connections and in culturally specific rationalities. For example, in the Middle East citizenries are entangled in concentric webs of belonging—notably families, as well as religious, ethnic, linguistic, and national communities, which may or may not match the identity of their states. In many Middle Eastern cultures connectivity affects the initial perception of self, to the degree that people feel that they are part of their significant others (Joseph 2005). And because almost without exception the various webs of belonging are patriarchal, citizenship is masculine by default, so that across the region women lack political personhood (Joseph 2000). Alternatively, as is the case among Israeli Jewish women, their inclusion through their roles as wives and mothers of the nation paradoxically blocks the possibility of their inclusion through the universal characteristics of citizenship (Berkovitch 1997).

The cultural implications of citizenship have been discussed mostly with respect to minorities (e.g., Rosaldo 1994; Stephen 2003; Wessendorf 2008) even though culture of course operates along the full ethnic continuum and shapes the hegemonic versions as much as it does the marginalized ones. One way or another, looking at citizenship through a cultural lens helps discern, besides particular forms of belonging and personhood, also the personal agency of subjects, as they maneuver their positions through multiple structures of power and different webs of signification. This dialectics of structure and agency implies, as Aihwa Ong (1996: 737) points out, that people are continuously "self-making and being-made by power relations that produce consent through schemes of surveillance, discipline, control, and administration." So besides a formal status and an ideological construct, citizenship is a lived concept. As such, its implications are never entirely certain. Its practical meanings are not identical to its formal meanings, and the gap between the lived and the perceived provides vital space for an ongoing process of subject making on the one hand and adjustments in the local discourses of citizenship on the other.

Besides social hierarchies internal to the state, the practical meanings of citizenship are also affected by international relations and transnational economies, which produce global routes of migration, tourism, business, and flight (e.g., Yuval-Davis 1997, 2010; Erel 2012; Lutz and Palenga-Mollenbeck 2012; Hanafi 2012). Under these conditions of late capitalism, nominal citizenship may remain bound to nation states, but its dividends—or lack of them—are contingent on multiple factors, including formal and informal memberships in more than one state, affiliations with collective entities within each country, or access to privatized health, educational, and security services. Ong, who has mapped the strategic maneuvering of transnational Asian subjects, offers the term *flexible citizenship,* to capture "the cultural logics of capitalist accumulation, travel, and displacement that induce subjects to respond fluidly and opportunistically to changing political-economic conditions" (Ong 1999: 6).

Another important aspect evinced by a multitiered paradigm is affective attachment. Carol Johnson (2010) argues that despite the apparent focus on rationality, citizenship has always had a significant affective component. Emotional regimes of citizenship are strongly sexed, gendered, and racialized. For example, emotional displays of pride, defiance, anger, or alienation, which are legitimate among members of the dominant groups, are used to dehumanize and criminalize members of ethnic and sexual minorities, as well as women from diverse social backgrounds. By the same token, the question of who is a legitimate object of empathy and who is a legitimate object of fear is closely entwined with race, ethnicity, religion, and gender. In this way, the politics of affect has major implications for determining who can pass as good citizens and who are more likely to fail.

Acknowledging the affective aspect of citizenship also immediately directs our attention to care, as a core *practice* of solidarity, cohesion maintenance, human upkeep, and intimacy. Care has always been a sensitive aspect of citizenship, igniting debates about the responsibility of the state as opposed to families and community-based charities, and about the boundaries of "the private" domain. Of course, as feminist scholars now largely agree, the initial idea of separate domains, and the common identification of the private with femininity and the public with masculinity, is a construct of Western bourgeois culture, not a universal truism. This *cultural* construct, however, is so deeply ingrained that it tends to be taken for granted not only by lay men and women but also by most mainstream political theorists, who conceive of "the private" as extrapolitical territory. Feminist theorists, by contrast (e.g., Pateman 1988; Walby 1994; Yuval-Davis 1997), argue that the private is political as much as the public is patriarchal, and that both domains have a direct—and combined—bearing on citizenship. In fact, as Hanna Herzog (1999) puts it, the symbolic split itself and the idea that women, but not men, face a role conflict when they step into the public domain serve as powerful ideological mechanisms that exclude women from positions of public power. The relegation of care to the realm of the domestic, a move that was reversed for several decades in socialist and some capitalist welfare states but is now becoming rapidly reinstated, has played a key role in the stratification of citizenship (Ehrenreich and Hochschild 2002; Zimmerman, Litt, and Bose 2006). In the preceding chapters I discussed at length the disempowering implications of the overlap of care, femininity, and minority status. In this chapter I look at the more specific implications of this disempowerment for the women's shaky and ambivalent citizenship. I will argue that their tendency to use an emotional love-work discourse, which I presented ethnographically in the previous chapter, at once reinforces their marginality and reinstates their agency, as those who voice a vital aspect of citizenship—care, on which the official discourses are largely silent.

Using this general outline as background, I now present three versions of economic citizenship. Two of these—the theoretically oriented feminist version and the action-oriented community economic-development version—echo the initial position that citizenship is inextricably entwined with structures of power and exclusion, primarily gender, ethnicity/race, and class. The third, free-market perspective is much closer to liberal platforms that see citizenship as a narrow, individualistic, and highly formalized construct, premised primarily on economic rationality and relatively detached from other dimensions of social life. Yet all of them see personal agency as pertinent to the actual fulfillment of citizenship.

Economic Citizenship

The idea of economic citizenship connotes several elements, to which different interpreters accord different weight. At the most general level, it means that earning a living is a basic component of citizenship, because it represents the dual essence of a right and an obligation. It represents the right to economic freedom and independence, the right to self-support, and by implication the right to participate in the most important activity of contemporary society. The flip side of the same coin is that capitalist democratic societies generally consider self-support an obligation of individual members of any community of citizens, and require them to be productive and actively to contribute to the overall good. This initial position, however, lends itself to quite diverse, even contradictory, interpretations in different ideological circles. Some focus on economic freedom while others emphasize economic independence; some stress that economic independence is inextricably connected to economic security while others still dwell on the component of self-fulfillment. Whatever the focus, the different articulations of economic citizenship usually acknowledge that the idea entails some basic tensions. The right-cum-obligation to economic independence, freedom, and security brings up dilemmas regarding the desirable balance between individualism and collective responsibility, and the most desirable extent of state intervention in private economic affairs (particularly the issues of welfare and taxation). It touches on boundaries, since contemporary workforces invariably include both citizens and noncitizens. Last but not least, it cannot escape the implications of structural inequalities for women, minorities, and the lower classes. The following outline of different perspectives of economic citizenship shows a broad range of preoccupations. The discourses below move between the abstract and the pragmatic, and stretch from radical through liberal to conservative worldviews. In their highly theoretical versions, these perspectives are anchored in very different ethical and moral positions. Yet as the actors representing them meet each other and collaborate in concrete projects, they engage in subtle but meaningful dialogues about justice, responsibility, and entitlement.

Feminist Perspectives

According to feminist historian Alice Kessler-Harris, to attain full citizenship women must have access to wage labor. Paradoxically, she argues, the expansion of women's social rights in the course of the twentieth century has hindered their civil inclusion, because it slowed down their integration into the workforce. Not wishing to reverse the wheel and obliterate social security, she nevertheless seeks to create a more comprehensive notion of citizenship that combines economic security and economic freedom. She offers the term *economic citizenship* to "capture those rights and obligations attendant to the daily struggle to reconcile economic well-being and household maintenance with the capacity to participate more fully in democratic societies" (Kessler-Harris 2003: 168) The idea builds on Thomas H. Marshall's (1964) typology of citizenship as composed of three categories: political (the right to political participation), civil (the right to liberty, freedom of speech, equality before the law, or property ownership), and social (the right to welfare, economic security, and education).[1] His primary interest was the relation of citizenship to social inequality, and the seemingly irreconcilable principles of democratic equality and social class. The emergence of modern citizenship closely bound up with capitalism and industrialization, he argued, entailed a deep-seated tension between citizenship rights and the class structure as a system of inequalities. It is against this tension that social rights, a twentieth-century addition to the political and civil components of citizenship, emerged as an attempt of citizenship to temper the antagonizing nature of capitalism by complementing the quest for economic independence with that of economic security. Kessler-Harris endorses this complexity, yet argues that the attempt to integrate economic freedom and economic security must take gender into account, since employment has radically different implications for women and for men. She points out that welfare policies are premised on cultural assumptions of women as natural caretakers, and that protective welfare mechanisms, particularly social benefits that signify the expansion of women's social rights, in effect weaken their economic rights, because they diminish their labor force participation and reinforce their symbolic and actual position as dependent. Rejecting the perceived opposition between the right to economic freedom and the right to economic security, she claims that the idea of economic citizenship offers a synthesis of these two basic rights. Hence the right to a job includes, ipso facto, the right to earn a decent salary, and "family wage" should be attainable by women as well as men. A gender-inclusive definition of economic citizenship, therefore, contains:

> the right to work at the occupation of one's choice (where work includes child-rearing and household maintenance), to earn wages adequate to the support of self and family, to a non-discriminatory job market, to the education and training that facilitates access to it, to the social benefits necessary to sustain and support labor-force participation. (Kessler-Harris 2003: 159)

Kessler Harris's idea is shared by other feminist scholars, such as Carole Pateman (1988), who in *The Sexual Contract* similarly argued that given the paramount duty of the citizen to work, the restrictions on women's work opportunities and their subjugated roles within the family assign them to secondary citizenship; or Vicky Schultz, who regards the official labor force as the single most important arena of civic participation, not simply because it affords economic independence but because "work is a site of deep self-formation that offers rich opportunities for human flourishing" (2000: 1883). According to Schultz, "everyone" has the right to participate meaningfully in life-sustaining work, with the social support necessary to do so. She writes: "Paid work is the only institution that can be sufficiently widely distributed to provide a stable foundation for a democratic order. It is also one of the few arenas in which *diverse groups of citizens* can come together and develop respect for each other due to shared experience" (2000: 1885, emphasis added). Like Kessler-Harris (particularly in Kessler-Harris 2003), Schultz is well aware that the emphasis on paid employment may undermine women's unpaid domestic labor, and may be used to downplay class and racial disadvantages in the official workforce. Still, grounding her analysis in the particular US legacy of "work" as a quintessential component of citizenship, she regards the framing of women as inauthentic workers as a major barrier to their civic participation. Both scholars also hold that it *is* possible to form a concept of economic citizenship that will not perpetuate but will eliminate historical disregard of women's labor.

Recently the idea of economic citizenship as a basic component of civil rights, particularly among poor and marginalized women, has also been adopted by scholars working on cultures other than North America. Building on Kessler-Harris's work, Valentine Moghadam (2011) advanced a definition of economic citizenship that emphasizes labor rights, social justice, and women's equality in the context of Middle East and North Africa (MENA). Moghadam's comprehensive definition includes, among other things, the right to gainful employment, along with public education, vocational training, fair wages, a healthy workplace, trade union organizing, social welfare, a workplace free of sexual harassment, paid maternity leave, and affordable quality childcare. She draws on feminist initiatives from various MENA countries to show that such a discourse is relevant also to that region. For Moghadam, Schultz, and Kessler-Harris alike, full citizenship entails access to economic independence *together with* economic security, which remains the responsibility of the state.

Despite its appeal, this version of economic citizenship has been criticized by feminist scholars in several respects. One line of criticism holds that the concept is not amenable to transposition to political settings other than the United States. For example, the emphasis on economic freedom, which is very specific to US political culture, is not as relevant in European countries that have a stronger legacy of state welfare. Arguably, Kessler-Harris's conceptual distinction between economic and social citizenship—and her attempt to collapse them—is irrelevant in Western European countries, where social policies emphasize precisely the interface of welfare and employment (Lewis 2003). Other complications arising from cross-country comparisons stem from the fact that institutional, cultural, and social diversity makes the actual empirical quantification of elements such as job quality or equitable wage hugely challenging (Guillén 2003). As Barbara Hobson (2003) asserts, it is true that supranational institutions such as the Organization for Economic Cooperation and Development, the International Labor Organization, or the European Union compile databases and devise cross-national surveys that become yardsticks for normative assessments of economic citizenship. These institutions produce epistemic communities, scientific experts, and technocrats that interpret and evaluate policy and make recommendations. Yet implementation still varies dramatically among the different member states of these organizations, whose labor forces include different blends of citizens, expatriates, guest workers, illegal migrants, asylum seekers, and refugees.

Another criticism holds that larger workforce participation and better employment conditions do not automatically ensure gender equality in pay and overall treatment; additional mechanisms are needed to ensure more jobs that are suitable for women, compensation for women's domestic work, etc. (Lewis 2003). Feminists, lastly, also debate the resistance, conveyed in the idea of economic citizenship, to remunerating homemaking labor, on the presumed grounds that this will reinforce the illegitimacy of women's official workforce participation and leave them dependent on state benefits and men's wages. For example, Martha Ertman (2002), in a reply to Schultz, disagrees with the initial assumption that wage labor is the most important path to full citizenship, and argues that compensating women for their homemaking work will actually buttress their citizenship claims. Similarly, Patemen, in an interview published more than a decade after *The Sexual Contract* (Puwar 2002), qualified her earlier position and suggested that employment and citizenship should be decoupled. The idea that democratic rights and benefits are contingent on financial contribution, she now stated, unduly underplays the contribution of women's domestic and care work.

Community Economic Development Perspective

Feminist ideas about justice, inclusion, and the value of women's invisible contribution resonate strongly in the discourse of community economic development (CED), of which the Israeli "social economy" is a culturally specific version. As presented in Chapter 1, CED refers to bottom-up initiatives to reduce poverty by combining economic self-help projects with mobilization of local communities. CED tends to be strongly holistic and participatory, encouraging the involvement of local businesses, fostering volunteer work, promoting education, and putting much emphasis on ideas such as community solidarity, local knowledge, and social sustainability. Such projects are often also characterized by a feminist perspective. Yet because CED is first and foremost an action-oriented approach, its discourse of economic citizenship is much less abstract or theoretical than the one presented above. Also, despite its radical potential, the strong emphasis on forging cross-sectorial partnerships creates some discursive affinity with the development and the business worlds.

Key concepts in CED discourse, which resonate directly with the idea of economic independence as a path to social inclusion, are "social capital," "capacity building," and an urgency to shift from a needs-based to an asset-based approach to poverty alleviation. Because of the pragmatic nature of CED, these concepts tend to act as empty signifiers (Walby 2012), open to radical, liberal, and neoliberal interpretations at one and the same time. For example, the concept of "capabilities," in the sense of opportunities, freedom, and the ability to choose, was offered by Amartya Sen (1999) as a humane substitute for the traditional focus on "outcomes" or "achievements." Yet as Sylvia Walby (2012) points out, despite Sen's explicit refusal to translate capabilities into fixed empirical measurements, so as not to reduce the value of human life to money and comparable currencies, his philosophical distinction between capabilities and functioning withers away when implemented on the ground. While development bodies have found the idea of capabilities attractive, their pragmatic orientation has conditioned them to measure it nevertheless, therefore effectively collapsing this qualitative, open-ended approach with a quantitative, fixed-categories one, and leaving little direct relevance for capability-as-freedom in measurements of justice, fairness, equality, and progress.

In a similar fashion, the notion of social capital too has become popular in diverse ideological environments. Among international development agencies, the idea of *social* capital, popularly defined as "local forms of association that express trust and norms of reciprocity" (Rankin 2002), has become widely accepted as pertinent to the accumulation of *financial* capital. The most famous example is "saving groups," in which women in the poorest regions of the world pool together weekly sums of money to create a collective credit against which they are entitled to receive individual loans from a microfinance institution. The attractiveness of social capital theory lies in its focus on the assets and capacities, as opposed to the needs, of poor people, and in its recognition of the value of social networks and associational life. It simultaneously acknowledges local traditions and indigenous agency, envisions an investment that is sustainable (as opposed to bottomless), and frames the poor as potentially self-sufficient. The following paragraph, quoted by Katharine Rankin (2002: 4) from the World Bank website, is characteristic:

> Social capital refers to the institutions, relationships, and norms that shape the quality and quantity of a society's social interactions. Increasing evidence shows that social cohesion is critical for societies to prosper economically and for development to be sustainable. Social capital is not just the sum of the institutions which underpin a society—it is the glue that holds them together.

But as Rankin notes, this understanding of social capital is very often blind to structural power. It tends to overlook hierarchies within local families and communities—particularly the subordination of women and members of lower castes—as well as the subordination of these communities within their states and the world capitalist system. Intentionally or not, it therefore often leads to development interventions reinforcing local hierarchies. Also, despite the importance accorded to "community," interventions guided by such a liberal understanding of social capital commonly continue to conflate development with economic growth and to embrace the rational, utility-maximizing individual as the locus of progressive change.

Alongside this widespread approach, though, CED literature also offers more critical interpretations of social capital and asset building. Alison Mathie and Gord Cunningham (2003) sketch an integrative summary of asset-building community development (ABCD). By their explanation, ABCD differs from World Bank and similar top-down perspectives in its focus on community mobilization rather than institutional reform, and in its linking of localized, community-driven initiatives to macroenvironmental policies. As distinct from finance-oriented development schemes, it puts great emphasis on *collective* assets and capacities, including cultural heritage and other forms of nonmonetary assets. It also encourages collective action, fosters local knowledge, and aims to eliminate stigmatic and negative collective images by cultivating communities' self-esteem. However, while Mathie and Cunningham mention power inequalities and the need to devolve political power, they acknowledge that the ABCD literature does not offer sufficient answers to economic discrimination based on gender and ethnic oppression.

Such answers are commonly found in more radical approaches. Marxist and feminist understandings, for example, treat social capital as embedded in communal and familial networks that are usually hierarchical and potentially oppressive. Structural inequalities mean that differently positioned individuals experience associational life differently, and the value of their social capital varies accordingly. The benefits and costs of participation are distributed unequally, with some benefitting at the expense of others (Rankin 2002). Interventions sensitive to such power differentials occur mostly on the margins of, or outside the more established industry of international development. They usually combine practical steps to increase the social capital of individual women (through education, vocational training, business initiatives, etc.), with political consciousness raising regarding the structural and historical mechanisms of their oppression.

We find an example of such an approach in the empowerment project that al-Tufula Center implemented in the recently recognized Bedouin villages in Galilee (documented in Chapter 3 as part of the Bedouin Village Study). Al-Tufula's idea of empowerment gave paramount importance to the role of the community in the lives of village women; it placed strong emphasis on their social and cultural capital (their historical knowledge, their productive contribution, their ingenuity, and their capacity to network); it aimed to reverse their framing as needy and passive by persistently talking about their capacities; and it interpreted their multiple disadvantages as a direct corollary of the state's discriminatory policies—the prolonged nonrecognition of the villages, and the overall discrimination of the Palestinian citizens. In keeping with the feminist intersectionality perspective, al-Tufula's approach targeted the complex intersection of patriarchal and ethnonational oppression. While it saw the institutions of the family and the village as oppressive to women, it did not aim to obliterate them or free the women *from* them. Instead, it aimed to resurrect the value of these institutions, which have stagnated as a result of oppressive manipulations by the state, and to empower women to become agents of change *within* them. This community-oriented feminist empowerment approach, in other words, acknowledged the political victimization of the community without downplaying its own oppressive agency.

It is possible that the radical and politically explicit tone of al-Tufula's initiative is connected to the fact that its platform did not include the term *economic development,* as do other ABCD programs. Although many of the projects' participants did testify to having undergone economic empowerment (they related their decision to join the waged workforce or to enroll in occupational training to the encouragement they received in the project), increasing women's economic independence was not one of al-Tufula's direct priorities. It therefore did not attempt to involve local businesses, and focused its fundraising efforts on general donors. By contrast, the common emphasis among CED initiatives on *economic* empowerment entails greater involvement of financial and business bodies.

Among such bodies, the concepts of social capital and asset building again resonate with the more liberal renditions that center on financial attainment and related quantifiable measurements, and reinforce individualistic perceptions of success despite the fascination with the term *community*. Here we encounter the terms *corporate responsibility, corporate citizenship,* or *financial citizenship.* According to Luis Moreno (2010) corporate social responsibility (CSR) refers to a commitment of private corporations to integrate social and environmental concerns in their interaction with their stakeholders and with society more generally. "It is generally assumed that a strong sense of business responsibility towards local communities, by means of formalizing partnerships, together with respect for the environment, is an important aspect of CSR" (2010: 684). CSR is premised on an assumed mutual dependency between the well-being of society and the well-being of business. Besides the ethical aspect, it is assessed as a strategic means for optimizing the public image of corporations. In fact, the promotion of CSR as a win-win strategy for optimizing the responsible civil participation of businesses while increasing their competitiveness and potential profitability has become de rigueur in business training. Donna Wood et al. (2002), who reviewed the curricula of 105 leading business schools in the United States, report that corporate involvement in community economic development (CI/CED) has become a popular topic in the discipline. Classifying such involvement as "corporate citizenship," they see the incorporation of CI/CED into the standard training of entrepreneurs and senior managers as a form of "citizenship studies." They therefore argue that by teaching managers to become involved and assume social responsibility, business schools effectively engage in citizenship education.

Against the liberal conviction that corporate involvement in CED strengthens democratic culture, critics have pointed out the countereffects of reinforcing neoliberal rationality. For example, Ronen Shamir (2008) argues that the moralization of the market—the increasing involvement of commercial enterprises in tasks that were once considered part of the civic domain of moral entrepreneurship and the political domain of the welfare state—has become an important part of the neoliberal global social order, which essentially grounds the very notion of moral duty within the rationality of the market. With the move away from legalistic, bureaucratic, top-down configurations of authority to a horizontal configuration, the idea of responsibility has become the practical master-key of reflexive, self-regulatory governance. In an ethnographic documentation of a nonprofit organization that promotes the idea of CSR, Shamir (2005) shows how the latter is transformed into a managerial tool, designed to enhance employee loyalty and improve brand loyalty. From a different angle, Adriana Kemp and Nitza Berkovitch (2013, n.d.) explore the effects the financialization of citizenship on actors at the grassroots level. They find that despite their explicit criticism of the neoliberal outlook, nongovernmental organizations actually replicate the rationale of finding market solutions to social and political problems. In this respect, the educational turn that many of these organizations have taken (as discussed in Chapter 3) proves particularly pertinent to their *active* production of norms and techniques that make the financial and entrepreneurial worlds look natural, necessary, and even progressive in gendered struggles against inequality. Kemp and Berkovitch also underscore the major role that microfinance NGOs play in transforming marginalized women into "financial subjects," who are competitive, self-reliant, and trained in opportunity spotting and calculated risk taking (see also Rankin 2001).

Free-Market Perspectives

Bringing this concise review full circle, ideas of economic citizenship are found also among those who believe that the market is the best regulator of all types of social problems. Somewhat similarly to the feminist discourse led by Kessler-Harris and Schultz, the free-market perspective of economic citizenship tends to be rather theoretical and replete with legalistic rationality. Thematically though, it is dominated by images of individuals as rational actors operating to maximize gains, leaving gender and ethnicity, and to a lesser degree also community, conspicuously out of the equation. To an extent, this discourse too acknowledges the problem of social inequalities, yet concerns about class disparities and economic security remain secondary to the value of individual freedom and economic growth.

A lucid example of a free-market approach to citizenship is found in discussions about the regulation of global work migration. For several decades now, economists in the United States have promoted the idea of selling citizenship rights as a way to allocate immigration certificates and permanent residency (Chiswick 1982; Borna and Stearns 2002). Versions of this idea are traceable back to notable economists such as Walter Adams (1968) or Gary Becker (1997). According to Adams, as long as human capital is free to seek the highest reward, and as long as it bears the cost of its own movement, it will tend to move into those regions and occupations where its productivity is high, and out of regions and occupations where its productivity is low. The combination of requesting immigrants to pay their way into the absorbing country and allowing citizens to sell their share in it is presumed to produce optimal results for all concerned. Operative proposals concerning the United States specifically (Borna and Stern 2002; Muaddi 2006) list the following benefits: poor US citizens will be able to "cash in" on the asset of their citizenship; they will use the money to relocate to countries with a lower cost of living, and thereby will relieve the American welfare system of the burden of their support. On the opposite side, among prospective immigrants the financial investment necessary to obtain a green card will put in motion a process of self-selection, attracting candidates who are either able-bodied and highly motivated to work, or wealthy, and discouraging the poor and the needy. Lastly, the federal state will supervise and tax the transactions, thus gaining an additional source of revenue, which at present circulates in the black market of green cards.

Despite their cost-effective and somewhat mechanistic tone, proposals of this sort do not necessarily ignore the ethical or moral aspects of citizenship. For one thing, as several authors note, the idea of selling citizenship rights merely taps into an already thriving illegal industry of visas and green cards. If anything, making the transactions legal and official will encourage a more sincere discussion of how to bring "citizenship" up to date with contemporary tensions between global population flows, vast economic disparities, and very heterogeneous workforces on the one hand, and a persistent conception of citizenship as bound to nation-states and geographical locations on the other. For another, at least some of the proposals include explicit acknowledgement that citizenship has emotional and collective components and not just calculated and individualistic elements, yet hold that the two aspects can be separated, at least for the sake of discussion. For example, Jawad Muaddi (2006) makes a distinction between alienable and inalienable aspects of citizenship. The right to permanent legal residency and the concomitant right to work, which represents the liberal aspect of citizenship, he argues, is alienable. This component, which is minimalist and individualistic by definition, happens also to be in very high demand in the international immigration market. Other components, by contrast, such as entitlement to social benefits, the right to be elected to high office, or the obligation to serve on juries, are inalienable. These are "republican and communitarian notions of political participation, identity, and solidarity" (2006: 230), which cannot be sold or bought.

Some free-market approaches to citizenship, lastly, include explicit reference to social inequalities. Francesca Strumia (2011) notes, with respect to EU citizenship, that this supranational construct entails social inequalities almost by definition. One of the elementary components of this citizenship is the right of legal nationals of the various member states to move freely between them, and to reside, work, and enjoy public services across the union. Yet the economic disparities between the various states—the dramatic differences in unemployment rates and in welfare mixes—give very different meanings to the freedom of movement of their respective subjects. While highly skilled persons largely benefit from this freedom, low-skilled people might more easily find relief from inequality in the right *not* to move, provided it is supported by protective supranational policies. Another important source of social inequality in EU citizenship is the presence of non-nationals who are economic actors in the union. These people are EU economic citizens in as much as they contribute to the operation of the internal market and benefit from the freedoms offered in it, yet most of them are denied the safety net available to legal nationals. This inclination to inequality, argues Strumia, seems to betray a fundamental premise of authentic common citizenship: shared status for the members of a same community.

Localizing Economic Citizenship

Many of the ideas that come up in the international or theoretical discussions of economic citizenship are relevant also to the Israeli field of social economy, and within it to the empowerment of low-income women. The sweeping shift, in poverty alleviation initiatives, from welfare- to work-oriented solutions, the restructuring of institutional interventions among poor people, the eagerness of the business community to help poor people transform their social capital into some sort of economic asset, the surging discourse on corporate social responsibility, the novel partnerships between radical grassroots activists and the capitalist and state establishments, or the financialization of the everyday life of low-income women and social change organizations—all testify to a seeming convergence of ideologies of justice and social solidarity on the one hand, and ideologies of economic self-sustainability on the other. At the same time, the assimilation of the globally circulating discourse of economic citizenship into a particular cultural and geopolitical context necessarily entails some measure of translation and adaptation. To understand how this process occurs, I ask first, how can the pecuniary approach to citizenship (Borna and Stearns 2002) be reconciled with the Israeli and Palestinian preoccupations with collective identity, history, and primordial belonging? Then, moving from the ideological to the pragmatic, I ask what are the practical meanings of economic citizenship that evolve in the field of social economy?

Israeli Citizenship as a Category of Collective Belonging

In Israel, the most important determinant of citizenship is national belonging. As detailed in Chapter 1, the Palestinians, who are formal citizens of the state, suffer manifold forms of exclusion and discrimination because they do not belong to the Jewish collective (see also Jabareen 2002). Within the Jewish majority group, degrees and forms of belonging are further determined according to local mythologies of contribution to the national good. These contributions are correlated primarily with ethnicity (Yonah and Saporta 2002a; Peled 2008), religiosity and fundamentalism (Stadler, Lomsky-Feder, and Ben-Ari 2008), and gender, which in turn intersects in complex ways with the other bases of stratification (Yuval-Davis 1987; Berkovitch 1997; Fogiel-Bijaoui 1997; Herzog 1999a; Helman 1999; Swirski 2000). In stark distinction from the globally circulating discourses on economic citizenship, in Israeli and Palestinian political traditions, economic productivity has played almost no role. The one exception is the public discourse that blames ultra-Orthodox Jews for not shouldering their equal share of national burden, which refers to the exemption from military service of men who enroll in *yeshivot* (religious schools), and by implication also exclude themselves from the job market for prolonged periods.

Of course, the liberal component of citizenship is not entirely absent from Israel. A narrative of universal individual rights has existed side by side with the collectivist narratives and has served as the primary framework that allows the Palestinians to become citizens. As mentioned in Chapter 1, scholars have debated the relative importance of this component in the Israeli regime. For example, Gershon Shafir and Yoav Peled (1998: 417) argue, "The historical trajectory of Israel's development since 1948 has consisted in the gradual decline of the republican discourse and the gradual transformation of the society from a colonial to a civil society." Yet they also emphasize the hierarchical and fragmented nature of Israeli citizenship: "different groups—citizens and noncitizens, Jews and Palestinians, Ashkenazim and Mizrahim, men and women, religious and secular—were placed in accordance with their conceived contribution to the Zionist cause" (Shafir and Peled 2002: 22). Sammy Smooha (2002) has contended that despite consistent and unambiguous domination of the Jewish majority, Israel should still be considered a democracy—an ethnic democracy. Opponents of this interpretation have argued that the scope and consistency of the exclusion of the Palestinians, and the overwhelming level of their policing, are such that the liberal component—the fact that they can vote and be elected to the Knesset, and that they fall under the nominal jurisdiction of an array of protective state laws—is too feeble to qualify the state as a democracy. These scholars have therefore termed Israel an ethnocracy (Rouhana and Ghanem 1998; Yiftachel 2006; Ghanem 2009), and an illiberal democracy (Sa'di 2002). Also Peled, who in the late 1990s concluded together with Shafir that the liberal discourse was gaining the upper hand, reversed his conclusion a decade later (Peled 2007, 2008) and argued that since October 2000 the status of the Palestinian citizens has been eroding; while the economic policy is now dominated by the liberal discourse, policy toward the Palestinian citizens is dominated increasingly by the exclusionary ethnonational discourse.

The ethnography presented in this book captures the moment at which, with the rapid penetration of ideas about inclusion-through-economic-participation, such framings of citizenship in terms of collective belonging and particularistic morality begin to undergo an *economic* shift. The offering of economic solutions to problems of social inequalities and social exclusion entails, willy-nilly, a seeming spillover of the liberal discourse, which as Peled (2008) convincingly contends, has taken over economic policies, into the management of ethnonational antagonisms. Recall, for example, the eagerness to include the Palestinian citizens in the economic empowerment projects and the use of terms such as "social" and "diversity" to depoliticize their difference. This "infiltration of market-driven truths and calculations into the domain of politics" (Ong 2006: 4) reflects a larger transformation of the liberal into a *neo*liberal. However, it does not necessarily mean that the normative logic of ethnonational exclusion is about to disappear. As Ong notes, "[t]he spread of neoliberal calculation as a governing technology is a historical process that unevenly articulates situated political constellations" (2006: 3). Hence it is more accurate to say that in Israel, as in the Asian settings documented by Ong, the neoliberal logic is incorporated as an exception to the dominant ethnonational logic, which remains as blatant as ever (Yonah and Saporta 2002b; Kemp 2004; Ram 2013).

In Chapter 1 I mentioned as an example the surge in racist legislation initiatives, which represents a popular sentiment among Jews that the Palestinian citizens are usurping their liberal rights to the point that they threaten to overturn the Jewish character of the state. This sentiment, which has been on the rise since the second Palestinian intifada in 2000, has become so prevalent that Nadeem Rouhana and Nimer Sultany (2003) call it "the New Zionist Hegemony," noting its traces on government policies, legislation, public opinion, and public discourse, and arguing that it has effected significant change in the meaning of citizenship for non-Jews in an ethnic Jewish state. In line with this assessment, one of the popular slogans of the political Right during recent election campaigns was "No citizenship without loyalty," which conveys a demand to condition the civic privileges of Palestinian Israelis upon their declared expression of loyalty to Zionism and the Jewish state. In the 2013 election campaign a slightly different slogan was added: "No rights without duties," to protest the exemption from military service of both Arabs and ultra-Orthodox Jews.

The Neoliberal Exception to Israeli Discourses of Citizenship

What are the implications of such heated ethnonational exclusionary sentiments for the seemingly inclusive orientations that flourish through the social economy field? How do this background and atmosphere affect the vernacularization of economic citizenship? As I was exploring these questions, during the January 2013 election campaign, I googled the "No citizenship without loyalty" and "No rights without duties" slogans, and discovered that even these quintessentially ethnonationalistic expressions have assumed interesting neoliberal overtones. For example, an Internet newspaper called "Patriotic Israeli—all that is Principled, Zionist, and Jewish" featured an article titled "No

Rights without Duties." Pressing the "about" button revealed that Patriotic Israeli is a business company that defines itself as "A leader and a coach of a business community. This community wants to grow and develop congenially, while bringing livelihood, welfare, and personal empowerment to itself and to thousands of others in the region."[2] A further exploration revealed that the juxtaposition of economic citizenship lingo—the introductory statement alone contains empowerment, community, welfare, and economic prosperity—and nationalistic, sharply exclusionary opinions, is consistent throughout the website. Far from this being a curiosity, a similar amalgam characterizes the public discourse of the Yesh Atid party, the big winner of the 2013 elections.[3] This self-defined center-stage party, whose main ticket is promoting the economic prosperity of the middle class, has nevertheless issued numerous statements that delegitimize the Palestinian citizens as partners to the coalition, reject territorial concessions in the negotiation with the Palestinian Authority, and similar messages, which align it quite clearly with the political right. It therefore appears that the tendency to address social problems using the lens of economic rationality is spreading throughout the political spectrum, and that in a manner reminiscent of, though not quite identical to, US neoconservatism, the Israeli versions of free-market economic citizenship are saturated with communitarian ideology.

One of the main characteristics of the social economy field is the space it creates for uncommon encounters and collaborations among actors from the business community, state agencies, grassroots organizations, and clients of the welfare system, as well as between ordinary Palestinians and Jews (ordinary in the sense that they are not necessarily invested in "coexistence efforts"). As they engage each other during the routine of empowerment projects, these actors bring with them varied understandings of what the projects are actually about, as well as diverse identities and identifications. Well aware of the social distances between them, individuals in concrete situations nevertheless often trust each other enough to develop sincere conversations and to pool together their distinct resources in order to achieve success. They self-censor some of the sentiments or habitual expressions they may use in their other, more segregated spaces, and they do not necessarily cultivate too much romance about bridging gaps and crossing social boundaries. In economic empowerment projects, as in any other work spaces, there are personal animosities, disappointments, focused self-interests, prejudices, or misunderstandings. But there *are* also dialogues.

Of the various perspectives presented earlier, the version of economic citizenship that resonates most strongly among government-organized nongovernmental organizations (GONGOs) and business-organized nonprofit organizations (BONPOs) is the one that characterizes community economic development. As shown in Chapter 1, the notions of corporate social responsibility, asset-based community development, and building social capital are quite popular particularly in these circles. The discourse here is characteristically pragmatic in orientation—most of the actors become interested through their actual involvement in the projects, which pushes it away from the ideological extremes. To a degree, the structural conditioning toward mainstream or even conservative worldviews of people well within the established elites gives some edge to liberal, free-market interpretations, yet for the most part these do not assume the calculated, mechanistic tone that was presented in the review above.

For many actors in these circles, the most meaningful aspect of CED is reaching across national, ethnic, and class divides. This too is done in a distinctly guarded, depoliticized style, as seen in the use of the terms "social" and "diversity." The gender component likewise serves as a mitigating factor in the process of reaching across the divides. Low-income women, in contrast to low-income men, are more easily imagined as needy than aggressive. As such, they often evoke a degree of identification among the professional/middle-class operators of the projects, who are mostly women. Alternatively, the framing of minority women as bearers of traditionalism and cultural oppression readily replaces their class, ethnic, and national oppression with a seemingly less antagonizing narrative.

At the level of grassroots activists, understandings of economic citizenship are much closer to the ideas articulated by feminists such as Kessler-Harris, albeit with some locally specific distinctions. Radical feminists posit that low-income and minority women have a *right* to work, as a counterargument to popular tendencies to stigmatize them for laziness, traditionalism, or parasitism. They also take issue with official tendencies to focus on statistical measurements of workforce participation and argue that efforts should concentrate on getting more women into good jobs, not just any jobs. In other words, local radical feminists' perspective on economic citizenship is that low-income and minority women are entitled to gainful, sustainable, and fulfilling employment, just like men and women of the dominant groups. Considering that the realistic prospects of low-income women rarely go beyond nonstandard jobs (low-paying, unstable, part-time, no benefits, bad treatment, frequent arbitrary dismissals, etc.), these expectations have a distinctly utopian aspect. Not coincidentally, therefore, the involvement of many grassroots activists in the projects is often fraught with ambivalence and intense reflexivity. While many of these actors are enthusiastic about the projects, they tend to see them as partial solutions at best. In their understanding, to achieve true economic security, many if not most of the women will still need long-lasting state support to supplement their independent income. None of the activists I met ever mooted the notion, as Kessler-Harris did, that state welfare should be reduced because it perpetuates women's economic dependence. If anything, most of them watched with alarm the shrinking of social benefits and sought to halt and even reverse the process; many also believed that women should be economically rewarded for their unpaid domestic labor.

Another specific concern of local feminists' discourse on women's right to make a respectable living is its distinctly political tone. Contrary to many of their partners in the BONPOs and GONGOs, who make a point of construing the projects as "social," actors at the grassroots level, as I showed ethnographically in Chapter 1, make direct links among what they take to be the class, ethnic, and national oppressions of women. They therefore regard their efforts to help these women improve their income-generating capacities as part of an overall struggle for social justice (*tsedek*), not charity (*tsdaka*). At the same time, there are different shadings among the grassroots activists also. Palestinian activists mostly frame their activity in the social economy field as part of their ongoing struggle against the national discrimination against the Palestinian minority. As shown in Chapter 1, the overwhelming funneling of funds in recent years to economic empowerment has left little choice for minority-rights groups but to join the stream. Some of them, coming with a solid socialist and communist background (an outcome of the hegemony of the Communist Party among the Palestinians during the early decades of Israeli statehood), give their participation a more specifically unionistic emphasis. The involvement of these actors in social economy projects is one way or another usually part of their broader involvement in civil society activism for human, minority, and women's rights, and of their broader immersion in the Israeli-Palestinian conflict.

To some extent this perspective is shared also by a hard core of radical Jewish activists. Yet Palestinians and Jews in grassroots organizations still differ in the level of their hostility to and alienation from the state, as well as in their personal histories of racist persecution. Outside the inner radical left-wing/feminist circles, activists again vary in the degree to which they see economic disempowerment as connected to ethnic or national oppression. In this respect, an important distinguishing factor among the operators of the projects at the grassroots level is age. As explained in Chapter 3 ("Empowerment"), younger women, both Jewish and Palestinian, who take on jobs as moderators and coordinators, do not always share the political passion of the older activists and founders of the organizations in which they work. These women characteristically have university degrees, sometimes they are still graduate students, and for them the feminist organizations are yet another "establishment," just like the BONPOs and GONGOs. While many of them like the activist character of their job, their professional training and aspirations tend to dominate their approach to the task of "empowering" low-income women. Together with their limited familiarity with the recent history of radical feminist activism and their strong individualistic career orientations, these attributes cause many of the younger NGO actors to veer away from the highly politicized discourse and move closer to mainstream interpretations. And while their discourse may sound akin to that of the grassroots environment in which they work, their perceptions of economic citizenship are often much less critical of "the neoliberal imaginary that seeks to subject all socio-cultural practices to the law of the market" (Rossiter, in Urciuoli 2010: 164).

This captivating effect of the neoliberal "imaginary" brings us, finally, to the clients of the projects. Like many of the other partners, their interpretations of the idea of wage-work as a right and a gateway to civil inclusion grow from their actual participation in the courses and workshops. The ethnography showed that low-income women are very keen to have a paying job. Their narratives and conversations revealed that beyond their obvious need for money, they wanted a job for a whole host of reasons. They imagined that in addition to economic independence it would give them identity, self-fulfillment, and respect, and that it would make their lives more interesting. This was striking, considering that most of these women had cumulative experiences of jobs that were plainly unfulfilling, often outright humiliating, with ridiculously low pay and a taxing work that won them very little appreciation, if any. Interestingly, more than these attitudes echo the discourse of the activists who run the projects, they seem to tap into the ideas of feminist theoreticians such as Kessler-Harris or Schultz, who despite full awareness of the manifold structural barriers awaiting low-income and minority women in the workforce, still see it as the foremost crucial arena that they need to conquer in order to realize their citizenship.

Another evident point in which the women's narratives differed from that of local grassroots activists was that their approach to economic citizenship was distinctly apolitical. They never discussed or analyzed government policies, for example. Also, in all the events that I witnessed, which brought together Jewish and Palestinian women, relations between the two communities or the Israeli-Palestinian conflict were consistently glossed over. With some exceptions, even Mizrahi identity politics, which is today widely consensual among low-income Mizrahim, came up mostly in response to remarks of workshop moderators, and was only rarely part of women's spontaneous talk. For the women, the quest to improve their economic situation was primarily a personal, individual journey. While they welcomed the companionship of other women who shared similar circumstances, they had no tendency to politicize it.

Within this generally apolitical approach, there was a fairly clear distinction between Jewish and Palestinian participants. Among the Jewish women, particularly the Mizrahiyot, identification with the state and with Zionism never came into question. Even though they were bitterly angry about the cutbacks in social benefits, they never expressed alienation from or hostility toward the state. Rather, the taken-for-granted political position in the workshops during my participant observations was center/right-wing, with occasional spontaneous expressions of explicit national sentiments. As for the ultra-Orthodox and recent immigrants, while their identification with the state was somewhat less obvious, this did not usually lead to any expressions of political criticism. The attitude of the Palestinian participants to the state was categorically different. The state, the Jews, and the Hebrew language were crucial factors to reckon with as they represented "hard facts" on the way to economic and workforce participation. Yet the state, let alone Zionism, evoked no identification. If anything, it was seen as hostile and threatening. At the same time, the women did not necessarily share the discourse of the moderators and project operators, who tended to be intellectuals and very political. They did, of course, share the basic defiant-proud sentiment of Palestinian belonging. In this close-knit society, the social distance between any individual woman and persons who are politically involved is never too wide, and none of the women was a stranger to Palestinian political discourse. Still, the dominant orientation among the workshops participants was first and foremost pragmatic.

Lastly, as shown in Chapter 4, the discourse of the women during the workshops was replete with emotional references. Talking about their involvement in waged work, participants abundantly voiced the words *love, care,* and *giving,* and at the same time eschewed comments on the practicalities of making money or on aggressive emotions. In my analysis of this discourse I pointed out more than one possible interpretation. On the one hand, I noted that this discursive style marked the women as unsophisticated and their attitudes as self-defeating; for while it resonated strongly with broader discourses of emotional capitalism, it also seemed to entrench even deeper their popular image as natural caretakers, hence as outsiders to the official workforce. I also noted, though, that the women's discourse may have had multiple effects, including subversive, nonconformist, and otherwise unsettling ones. Among other things, I suggested that it might have the capacity to enchant, inspire, and energetically recharge them during the dreary and often daunting process of "economic empowerment." Linking this to the topic of the present chapter, it is possible to add that through their emotional discourse, the workshops participants vocalize a component of economic citizenship that is conspicuously absent in the different versions that circulate in the field.

The discourse on economic citizenship that is evolving in the field of social economy creates intriguing "dialogues" among radical, liberal, and ethnonationalistic perceptions of citizenship. On a different level, it also articulates the forces of separation and attachment, an elementary pair in the constitution of self and concomitantly also of citizenship. Separation and individuation are represented in the emphasis on economic independence and on money, the typical symbol of negative exchange and abstract relationships; attachment is represented in the counteremphasis on economic *security* and communal solidarity. The clients of the projects, by steering away from the explicitly ideological components that all the other partners seem to be preoccupied with, talk directly to this other, more universal, dilemma of citizenship. In their focus on relationships of support and intimacy, they express in no uncertain terms the relevance of care and emotional attachment to the practice of active citizenship.

So while to the hegemonic ear the women's excessive talk about love and care may sound off-key, and therefore seem to reinforce their marginalization, it does not necessarily represent failure to grasp and internalize the "right" narrative of economic success. Such an interpretation, to borrow Jane Goodman's (2010: 206) perceptive observation, would "presume that positive agency under neoliberal regimes can only be construed in terms of a transparent and singular alignment between politics, social conduct, and subjectivity." Instead, the ritualistic emotional talk of the workshop participants can be said "to demonstrate a flexible and pragmatic sensitivity to the imbricated social contexts" in which they find themselves (2010: 206). In a still deeper symbolic sense, this pragmatic sensitivity may also be said to render them agents in bringing the conversation on citizenship to bear on the uncanny elements of mundane vulnerability (as opposed to heroic sacrifice) and plain neediness, which the self-important, official renditions prefer to leave out of the discussion.

Conclusion: Affective Citizenship, Low-Income Women, and Claims for Inclusion

Economic citizenship can be thought of as a conceptual vessel, which contains a mixture of attitudes to strategies of inclusion in the contemporary moment of late capitalism. This moment entails increasing polarization on several fronts—social, economic, and political, which leaves mounting numbers of people vulnerable, and a minority fantastically rich. The chance of the latter releases an avalanche of messages that promise opportunities for growth and prosperity, and creates acute pressures to engage in perpetual self-invention. A corollary of these contradictions, organized efforts to empower the poor and the marginalized feed simultaneously on the seemingly contrary narratives of justice, charity, and self-sufficiency. It cultivates images of self-sustained individuals comfortable in the embrace of supportive communities. In the field of social economy, abstract intellectual ideas about "giving fishing rods to the poor" or radical demands to grant women due opportunity to become truly independent translate into pragmatic action plans. The result is a hybrid discourse of entitlement, with dialogues across political, sectorial, and social boundaries.

I have identified several strands of this discourse as it appears in the scholarly literature—feminist, CED, and free-market, and then examined the correspondence between these and the bottom-up ideas that evolve in the field. I showed that in the process of its localization, the general notion of economic self-sufficiency as a route to civil participation is ultimately supplemented by certain aspects of citizenship—embedment, attachments, and essentialized differences, which are absent from scholarly discourses on economic citizenship. I concluded that in the Israeli case economic citizenship as a neoliberal position is an exception to, not a substitute for, the cultural blueprint of citizenship, albeit one that agitates it and challenges it to accommodate. Not surprisingly, the process of accommodating the exception generates tensions and paradoxes, which the different participants handle according to their particular standpoints.

Actors in the BONPO and GONGO sectors primarily endorse the ideas of social capital, social corporate responsibility, asset building, and community building, which are milder versions of free-market perspectives of economic citizenship—unapologetically capitalistic yet relatively moderate. Their appeal lies in their distinctly apolitical ring, which makes it easier for people firmly within the state and business establishments to collaborate with grassroots activists despite their sharp and critical language that purports to take hegemonic power relations to task. The apolitical discourse also facilitates their collaboration with low-income Mizrahim and Palestinians, who embody the attractive-scary outer circumference of their social world. Where free-market lingo blends with that of social solidarity, the operation of BONPO and GONGO actors is favored; it is a reasonably reassuring place, although it exceeds their customary comfort zone. They employ words such as "social" and "diversity" to neutralize potentially explosive encounters.

Grassroots activists generally endorse a much more justice-oriented and explicitly feminist version of economic citizenship, one reminiscent of what I called the "theoretical" feminist position on economic citizenship, to which they nevertheless add some locally specific ideological elements. Their language is explicitly political, setting them apart from both the English-speaking feminist theoretical discourse and that of BONPO and GONGO actors, which frame economic empowerment as "social." Another point on which they part company with feminist theoreticians such as Kessler-Harris and Schultz is their wish to see a revival, not the elimination, of state welfare. Lastly, activists' holding that work and economic independence should be conceived as rights may further complicate matters, as discourses on rights risk backfiring (see, e.g., Choo 2013; Joseph 2000). Applying rights narratives to local feminist struggles may unintentionally trap women in essentialized versions of "culture," or may have the opposite effect of imposing on them an unduly universalistic perception. As Ong (2006: 31) writes, "mantras from the north like 'women's rights are human rights' propose global human standards without regard to other moral systems and visions of ethical living." The language of rights has a powerful grip, particularly on activists with university education and professional training—recall the component of legal advocacy in the local feminist and workers' rights scene, documented in Chapter 3. So has the language of capacities and assets. Indeed, activists are aware of the potential slippages, and as mentioned try to offset what they perceive as biases by keeping busy with political and social-protest activism.

However, for the grassroots activists and for actors in the BONPO and GONGO sectors alike, I should note that despite the ideological distances and symbolic "breaks" that they each use to keep their worlds in order, their involvement in the social economy field tends to make them flexible. Through their routine contacts in the field, these actors are continuously challenged to mold and adjust their perspectives on economic citizenship.

And lastly, the women at the receiving end: Kessler-Harris encourages us to use the category of economic citizenship as a way to begin to imagine an equitable and fair society "that can effectively meld care-giving interests (for children as well as elderly and ill relatives and partners) with market-driven self-interest" (2003: 158). As the mapping of the various versions of economic citizenship that circulate in the social economy field revealed, the one closest to this interpretation was that of the women who participated in the workshops. In their unapologetic interweaving of words like *love, care,* and *giving* into the very training that aimed to make them more adept economic actors, these women brought their own understanding of the type of work that is valuable and the type of participation that should count. They thereby tapped at once into a distinctly local attitude to citizenship—one highly emotional and oblivious to detached economic rationality, and they added a markedly universal layer—care, which was entirely their own. So from their standpoint on the margins, and with their somewhat discordant discourse, these women shed light on the aspect of citizenship that official discourses prefer to evade: the practice of care and the unmediated contact that it generates with messy, bodily, and emotional needs. These uncanny practices—uncanny because they represent the innermost part of "the private" and therefore the alleged antithesis of "public" civility, and because they are potentially unruly—are readily marginalized; much like the women who perform them. However, as Yael Navaro-Yashin (2012) argues, the uncanny is in some way a species of the familiar.

The incorporation of care into discourses of citizenship poses a theoretical dilemma. It seems to aggravate the already existing tension between universalism (the principle of personal equality and freedom from primordial ties, which is premised on separation) and particularism (the passion for difference and group identification, premised on attachment). The vocabulary of care, moreover, is not identical to the emotional vocabulary already in use in particularistic discourses, with their stress on collective belonging and loud masculine overtones. The incorporation of care into discourses of citizenship also poses a political dilemma for feminists, who struggle to acknowledge women's care-work, but also to liberate them from its essentializing grip (e.g., Walby 1994). Pnina Werbner and Nira Yuval-Davis, in an attempt to overcome this impasse, invoke the idea of encompassment, and argue that while attachment should not eliminate universal individual rights, it needs to be encompassed by an ethic of care, compassion, and responsibility:

> For democracy to work, universalism must transcend difference, defining all subjects in abstract terms as equal before the law. But difference is then reinstated as a higher-order value, which encompasses equality through a relational and dialogical ethic of care, compassion, and responsibility. This higher-order stress upon difference therefore encompasses and subsumes universal and inclusive ideas about equality within it, without denying them. Hence, rather than a model that posits opposition between … a "liberal" individualist and a "republican" communitarian—feminist scholars seek to formulate models that highlight citizenship and civic activism as dialogical and relational, embedded in cultural and associational life. (Werbner and Yuval-Davis 1999b: 10)

By insisting on a vocabulary of care, and ultimately succumbing into the nonprofitability of the caretakers' position, the women therefore present an interpretation of economic citizenship that resists the attempt of the *economic* to overtake the *civic*, and urges restoration of the broad, humanistic sense of citizenship.

Notes

1. Another clear source of inspiration for feminist perspectives of economic citizenship is the International Covenant on Economic, Social and Cultural Rights (resolution 2200A XXI), which was ratified by the United Nations General Assembly in 1966 and entered into force ten years later.
2. "No rights without duties," Patriotic Israeli, accessed January 2013, http://www.kr8.co.il/BRPortal/br/P102.jsp?arc=456353.
3. This completely new party, headed by a popular TV presenter with no previous parliamentary experience, came second and promptly became the senior partner to the Netanyahu right-wing government coalition.

Conclusion

This book has explored the journeys of low-income women in Israel, Jewish and Palestinian, to economic self-sufficiency, and the institutional field of economic empowerment projects meant to help them achieve this goal. By including both Jewish and Palestinian women, and by paying attention to their distinct positioning but also to the contact zones between them, the book offers a grounded analysis of the intersections of gender, class, and ethnonationality. It has shed light on the tapestry of opportunities and blockages, and on how real women navigate them in their ongoing production of meaningful lives and meaningful femininities. The second layer of the book, the ethnography of social economy, describes the political economic context within which these personal experiences evolve. Analyzing the unusual collaborations among agents with very different subject positions, and their subsequent hybrid discourse on inclusion and entitlement, has allowed me to expose the context-bound effects of neoliberalism, or more specifically, the paradoxes that ensue as an ethnonational-cum-patriarchal logic of belonging gets infiltrated by the idea that the market is the best mediator of morality, justice, and identity.

Part I, *Paradoxes of the Pursuit of Solidarity amid Polarizing Social Inequalities,* introduced the global, paradox-ridden discourse on social justice in a neoliberal age, followed by an ethnographic description of the structure and texture of the Israeli social economy field. It featured a discourse full of paradoxes, which appears to bridge social and ideological oppositions without actually challenging the local structure of power. One of the confusing effects that emerged in the ethnographic description is encapsulated in the idea of "diversity" that informs much of the activity in the field. In seeming contrast to a hoary tradition of ethnic, national, and class rivalries, social economy projects entail a commitment of Zionist bodies to empower Palestinian citizens, inspire partnerships between social-change activists and state functionaries, and foster a newfound sense of sisterhood between Palestinian and Jewish low-income women. However, we have seen that despite a certain eagerness in members of the old elites to embrace Palestinians, Mizrahim, ultra-Orthodox, and other Others, the new language of "diversity" does not pose a fundamental challenge to the existing ethnic division of power. Rather, those in positions of social domination seek out the colorfulness and thick social fabric that diversity seems to offer. And while they do not recoil at the provocative tones of identity politics that many minority groups in Israel now communicate, they typically treat the proud, defiant language of those who embody "diversity" as a badge of exoticism, and thus neutralize its radical potential. This general effect of a seemingly drastic redefinition of the criteria for civil inclusion, which does not actually undermine the intractable nature of existing social divisions, is characteristic of the shift to neoliberal rationality more generally. I explored this effect systematically in the last chapter of the book, where I analyzed the penetration of the idea that entitlement should be mediated by economic productivity to a political setting that is premised on completely different measurements of belonging.

Part II, *Women Making Sense of the Demand to Make Money*, was dedicated to the women at the receiving end, the clients of economic empowerment projects. Chapter 2 presented a collective portrait of the women, framed within the idea of intersectionality, in which gender works in multiple ways with other mechanisms of power and exclusion, notably class, ethnicity, and—in the case at hand—ethnonationality. I explored how various subgroups are similar and different, and dwelt on the interplay of structural barriers, particular locations, and personal agency. I described the main sources of women's vulnerabilities, with an emphasis on their structural disadvantages in the labor force and the implications of economic liberalization, then looked closer at the particular situations of Palestinian women, new immigrant women, ultra-Orthodox Jewish women, and single mothers. I used lengthy excerpts from women's interviews to draw a complex profile of their vulnerabilities and agency.

Next I turned to empowerment, which is a key scenario in the field. Chapter 4 highlighted the deep contrariety of the term in the academic scholarship and dwelt on some unintended consequences of its implementation, resulting from the capitalistic embedment of social activism. The ethnography revealed that despite significant grassroots and scholarly critiques, the idea of empowerment remains highly popular in the field—although differently positioned actors invest it with very different meanings. In Israel *empowerment* is a term in constant flux, serving radical, liberal, and conservative circles, and appearing concurrently in the political, activist, professional, and consumerist domains. As such, I argued, it is a lingua franca that mediates competing definitions of reality and plays an important part in the emerging vernacular of entitlement. One prominent feature of empowerment that emerged from the ethnography was the extensive use of emotional talk, and the evident satisfaction that many participants derived from the workshops even when they did not get tangible economic benefits. I suggested that the opportunity to experiment with emotional talk might have value in and of itself, a point I continued to develop in Chapter 4, as part of my exploration of the ways in which the women perceived entitlement.

The main argument in Chapter 4 was that in their approach to work, low-income women are guided by a deep-seated cultural schema of a "gender contract," which expects them to be caretakers. While more and more of the women do want—and are even expected—to become wage earners, they do not wish to become primary breadwinners. In practice though, this schema does not work for most of them because the men they marry cannot earn enough to be the sole or even primary provider, and because they face a high probability of divorce. Gender contracts vary historically across social classes and ethnic groups, according to their degree of embedment in cash economy, their access to state services, and the scope of their civil prerogatives. Most relevant, in the case at hand, is the distinction between Jewish and Palestinian women, who operate within rather different structures of opportunities, despite some important common denominators. I used ethnographic materials to explore how low-income women of each respective group interpreted their opportunities, how they maneuvered between cash work and care work, and how they acted on these understandings to increase their income.

Besides the effects of anchoring normative femininity to the capacity to care (the gender contract), women were highly susceptible to the discourse of emotional capitalism, with its glorification of love as a motivation and a reward for income-generating work. Chapter 4 documented how, when challenged to think about how to increase their income, women preferred to talk about their capacity to care and love and avoided talking about money and financial interests. They talked about their work in altruistic terms even during business training workshops or when reflecting on their job market experiences in personal interviews. I suggested that while such love-work talk potentially reinforced their framing as those who do not really belong in the official working world—as somehow incapable of rational economic thinking—there was more to this phenomenon than simply self-defeating behavior. The workshop participants, I argued, may be using social economy projects as opportunities to experiment with a particular cultural style that makes extensive use of narratives of self and reflexivity, which is characteristically middle class and therefore not within their traditional reach. And they may be using the workshops, which purport to help them increase their income without facilitating too many tangible resources, as spaces on the margins where they exercise affective engagements and generate everyday forms of charisma.

Lastly, Part III, *Economic Citizenship—Between the Right to Work and the Obligation to Be Productive,* is a discussion of the notions of inclusion that emerged in the ethnography, using the concept of "economic citizenship." Unlike *empowerment, social economy,* or *diversity, economic citizenship* is not an emic term. It is an analytical concept that I chose because it resonates with some of the main ideas that circulate in the field. I reviewed the different meanings given to economic citizenship in the scholarly literature, and explored the echo of these various meanings in the local Israeli context. Emblematic of social economy's tendency to create strange bedfellows, the ways local actors think about economic citizenship—the idea that civil rights can be earned and measured according to economic self-sufficiency—are rooted in different and even conflicting ideological worldviews: feminists argue that access to gainful employment should be treated as a basic civil right; free market advocates see economic self-sufficiency as an obligation—poor people must earn their keep—as well as a justification for extended prerogatives for particularly high-income people; community economic development supporters emphasize social capital and collective capacity building as important enhancers of economic productivity. Yet despite ideological distances, on the ground understandings of economic citizenship reflect subtle but meaningful dialogues between bearers of these different perspectives, since they develop through the hands-on involvement of actors from very different social backgrounds.

Besides looking at how an idea is made meaningful in the process of crossing social and ideological spheres within a single polity (Israel), my exploration of economic citizenship also looked at how this globally circulating concept travels across regional and cultural borders. In this respect I asked how the idea of economic citizenship, with its distinctly individualistic and pecuniary emphases, integrates into the Israeli context, where citizenship is imagined, first and foremost, in collective and primordial terms. How, in other words, does the rapidly disseminating idea that rights and obligations in a polity should be earned and measured in capitalistic tokens settle and adapt into a particular locale? I argued that the vernacular version of economic citizenship comprises a neoliberal exception to local understandings of citizenship, rather than replaces the cultural blueprint: this remains deeply essentialist, collectivist, and exclusionary. I likewise considered the subtle contribution of low-income women to this emerging discourse. By insisting on a vocabulary of care, and ultimately conceding the nonprofitability of the caretakers' position, they present an interpretation of economic citizenship as resisting the attempt by the *economic* to overtake the *civic,* and urge restoration of the broad, humanistic sense of citizenship.

In more general terms, this ethnography aimed to shed light on some of the main ironies that result from shifting responsibility to reduce poverty and social inequalities from the state to the market. Many of the developments described are familiar in other countries as well: we have seen a disproportionate investment in pedagogy—teaching women how to do business or apply for jobs—without comparable investments in the creation of new jobs or supportive infrastructure, such as subsidized childcare or proper transportation. We have seen how despite the best intentions of their operators, the projects effectively reinforce the focus on women as individuals rather than members of structural categories, how they willy-nilly endorse the idea that economic success depends on women's capacity to connect to their true selves, how they encourage women to want to fulfill themselves through jobs that will never yield sufficient monetary returns, and how they irradiate them with everyday forms of charisma, which is rewarding and meaningful but also distinctly apolitical. At the same time, we have also seen that the agency of the participants in social economy initiatives cannot be dismissed out of hand, despite the formidable dynamics of exclusion, co-optation, and entrenched structural violence. Careful documentation of the motivations, the meaning making, and the emotional investment of the actors provided insights into the complex operation of neoliberal rationality, as the ravaging forces of economic globalization assume distinct shapes in culturally specific settings, with particular histories and particular articulations of social inequalities.

Not an Aloof Observer: Engaging Activists' Spirit of Hope

During the decade that I spent researching social economy and women's empowerment, I had many conversations and exchanges with actors within and outside the field. In addition to long periods of participant observations that I conducted in courses, study days, general assemblies, etc., and dozens of personal interviews with a wide array of people, I was invited to give talks, join steering committees, write reports, comment on other people's reports and policy papers, and advise project operators during various phases of their work. Later, as I was writing this book, I presented chapters at academic seminars in Israel and abroad. Often, these very meaningful engagements, in which I presented my work to diverse kinds of informed audiences, generated some confusion regarding my position vis-à-vis the grand task of empowering economically vulnerable women. In particular, my focus on unintended consequences, internal paradoxes, and the contradictory meanings of concepts such as "empowerment," "economic citizenship," "social capital," or "diversity," was frequently met with discomfort. To activists and practitioners, who expected my advice regarding best practices, my fascination with contradictions was not particularly fruitful. By contrast, some politically radical activists and critical scholars thought I was not decisive enough in stating the inherent fallacies of empowerment schemes that are rooted in a racist-classist regime. Then again, some colleagues inferred that I was advocating the ideas of economic citizenship, empowerment, or diversity: they ignored or missed my argument that these are conceptual vessels that, at one and the same time, facilitate dialogues across vast social and ideological divides and trap ideas about social justice in an all-encompassing neoliberal logic.

In large measure, these responses reflected my own complex position. Throughout this research project I have swung between dismay at the gripping force with which capitalism co-opts even the most innovative attempts to create a more balanced, solidary, and just society, and awe at the vision and passion with which people leap into action, reach outside their comfort zones, and produce meaningful results for real-life women. Incidentally, this complexity besets many social economy practitioners also. As I have described in detail, many actors in the field are reflexive, very well informed, and sophisticated in the ways they think about what they are doing. In particular, people in the field are concerned with the implications of NGOization—the fact that social change activism has shifted from the old labor unions/social movements patterns to civil society organizations that are tied to donor money, committed to predesigned and inflexible work plans, encourage professionalization, and are bound by a specific form of economic accountability. Yet as also described, these are often the same people who continue to be active for peace, feminism, labor rights, and democracy also outside the NGO frameworks. They are intensely alert to the forces of co-optation that intervene in their work in social economy, but are also wary of perpetuating the dogmatism of the old Israeli political left; they understand the benefits of cross-sectorial alliances; and are capable of admitting their own complex motivations.

I want to end this brief conclusion by applauding the spirit of these activists. As I write, in mid-2014, many of them are debating the limits of NGOization and are using Information Technology to form new types of alliances, to loosen the grip of business philanthropists, and to disseminate knowledge and create new resources. Some of them opt to resurrect labor unionism, and practically all of them aim to reassert collective subjectivity as a counterforce to the strong individualizing influences of the era. And they are producing insightful counternarratives, even as their speech style converges with the latest emotional fashion. These activists, in other words, are using and developing their capabilities as thinking, moral subjects, and treating the women they work with in the same way. These are the very qualities that scholars of development have identified as essential to the fulfillment of social justice and human freedom (Sen 1999; Nussbaum 2003; Walby 2005; Moghadam and Senftova 2005; Kabeer 1994). I am inspired by the capabilities of these actors and by the hopeful, creative spirit that drives them. By presenting their stories, and those of the women they work with, this book hopes to shed light on the thick layers of meaningful action, care, and dedication that strive on, even at the heart of rapacious capitalism.

References

Abdo-Zubi, Nahla. 2011. *Women in Israel: Race, Gender and Citizenship.* London and New York: Zed Books.
Abdu, Janan. 2008. *Palestinian Women's and Feminist NGOs within the 1948 Green Line.* Haifa: Mada al-Carmel. (Arabic)
Aboim, Sofia. 2010. "Gender Cultures and the Division of Labour in Contemporary Europe: A Cross-national Perspective." *Sociological Review* 58(2): 171–96.
Abu-Lughod, Lila, and Catherine A. Lutz. 1990. "Introduction: Emotion, Discourse, and the Politics of Everyday Life." In *Language and the Politics of Emotion,* edited by Catherine Lutz and Lila Abu-Lughod, vol. 1, 1–23. Cambridge: Cambridge University Press.
Abu-Rabia-Queder, Sarab. 2007. "The Activism of Bedouin Women: Social and Political Resistance." *HAGAR: Studies in Culture Polity and Identities* 7: 67–85.
Adams, Walter. 1968. *The Brain Drain.* New York: Macmillan.
Abutbul, Guy, Lev Grinberg, and Pnina Motzafi-Haller, eds. 2005. *Mizrahi Voices: Towards a New Discourse on Israeli Society and Culture.* Tel Aviv: Massada. (Hebrew)
Ailon, Galit. 2011. "Mapping the Cultural Grammar of Reflexivity: The Case of the Enron Scandal." *Economy and Society* 40(1): 141–66.
Ajzenstadt, Mimi. 2009. "Moral Panic and Neo-Liberalism the Case of Single Mothers on Welfare in Israel." *British Journal of Criminology* 49(1): 68–87.
Al-Haj, M. 1995. *Education, Empowerment and Control: The Case of the Arabs in Israel.* Albany: State University of New York Press.
Almagor-Loten, Orly. 2008. "Employment of Women in the Arab Sector." Jerusalem: Israeli Knesset, Center of Research and Information. Accessed January 2013. (Hebrew) http://www.knesset.gov.il/mmm/data/pdf/m01983.pdf.
Almog-Bar, Michal, and Mimi Ajzenstadt. 2010. "Women, Welfare and Civil Society Organizations: Creating an Alternative Women's Welfare Sphere in Israel." *Social Policy & Administration* 44(6): 673–88.
Anitha, Sundari. 2011. "Legislating Gender Inequalities: The Nature and Patterns of Domestic Violence Experienced by South Asian Women with Insecure Immigration Status in the United Kingdom." *Violence against Women* 17(10): 1260–85.
Anthias, Floya. 1998. "Rethinking Social Divisions: Some Notes Towards a Theoretical Framework." *Sociological Review* 46(3): 505–35.
Barak-Erez, Daphne. 2008. "Israel: Citizenship and Immigration Law in the Vise of Security, Nationality, and Human Rights." *International Journal of Constitutional Law* 6: 184–92.
Bartram, David V. 1998. "Foreign Workers in Israel: History and Theory." *International Migration Review* 32(2): 303–25.
Batliwala, Srilatha, and Deepa Dhanraj. 2004. "Gender Myths that Instrumentalise Women: A View from the Indian Frontline." *Ids Bulletin* 35(4): 11–18.

Baum, Dalit. 2006. "Women in Black and Men in Pink: Protesting Against the Israeli Occupation." *Social Identities* 12(5): 563–74.

Becker, Gary. 1997. "Why Not Let Immigrants Pay for Speedy Entry?" In *The Economics of Life: From Baseball to Affirmative Action to Immigration, How Real-World Issues Affect our Everyday Life*, edited by Gary Becker and Guity Nashat Becker, 58–60. New York; McGraw Hill Professional.

Benjamin, Orly. 2002. "The Duality in the Relations between the State and Women in Israel: The Case of Public Sector Employees Working through Manpower Agencies." *Society and Welfare: A Social Work Quarterly* 22(4): 455–80. (Hebrew)

———. 2006. "In the Downslopes of the Labor Market: Marketing the Female Labor Force in Israel." *Democratic Culture* 10: 63–96.

Bennett, Jane. 1997. "The Enchanted World of Modernity: Paracelsus, Kant, and Deleuze." *Journal for Cultural Research* 1(1): 1–28.

———. 2001. "Commodity Fetishism and Commodity Enchantment." *Theory & Event* 5(1).

Ben-Porat, Guy. 2004. "Business and Peace: The Rise and Fall of the New Middle East." In *The Power of Property: Israeli Society in the Global Age*, edited by Dani Filc and Uri Ram, 181–96. Jerusalem: Van Leer and HaKibuts Hame'uhad. (Hebrew)

———. 2005. "Business and Peace: The Rise and Fall of the New Middle East." *World Political Science Review* 1(1).

Berkovitch, Nitza. 1997. "Motherhood as a National Mission: The Construction of Womanhood in the Legal Discourse in Israel." *Women's Studies International Forum* 20(5–6): 605–19.

Berkovitch, Nitza and Adriana Kemp. 2010. "Economic Empowerment of Women as a Global Project: Economic Rights in the Neo-Liberal Era." In *Confronting Global Gender Justice: Women's Lives, Human Rights*, edited by Debra bergoffen, Paula Ruth Gilbert, Tamara Harvey and Connie L. NcNeely, 158–179. Oxford, UK: Routledge.

Bernstein, Deborah, Orly Benjamin, and Pnina Motzafi-Haller. 2011. "Diversity in an Israeli Intersectional Analysis: The Salience of Employment Arrangements and Inter-Personal Relationships." *Women's Studies International Forum* 34(3): 220–31.

Bernstein, Deborah, and Shlomo Swirski. 1982. "The Rapid Economic Development of Israel and the Emergence of the Ethnic Division of Labour." *British Journal of Sociology* 33(1): 64–85.

Birenbaum-Carmeli, Daphna. 2008. "Your Faith or Mine: A Pregnancy Spacing Intervention in an Ultra-Orthodox Jewish Community in Israel." *Reproductive Health Matters* 16(32): 185–91.

Blumen, Orna. 2007. "The Gendered Display of Work: The Midday Scene in an Ultra-Orthodox Street in Israel." *Nashim: A Journal of Jewish Women's Studies & Gender Issues* 13 (1): 123–154.

Blumberg, Rae Lesser. 1991. *Gender, Family and Economy: The Triple Overlap*. Newbury Park, London, New Delhi: Sage.

Boje, David M., and Grace A. Rosile. 2001. "Where's the Power in Empowerment? Answers from Follett and Clegg." *Journal of Applied Behavioral Science* 37(1): 90–117.

Boltanski, Luc, and Eve Chiapello. 2005. "The New Spirit of Capitalism." *International Journal of Politics, Culture, and Society* 18(3–4): 161–88.

Borna, Shaheen, and James M. Stearns. 2002. "The Ethics and Efficacy of Selling National Citizenship." *Journal of Business Ethics* 37(2): 193–207.

Bornstein, Avram S. 2002. "Border Enforcement in Daily Life: Palestinian Day Laborers and Entrepreneurs Crossing the Green Line." *Human Organization* 22(2): 201–20.

Boserup, Ester. 1970. *Woman's Role in Economic Development*. London, Allen & Unwin.

Bourdieu, Pierre. 1977. *Outline of a Theory of Practice*. Trans. Cambridge: Cambridge University Press.
Broomhill, Ray, and Rhonda Sharp. 2005. "The Changing Male Breadwinner Model in Australia: A New Gender Order?" *Labour & Industry* 16(1): 103–27.
Budig, Michelle J., Joya Misra, and Irene Boeckmann. 2012. "The Motherhood Penalty in Cross-National Perspective: The Importance of Work–Family Policies and Cultural Attitudes." *Social Politics: International Studies in Gender, State & Society* 19(2): 163–93.
Buksbaum, Ya'ara, and Michal Dagan. 2010. *Women Entrapped between Age and Employment*. Haifa: Mahut Centre. (Hebrew)
Buksbaum, Ya'ara, Michal Dagan, Umayma Diab, and Dorit Avramovitch. 2009. *Women Workers in a Precarious Employment Market*. Haifa: Mahut Centre. (Hebrew)
Bunch, Charlotte, and Roxanna Carrillo. 1990. "Feminist Perspectives on Women in Development." In *Persistent Inequalities: Women and World Development*, edited by Irene Tinker, 70–82. New York: Oxford University Press.
Butler, Judith. 1993. *Bodies That Matter: On the Discursive Limits of "Sex."* New York: Routledge.
Canadian Women's Foundation. 2010. "Beyond Survival: Helping Women Transition Out of Poverty." Accessed 8 April 2013. http://www.canadianwomen.org/sites/canadian women.org/files/PDF%20-%20Beyond%20Survival%20-%20Report%20FINAL%20 EN.pdf.
Chaskin, Robert J., and Jona M. Rosenfeld. 2008. *Research for Action: Cross-National Perspectives on Connecting Knowledge: Policy and Practice for Children*. Oxford: Oxford University Press.
Chetrit, Sami Shalom. 2004. *The Mizrahi Struggle in Israel 1948–2003*. Tel Aviv: Am Oved. (Hebrew)
Chiswick Barry R. 1982. "The Impact of Immigration on the Level and Distribution of Economic Well-Being." In *The Gateway: U.S. Immigration Issues and Policies*, edited by Barry R. Chiswick, 289–313. Washington, DC: American Enterprise Institute for Public Policy Research.
Choo, Hae Yeon. 2013. "The Cost of Rights: Migrant Women, Feminist Advocacy, and Gendered Morality in South Korea." *Gender & Society* no. 27: 445–68.
Cockburn, Cynthia. 2004. *The Line: Women, Partition and the Gender Order in Cyprus*. London: Zed Books.
Coker, Jeffrey W. 2002. *Confronting American Labor: The New Left Dilemma*. Columbia: University of Missouri Press.
Colen, Shellee. 1995. "'Like a Mother to Them': Stratified Reproduction and West Indian Childcare Workers and Employers in New York." In *Conceiving the New World Order: The Global Politics of Reproduction*, edited by Faye D. Ginsburg and Rayna Rapp, 78–102. Berkeley: University of California Press.
Collins, Patricia Hill. 1990. *Black Feminist Thought: Knowledge, Consciousness, and the Politics of Empowerment*. Boston: Unwin Hyman.
Comaroff, Jean, and John Comaroff, eds. 2001. *Millennial Capitalism and the Culture of Neoliberalism*. Durham, NC: Duke University Press.
———. 2001a. Millennial capitalism: first thoughts on a second coming." In *Millennial Capitalism and the Culture of Neoliberalism*, edited by Jean Comaroff and John Comaroff, 1–56. Durham, NC: Duke University Press.
———. 2003a. "Ethnography on an Awkward Scale: Postcolonial Anthropology and the Violence of Abstraction." *Ethnography* 4(2): 147–79.
———. 2003b. "Reflections on Liberalism, Policulturalism, and ID-Ology: Citizenship and Difference in South Africa." *Social Identities* 9(4): 445–73.

Combahee River Collective. 1983. "Combahee River Collective Statement." In *Home Girls: A Black Feminist Anthology*, edited by Barbara Smith, 272–82. New York: Kitchen Table—Women of Color Press.
Connell, R. W. 1996. "New Directions in Gender Theory, Masculinity Research, and Gender Politics," *Ethnos* 3–4(61): 157–76.
Connell, R. W. 2000. "Arms and the Man." In *Male Roles, Masculinities and Violence: A Culture of Peace Perspective*, edited by Ingeborg Breines, Robert Connell, and Ingrid Eide, 21–34. Paris: UNESCO.
Crenshaw, Kimberle. 1989. "Demarginalizing the Intersection of Race and Sex: A Black Feminist Critique of Antidiscrimination Doctrine, Feminist Theory and Antiracist Politics." *University of Chicago Legal Forum* 140: 139–67.
Cruikshank, Barbara. 1993. "The Will to Empower: Technologies of Citizenship and the War on Poverty." *Socialist Review* 23(4): 29–55.
———. 1999. *The Will to Empower: Democratic Citizens and Other Subjects*. Ithaca, NY: Cornell University Press.
Curtis, Richard F. 1986. "Household and Family in Theory on Inequality." *American Sociological Review* 51: 168–83.
Cushman, Philip. 1995. *Constructing the Self, Constructing America: A Cultural History of Psychotherapy*. Boston, MA: Addison-Wesley.
Cwikel, Julie, and Nurit Barak. 2002. "Health and Welfare of Bedouin Women in the Negev." Be'er Sheva: Center for Bedouin Studies and Development, Ben Gurion University of the Negev.
Dagan-Buzaglo, Noga, Yael Hasson, and Arian Ophir. 2014. *Gender Salary Gaps in Israel*. Tel Aviv: Adva Center. (Hebrew)
Dahan-Kalev, Henriette. 2001. "Tensions in Israeli Feminism: The Mizrahi Ashkenazi Rift." *Women's Studies International Forum* 24(6): 669–84.
Dalal, K., and K. Lindqvist. 2012. "A National Study of the Prevalence and Correlates of Domestic Violence among Women in India." *Asia-Pacific Journal of Public Health/Asia-Pacific Academic Consortium for Public Health* 24(2): 265–77.
Damary-Madar, Vered, ed. 2002. *Mizrahi Feminism*. Jerusalem: Hillel, the Hebrew University and Students for Social Justice. (Hebrew)
Davis, Kathy. 2008. "Intersectionality as Buzzword A Sociology of Science Perspective on what Makes a Feminist Theory Successful." *Feminist Theory* 9(1): 67–85.
Dominguez, Virginia R. 1989. *People as Subject, People as Object: Selfhood and Peoplehood in Contemporary Israel*. Madison: University of Wisconsin Press.
Doron, Avraham. 2004. "The Annual Publication of Israel's Poverty Report: The Media and the Reactions in the Political System." In *The Power of Property: Israeli Society in the Global Age*, edited by Dani Filc and Uri Ram, 164–80. Jerusalem: Van Leer and HaKibuts Hame'uhad. (Hebrew)
———. 2007. "Multiculturalism and the Erosion of Support for the Universalistic Welfare State: The Israeli Experience." *Israel Studies* 12(3): 92–108.
Drori, Israel. 2000. *The Seam Line: Arab Workers and Israeli Managers in the Israeli Textile Industry*. Princeton, NJ: Princeton University Press.
Dwyer, Daisy, and Judith Bruce. 1988. *A Home Divided: Women and Income in the Third World*. Palo Alto, CA: Stanford University Press.
Ehlers, Tracy Bachrach, and Karen Main. 1998, "Women and the False Promise of Microenterprise." *Gender & Society* 12(4): 424–40.
Ehrenreich, Barbara, and Arlie Russell Hochschild. 2002. *Global Woman: Nannies, Maids, and Sex Workers in the New Economy*. New York: Metropolitan Books.

Elder, Glen H. 1978. "The Family Cycle and the Life Course." In *Transitions: The Family and the Life Course in Historical Perspective*, edited by Tamara Hareven, 57–64. New York: Academic Press.
El-Or, Tamar. 1994. *Educated and Ignorant: Ultraorthodox Jewish Women and Their World*. Boulder, CO: Lynne Rienner.
———. 1997. "Visibility and Possibilities: Ultraorthodox Jewish Women between the Domestic and Public Spheres." *Women's Studies International Forum Journal* 20(5): 665–73.
Elyachar, Julia. 2002. "Empowerment Money: The World Bank, Non-Governmental Organizations, and the Value of Culture in Egypt." *Public Culture* 14(3): 493–513.
———. 2005. *Markets of Dispossession: NGOs, Economic Development, and the State in Cairo*. Durham, NC: Duke University Press.
Endeweld, Miri, Netanela Barkali, Daniel Gottlieb, and Alex Fruman. 2012. *Poverty and Social Gaps Report—Poverty and Social Gaps in 2011, Annual Report*. Jerusalem: National Insurance Institute, Research and Planning Administration. (Hebrew)
Erel, Umut. 2012. "Introduction: Transnational Care in Europe Changing Formations of Citizenship, Family and Generation." *Social Politics* 19(1): 1–14.
Ertman, Martha M. 2002. "Love and Work: A Response to Vicki Schultz's 'Life's Work.'" *Columbia Law Review* 102(3): 848–64.
Faier, Elizabeth. 2005. *Organizations, Gender and the Culture of Palestinian Activism in Haifa, Israel*. New York: Routledge.
Farminger, Jonathan. 2010. "Manpower Subcontractors in Israel: Government Interests in the Development of a Dual Labor Force." *Public Space* no. 4: 131–55.
Feder, Kittay Eva. 1999. *Love's Labor: Essays on Women, Equality and Dependency*. New York: Routledge.
Filc, Dani. 2004. "Israel Model 2000: Neo-Liberal Post-Fordism." In *The Power of Property: Israeli Society in the Global Age*, edited by Dani Filc and Uri Ram, 31–56. Jerusalem: Van Leer and HaKibuts Hame'uhad. (Hebrew)
Fogiel-Bijaoui, Sylvie. 1997. "Women in Israel: The Politics of Citizenship as a Non-Issue." *Israel Social Science Research* 12(1): 1–30.
Folbre, Nancy. 1991. "The Unproductive Housewife: Her Evolution in Nineteenth-Century Economic Thought." *Signs* 3: 463–84.
Fried, Devora, Ronit Harris, and Osnat Fichtelberg-Barmats. 2009. "Characteristics of the Employees of Tender-Age Daycare Services Certified by the Ministry of Industry, Trade, and Labor. Findings Form a Special Survey." (Hebrew) Accessed 20 May 2013. http://www.moital.gov.il/NR/rdonlyres/922BBEE4-844E-4F1B-BFDB-BDBBD5B0 D052/0/X9463A.pdf.
Ghanem, As'ad. 2009. "Democratizing "Ethnic States": The Democratization Process in Divided Societies–with a Special Reference to Israel." *Constellations* 16(3): 462–75.
Goldstein-Gidoni, Ofra. 2012. *Housewives of Japan: An Ethnography of Real Lives and Consumerized Domesticity*. Basingstoke: Palgrave Macmillan.
Goodman, Jane E. 2010. "Performing Laicite: Gender, Agency, and Neoliberalism among Algerians in France." In *Ethnographies of Neoliberalism*, edited by Carol J. Greenhouse, 195–206. Philadelphia: University of Pennsylvania Press.
Gottfried, Heidi. 2000. "Compromising Positions: Emergent neo-Fordisms and Embedded Gender Contracts." *British Journal of Sociology* 51(2): 235–59.
———. 2013. *Gender, Work, and Economy: Unpacking the Global Economy*. Cambridge: Polity.
Gottfried, Heidi, and Jecqueline O'Reilly. 2002. "Regulating Breadwinner Models in Socially Conservative Welfare Systems: Comparing Germany and Japan." *Social Politics* 9(1): 29–59.

Greenhouse, Carol J. 2010. *Ethnographies of Neoliberalism*. Philadelphia: University of Pennsylvania Press.
Grinberg, Lev L. 1993. *The Histadrut Above All*. Jerusalem: Nevo Publications. (Hebrew)
Guillén, Ana M. 2003. "Measuring Economic Citizenship: A Comment on Alice Kessler-Harris." *Social Politics: International Studies in Gender, State and Society* 10(2): 186–95.
Gutmann, Amy. *Democracy and the Welfare State*. Princeton, NJ: Princeton University Press, 1988.
Guyer, Jane. 1988. "Dynamic Approaches to Domestic Budgeting: Cases and Methods from Africa." In *A Home Divided: Women and Income in the Third World*, edited by Daisy Dwyer and Judith Bruce, 155–72. Palo Alto, CA: Stanford University Press.
Haidar, Aziz, ed. 2005. *The Arab Society in Israel Book*. Jerusalem: Van Leer Institute. (Hebrew)
Hanafi, Sari. 2012. "Flexible Citizenship and the Inflexible Nation-State: New Framework for Appraising the Palestinian Refugees' Movements." *Journal of International Migration and Integration* 13(4): 441–58.
Harker, Richard K., Cheleen Mahar, and Chris Wilkes, eds. 1990. *An Introduction to the Work of Pierre Bourdieu: The Practice of Theory*. New York: Martin's Press.
Hartsock, Nancy C. M. 1983. "The Feminist Standpoint: Developing the Ground for a Specifically Feminist Historical Materialism." In *Discovering Reality: Feminist Perspectives on Epistemology, Metaphysics, Methodology, and Philosophy of Science*, edited by Sandra Harding and Merrill B. Hintikka, 283–310. New York: Kluwer Academic.
Harvey, David. 2005. *A Brief History of Neoliberalism*. Oxford: Oxford University Press.
Hasson, Yael. 2006. *Three Decades of Privatization*. Tel Aviv: Adva Center. (Hebrew)
Helman, Sara. 1999. "From Soldiering and Motherhood to Citizenship: A Study of Four Israeli Peace Protest Movements." *Social Politics: International Studies in Gender, State & Society* 6(3): 292–313.
———. 2013. "How Cashiers, Cleaning Workers and Caretakers Turned into Entrepreneurs: Workfare Programs and the Construction of the Construction of the Entrepreneurial Self." *Israeli Sociology* 14(2): 312–35. (Hebrew)
Herbst, Anat. 2012. "Discourse of Need: The Case of Child Support (Payment Assurance)." *Women's Studies International Forum* 35(4): 214–22.
———. 2013. "Welfare Mom as Warrior Mom: Discourse in the 2003 Single Mothers' Protest in Israel." *Journal of Social Policy* 42(1): 129–45.
Herzog, Hanna. 1999a. *Gendering Politics: Women in Israel*. Ann Arbor: University of Michigan Press.
———. 1999b. "A Space of Their Own: Social-Civil Discourses among Palestinian-Israeli Women in Peace Organizations." *Social Politics: International Studies in Gender, State & Society* 6(3): 344–69.
———. 2004. "'Both an Arab and a Woman': Gendered, Racialised Experiences of Female Palestinian Citizens of Israel." *Social Identities* 10(1): 53–82.
———. 2008. "Re/visioning the Women's Movement in Israel." *Citizenship Studies* 12(3): 265–82.
Hever, Hannan, Yehouda Shenhav, and Pnina Mutzafi-Haller, eds. 2002. *Mizrahim in Israel: A Critical Observation into Israel's Ethnicity*. Jerusalem: Van Leer and Hakibutz Hameuhad. (Hebrew)
Hobson, Barbara. 2003. "Some Reflections and Agendas for the Future." *Social Politics: International Studies in Gender, State and Society* 10(2): 196–204.
Hochberg, Gil Z., Haneen Maikey, and Samira Saraya. 2010. "No Pride in Occupation a Roundtable Discussion." *GLQ: A Journal of Lesbian and Gay Studies* 16(4): 599–610.

Hochschild Arlie R. 1983. "The Managed Heart: Commercialization of Human Feeling." Berkeley, University of California Press.
———. 1989. *The Second Shift: Working Parents and the Revolution at Home*. New York: Viking.
———. 1997. *The Time Bind*. New York: Henry Holt.
———. 2003. *The Commercialization of Intimate Life: Notes from Home and Work*. Berkeley: University of California Press.
———. 2011. "Emotional Life on the Market Frontier." *Annual Review of Sociology* 37: 21–33.
Hoodfar, Homa. 1988. "Household Budgeting and Financial Management in a Lower-Income Cairo Neighborhood." In *A Home Divided: Women and Income in the Third World*, edited by Daisy Dwyer and Judith Bruce, 120–42. Palo Alto, CA: Stanford University Press.
Horev, Tuvia, and Nir Keidar. 2010. "Light and Shadow in the Development and Implementation of the Law of National Health Insurance." (Hebrew) Accessed 25 April 2013. http://www.health.gov.il/PublicationsFiles/econ_light_shadow.pdf.
Hossein, Johayna, ed. 2012. *Kuluna Hikaya (We Are All a Story): Action Oriented Research on Al-Tufula Center's Empowerment Approach to Engaging Women in Social Change*. Nazareth: Al-Tufula Center. (Arabic)
Humphrey, Hubert H. "The War on Poverty." *Law and Contemporary Problems* (1966): 6–17.
Ilany, Ayelet. 2005. *Growth from a Different Direction: Mapping Strategies for Community Economic Development and Observing the Development of Social Economy in Israel*. Jerusalem: Shatil. (Hebrew)
Illouz, Eva. 1997. *Consuming the Romantic Utopia: Love and the Cultural Contradictions of Capitalism*. Berkeley: University of California Press.
———. 2007. *Cold Intimacies: The Making of Emotional Capitalism*. Cambridge: Polity.
Ivry, Tsipy, Elly Teman, and Ayala Frumkin. 2011. "God-Sent Ordeals and Their Discontents: Ultra-Orthodox Jewish Women Negotiate Prenatal Testing." *Social Science & Medicine* 72(9): 1527–33.
Jabareen, Hassan. 2002. "The Future of Arab Citizenship in Israel: Jewish-Zionist Time in a Plce with No Palestinian Memory." In *Challenging Ethnic Citizenship: German and Israeli Perspectives on Immigration*, edited by Daniel Levy and Yfaat Weiss, 196–220. New York: Berghahn.
Jenkins, Richard. 2012. "Disenchantment, Enchantment and Re-Enchantment: Max Weber at the Millennium." *Mind and Matter* 10 (2): 149–168.
Johnson, Carol. 2010. "The Politics of Affective Citizenship: From Blair to Obama." *Citizenship Studies* 14(5): 495–509.
Joseph, Suad. 2000. "Gender and Citizenship in the Middle East." In *Gender and Citizenship in the Middle East*, edited by Suad Joseph, 3–30. Syracuse, NY: Syracuse University Press.
———. 2005. "The Kin Contract and Citizenship in the Middle East." In *Women and Citizenship*, edited by Marilyn Friedman, 149–69. New York: Oxford University Press.
Kabeer, Naila. 1994. *Reversed Realities: Gender Hierarchies in Development Thought*. Verso.
———. 1999. *The Conditions and Consequences of Choice: Reflections on the Measurement of Women's Empowerment*. United Nations Research Institute for Social Development Discussion Paper no. 108. Geneva: UNRISD.
Kalekin-Fishman, Devorah, and Karlheinz Schneider. 2007. *Radicals in Spite of Themselves: Ultra-Orthodox Women Working Outside the Haredi Community*. Rotterdam: Sense Publishers.

Kalleberg, Arne L., Barbara F. Reskin, and Ken Hudson. 2000. "Bad Jobs in America: Standard and Nonstandard Employment Relations and Job Quality in the United States." *American Sociological Review*: 256–78.
Kanaaneh, Hatim, Fiona McKay, and Emily Sims. 1995. "A Human Rights Approach for Access to Clean Drinking Water: A Case Study." *Health and Human Rights* 1(2): 190–204.
Kanaaneh, Rhoda Ann. 2002. *Birthing the Nation: Strategies of Palestinian Women in Israel*. Berkeley, CA: University of California Press.
Kandiyoti, Deniz. 1988. "Bargaining with Patriarchy." *Gender & Society* 2(3): 274–90.
———., ed. 1991. *Women, Islam, and the State*. Temple University Press.
Kaneh-Shalit, Tamar. 2015. "Positive Thinking without a Smile: Self and Care in Israeli Life Coaching." PhD diss., University of Haifa.
Karim, Lamia. 2011. *Microfinance and Its Discontents: Women in Debt in Bangladesh*. Minneapolis: University of Minnesota Press.
Katriel, Tamar. 2004. *Dialogic Moments: From Soul Talks to Talk Radio in Israeli Culture*. Detroit, MI: Wayne State University Press.
Katz, Hagai, and Hila Yogev-Keren. 2013. "The Labor Market of the Third Sector in Israel: Data and Orientations 2000–2009." The Israeli Center for the Study of the Third Sector. Accessed 6 May 2013. http://web.bgu.ac.il/NR/rdonlyres/67CD3063-7886-4F9F-99D8-F0D87D465BD2/127742/ShukHaAvoda_SMALL_180413.pdf.
Kemp, Adriana. 2002. "'Peoples' Migration': State Control and Resistance in the Israeli Frontier." In *Mizrahi Voices: Towards a New Discourse on Israeli Society and Culture*, edited by Guy Abutbul, Lev Grinberg and Pnina Motzafi-Haller, 309–319. Tel Aviv: Massada. (Hebrew)
Kemp, Adriana. 2004. "Labour Migration and Racialisation: Labour Market Mechanisms and Labour Migration Control Policies in Israel." *Social Identities* 10(2): 267–92.
Kemp, Adriana, and Nitza Berkovitch. n.d. "The Making of Financial Citizenship: Economic Empowerment of Women in Israel."
———. 2013. "Pedagogic Governance and the Financialization of Everyday Life the Making of Micro Finance for Marginalized Women in Israel." In *Neo-liberal Bureaucratisation*, edited by Béatrice Hibou. Paris: La Découverte. (French)
Kessler-Harris, Alice. 2003. *In Pursuit of Equity: Women, Men, and the Quest for Economic Citizenship in 20th Century America*. Oxford University Press.
———. 2006. "The Wages of Patriarchy: Some Thoughts about the Continuing Relevance of Class and Gender." *Labor* 3(3): 7–21.
Khamaisi, Rasem. 2009. *The Arab Society in Israel Book 3*. Jerusalem: Van Leer Institute. (Hebrew)
Khattab, Nabil. 2002. "Ethnicity and Female Labour Market Participation: A New Look at the Palestinian Enclave in Israel." *Work, Employment & Society* 16(1): 91–110.
Khazzoom, Aziza. 2005. "Did the Israeli State Engineer Segregation? On the Placement of Jewish Immigrants in Development Towns in the 1950s." *Social Forces* 84(1): 115–34.
Kimmerling, Baruch. 2001. *The End of Ashkenazi Hegemony*. Jerusalem: Keter. (Hebrew)
King, Judith, Deniz Neon, Wolde-Tsadick Abraham, and Jack Habib. 2009. "Employment of Arab Women Aged 18–64." Myers-JDC-Brookdale Institute. (Hebrew) Accessed July 2010. http://brookdale.jdc.org.il/?CategoryID=192&ArticleID=39.
Kretzmer, David. 1990. *The Legal Status of the Arabs in Israel*. Boulder, CO: Westview Press.
Lavie, Noa. 2006. "Sawing Globalization: Globalization, the State, and the Textile Industry." *Theory and Criticism* no. 29: 103–23. (Hebrew)
Lavie, Smadar. 2011. "Mizrahi Feminism and the Question of Palestine." *Journal of Middle East Women's Studies* 7(2): 56–88.

———. 2014. *Wrapped in the Flag of Israel: Mizrahi Single Mothers and Bureaucratic Torture.* New York: Berghahn Books.
Lee, Raymond L. M. 2010. "Weber, Re-Enchantment and Social Futures." *Time & Society* 19(2): 180–92.
Levi, Andre. 1999. "Towards a Politics of Identities: The Struggle of Oriental Culture for Recognition and Support." *Panim: Quarterly for Society, Culture, and Education* 10: 31–40. (Hebrew)
Levi, Shelly. 2010. "Sexual Harassment in the Work Place." Jerusalem: Israeli Knesset. Accessed June 2013. http://www.knesset.gov.il/mmm/data/pdf/m02565.pdf.
Levi-Faur, David. 1995. "Economic Policy and Nationalism: The Textile Industry in the 1950s and 1960s." *Cathedra* no. 77: 139–160. (Hebrew)
———. 1998. "The Developmental State: Israel, South Korea, and Taiwan Compared." *Studies in Comparative International Development* 33 (1): 65–93.
———. 2001. *The Visible Hand: State-Directed Industrialization in Israel.* Jerusalem: Yad Ben-Zvi. (Hebrew)
Levy, Peter B. 1994. *The New Left and Labor in the 1960s.* Urbana and Chicago: University of Illinois Press.
Levy, Yair. 2004. *There Is Another Economy, There Is Another Society: Social Economy and the Third Sector in the Age of Globalization.* Ramat Ef'al: Yad Tabenkin. (Hebrew)
Lewin, Alisa C. and Haya Stier. 2002. "Who Benefits the Most? The Unequal Allocation of Transfers in the Israeli Welfare State." *Social Science Quarterly* 83 (2): 488–503.
———. 2003. "Immigration, State Support, and the Economic Well-being of the Elderly in Israel." *Research on Aging* 25 (3): 195–223.
Lewin, Alisa C., Haya Stier, and Dafna Caspi-Dror. 2006. "The Place of Opportunity: Community and Individual Determinants of Poverty among Jews and Arabs in Israel." *Research in Social Stratification and Mobility* 24 (2): 177–191.
Lewin-Epstein, Noah, Amit Kaplan, and Asaf Levanon. 2003. "Distributive Justice and Attitudes Toward the Welfare State." *Social Justice Research* 16 (1): 1–27.
Lewis, Jane. 2001. "The Decline of the Male Breadwinner Model: Implications for Work and Care." *Social Politics: International Studies in Gender, State & Society* 8 (2): 152–169.
———. 2003. "Economic Citizenship: A Comment." *Social Politics: International Studies in Gender, State and Society* 10 (2): 176–185.
Lindholm, Charles. 1990. *Charisma.* Basil Blackwell.
———. 2008. *Culture and Authenticity.* Malden, MA: Blackwell.
———. 2013. "The Rise of Expressive Authenticity." *Anthropological Quarterly* 86 (2): 361–395.
Lutz, Catherine A. 1990. "Engendered Emotion: Gender, Power, and the Rhetoric of Emotional Control in American Discourse." In *Language and the Politics of Emotions,* edited by Catherine Lutz and Lila Abu-Lughod, 69–91. Cambridge, UK: Cambridge Univ. Press.
Lutz, Helma, and Ewa Palenga-Möllenbeck. 2012. "Care Workers, Care Drain, and Care Chains: Reflections on Care, Migration, and Citizenship." *Social Politics* 19(1): 15–37.
Mada al-Carmel. 2012. "Israel and the Palestinian Minority Political Monitoring Report 16." Mada al-Carmel. Accessed May 8, 2013. http://mada-research.org/en/files/2013/05/pmr16.pdf.
Maman, Daniel, and Zeev Rosenhek. 2012. "The Institutional Dynamics of a Developmental State: Change and Continuity in State–Economy Relations in Israel." *Studies in Comparative International Development* 47(3): 342–63.
Maron, Asa, and Sara Helman. 2015. "Unravelling the Politics of Activation Reforms: Exploring the Unusual Israeli Trajectory." *Social Policy & Administration.*

Marsh, Clifton E. 1993. "Sexual Assault and Domestic Violence in the African American Community." *Western Journal of Black Studies* 17(3): 149–55.
Marshall, Thomas H. 1964. *Class, Citizenship and Social Development*. Garden City, NY: Doubleday.
Masarwah-Srour, Afnan. 2013. "Gender, Religion and Knowledge: Islamic Palestinian Women Prompt Social Action." PhD diss., School of Education, Hebrew University, Jerusalem. (Hebrew)
Mathie, Alison, and Gord Cunningham. 2003. "From Clients to Citizens: Asset-Based Community Development as a Strategy for Community-Driven Development." *Development in Practice* 13(5): 474–86.
Maurer, Martin and Rod P. Githens. 2010. "Toward a Reframing of Action Research for Human Resource and Organization Development Moving Beyond Problem Solving and Toward Dialogue." *Action Research* 8 (3): 267–292.
McCracken, Molly, Kate Dykman, Francine Parent, and Ivy Lopez. 2005. *Young Women Work: Community Economic Development to Reduce Women's Poverty and Improve Income*. Winnipeg: Prairie Women's Health Centre of Excellence.
Mencher, Joan. 1988. "Women's Work and Poverty: Women's Contribution to Household Maintenance in South India." In *A Home Divided: Women and Income in the Third World*, edited by Daisy Dwyer and Judith Bruce, 99–119. Palo Alto, CA: Stanford University Press.
Moghadam, Valentine M. 1995. "WID, WAD, GAD Integration of Gender in Development." *Gender and Society, Working Paper 3 in Series Gender and Development*: 1–30.
———. 1998. *Women, Work, and Economic Reform in the Middle East and North Africa*. Boulder, CO: Lynne Rienner.
———. 2005a. *Globalizing Women: Transnational Feminist Networks*. Baltimore: Johns Hopkins University Press.
———. 2005b. "Women's Economic Participation in the Middle East: What Difference Has the Neoliberal Policy Turn Made?" *Journal of Middle East Women's Studies*: 110–46.
———. 2008. "Feminism, Legal Reform and Women's Empowerment in the Middle East and North Africa." *International Social Science Journal* 59(191): 9–16.
———. 2011. "Toward Economic Citizenship: The Middle East and North Africa." *Making Globalization Work for Women: The Role of Social Rights and Trade Union Leadership*, edited by Valentine M. Moghadam, Suzanne Franzway, and Mary Margaret Fonow, 25–46. Albany: State University of New York Press.
Moghadam, Valentine M., and Lucie Senftova. 2005. "Measuring Women's Empowerment: Participation and Rights in Civil, Political, Social, Economic, and Cultural Domains." *International Social Science Journal* 57(184): 389–412.
Mohanty, Chandra T. 1999. "Women Workers and Capitalist Scripts." In *Feminist Approaches to Theory and Methodology*, edited by Sharlene Hesse-Biber, Christina Gilmartin, and Robin Lydenberg, 362–85. New York and Oxford: Oxford University Press.
Moreno, Luis. 2010. "Welfare Mix, CSR and Social Citizenship." *International Journal of Sociology and Social Policy* 30 (11/12): 683–696.
Morginstin, Brenda, Sarit Baich-Moray, and Allan Zipkin. 1991. *The Long-Term Care Insurance Law: Data from the First Two Years*. Jerusalem: National Insurance Institute, Research and Planning Administration.
Morin, Richard, and Jill Hanley. 2004. "Metropolization: A Comparison of Four North American Cities" *International Journal of Urban and Regional Research* 2(28): 369–83.
Motzafi-Haller, Pnina. 2001. "Scholarship, Identity, and Power: Mizrahi Women in Israel." *Signs* 697–734.

———. 2012. *Inside Cement Boxes: Mizrahi Women in the Israeli Periphery*. Jerusalem: Magnes. (Hebrew)
Muaddi, Jawad B. 2006. "The Alienable Elements of Citizenship: Can Market Reasoning Help Solve America's Immigration Puzzle?" *Emory Law Journal* 56: 229.
Nadiv, Ronit. 2003. *Employment through Manpower Agencies, Israel 2000*. Israel: Ministry of Labor, Authority of Manpower Planning. (Hebrew)
Nagar, Asaf, and Noam Zussman. 2006. *Survey of Welfare Organizations That Gave Financial and Material Assistance in 2005*. Jerusalem: Bank of Israel Research Department. (Hebrew)
Nathan, Gilad. 2010. *Issues Regarding the Employment of Foreign Workers in Agriculture*. Jerusalem: Israeli Knesset, Center of Research and Information. (Hebrew)
Navaro-Yashin, Yael. 2012. *The Make-Believe Space: Affective Geography in a Postwar Polity*. Durham, NC: Duke University Press.
Nidhal. 2013. "Queer Transformations in Palestine." Accessed June 2013. http://www.aswatgroup.org/en/article/queer-transformations-palestine-2013.
Numerato, Dino. 2009. "Revisiting Weber's Concept of Disenchantment: An Examination of the Re-Enchantment with Sailing in the Post-Communist Czech Republic." *Sociology* 43(3): 439–56.
Nusair, Isis. 2009. "Gender Mainstreaming and Feminist Organizing in the Middle East and North Africa." In *Women and War in the Middle East*, edited by Nadje Al-Ali and Nicola Pratt, 131–57. London: Zed Books.
Nussbaum, Martha. 2003. "Capabilities as Fundamental Entitlements: Sen and Social Justice." *Feminist Economics* 9(2–3): 33–59.
Oakley, Ann. 1974. *The Sociology of Housework*. New York: Pantheon.
Olmsted, Jennifer C. 2005. "Gender, Aging, and the Evolving Arab Patriarchal Contract." *Feminist Economics* 11 (2): 53–78.
Ong, Aihwa. 1996. "Cultural Citizenship as Subject-Making: Immigrants Negotiate Racial and Cultural Boundaries in the United States [and Comments and Reply]." *Current Anthropology* 37(5): 737–62.
Ong, Aihwa. 1999. *Flexible Citizenship: The Cultural Logics of Transnationality*. Durham, NC: Duke University Press.
———. 2006. *Neoliberalism as Exception: Mutations in Citizenship and Sovereignty*. Duke University Press.
Ortner, Sherry B. 1973. "On Key Symbols." *American Anthropologist* 75 (5): 1338–1346.
Pateman, Carole. 1988. *The Sexual Contract*. Palo Alto, CA: Stanford University Press.
Payes, Shany. 2005. *Palestinian NGOs in Israel: The Politics of Civil Society*. London: I.B. Tauris.
Pearson, Ruth. 2004. "Women, Work and Empowerment in a Global Era." *Ids Bulletin* 35(4): 117–20.
Peled, Yoav. 2007. "Citizenship Betrayed: Israel's Emerging Immigration and Citizenship Regime." *Theoretical Inquiries in Law* 8(2): 603–28.
———. 2008. "The Evolution of Israeli Citizenship: An Overview." *Citizenship Studies* 12(3): 335–45.
Puwar, Nirmal and Carole Pateman. 2002. "Interview with Carole Pateman: "the Sexual Contract," Women in Politics, Globalization and Citizenship." *Feminist Review* 70: 123–133.
Peteet, Julie, and Joe Stork.1995. "The NGO Phenomenon in the Arab World." *Middle East Report* 193: 26–27.
Pope, Jacqueline. 1992. "The Colonizing Impact of Public Service Bureaucracies in Black Communities." *Race, Politics, and Economic Development: Community Perspectives*, edited by James Jennings. New York: Verso.

Puwar, Nirmal, and Carole Pateman. 2002. "Interview with Carole Pateman: The Sexual Contract, Women in Politics, Globalization and Citizenship." *Feminist Review* 70: 123–33.
Raijman, Rebeca, and Adriana Kemp. 2004. "State and Non-State Actors: A Multi-Layered Analysis of Work-Migration Policy in Israel." In *The Power of Property: Israeli Society in the Global Age*, edited by Filc Dani and Uri Ram, 222–38. Jerusalem: Van Leer and HaKibuts Hame'uhad.
———. 2011. "Labor Migration in Israel: The Creation of a Non-Free Workforce." *Protosociology* no. 27: 177–93.
Raijman, Rebeca, and Adriana Kemp. 2007. "Labor Migration, Managing the Ethno-National Conflict, and Client Politics in Israel." *Transnational Migration to Israel in Global Comparative Context*: 31–50.
Raijman, Rebeca, and Nonna Kushnirovich. 2012. *Labor Migrant Recruitment Practices in Israel: Final Report*. Jerusalem: CIMI, Center for International Migration and Integration, and Rupin Academic Center. http://lib.ruppin.ac.il/multimedia_library/pdf/38849.pdf.
Ram, Uri. 2013. *The Globalization of Israel: McWorld in Tel Aviv, Jihad in Jerusalem*. London: Routledge.
Rankin, Katharine N. 2001. "Governing Development: Neoliberalism, Microcredit, and Rational Economic Woman." *Economy and Society* 30(1): 18–37.
———. 2002. "Social Capital, Microfinance, and the Politics of Development." *Feminist Economics* 8(1): 1–24.
Reber, Dierdra. 2012. "Headless Capitalism: Affect as Free-Market Episteme." *Differences* 23(1): 62–100.
Reddy, William M. 1999. "Emotional Liberty: Politics and History in the Anthropology of Emotions." *Cultural Anthropology* 14(2): 256–88.
Rieff, Philip. 1966. *The Triumph of the Therapeutic: Uses of Faith After Freud*. Chicago: University of Chicago Press.
Roberts, C., and J. Martin. 1984. "Women and Employment: A Lifetime Perspective." *The Report of the 1980 DE/OPCS Women and Employment Survey, London*: 23.
Rodó-de-Zárate, Maria, and Marta Jorba. 2005. "The Complexity of Intersectionality." *Humanamente* 30(3): 189.
Ron, Tikva, and Yaniv Ronen. 2005. *Care for Tender Age Children—A Background Paper for the Committee on Children's Rights*. Jerusalem: Israeli Knesset, Center of Research and Information. (Hebrew)
Rosaldo, Renato. 1994. "Cultural Citizenship and Educational Democracy." *Cultural Anthropology* 9(3): 402–11.
Rose, Colin Penfield, and Malcolm J. Nicholl. 1998. *Accelerated Learning for the 21st Century: The Six-Step Plan to Unlock Your Master-Mind*. New York: Dell Books.
Rose, Nikolas. 1990. *Governing the Soul: The Shaping of the Private Self*. Taylor & Frances/Routledge.
Rose, Nikolas, Pat O'Malley, and Mariana Valverde. 2006. "Governmentality." *Annual Review of Law and Social Science* 2: 83–104.
Rosenfeld, Henry. 1978. "The Class Situation of the Arab National Minority in Israel." *Comparative Studies in Society and History* 20(3): 374–407.
Rosenhek, Zeev. 1998. "Policy Paradigms and the Dynamics of the Welfare State: The Israeli Welfare State and the Zionist Colonial Project." *International Journal of Sociology and Social Policy* 18(2/3/4): 157–202.
———. 1999. "The Exclusionary Logic of the Welfare State Palestinian Citizens in the Israeli Welfare State." *International Sociology* 14(2): 195–215.

———. 2003. "The Political Dynamics of a Segmented Labour Market: Palestinian Citizens, Palestinians from the Occupied Territories and Migrant Workers in Israel." *Acta Sociologica* 46(3): 231–49.
Rouhana, Nadim, and Ased Ghanem. 1998. "The Crisis of Minorities in Ethnic States: The Case of Palestinian Citizens in Israel." *International Journal of Middle East Studies* 30(3): 321–46.
Rouhana, Nadim N., and Nimer Sultany. 2003. "Redrawing the Boundaries of Citizenship: Israel's New Hegemony." *Journal of Palestine Studies* 33(1): 5–22.
Sa'ar, Amalia. 1998. "Carefully on the Margins: Christian Palestinians in Haifa between Nation and State." *American Ethnologist* 25(2): 215–39.
———. 2005. "Postcolonial Feminism, the Politics of Identification, and the Liberal Bargain." *Gender & Society* 19(5): 680–700.
———. 2006a. "Cooperation and Conflict in the Zone of Civil Society: Arab-Jewish Activism in Jaffa." *Urban Anthropology and Studies of Cultural Systems and World Economic Development* 35(1): 105–40.
———. 2006b. "Feminine Strength: Reflections on Power and Gender in Israeli-Palestinian Culture." *Anthropological Quarterly* 79(3): 397–430.
———. 2007a. "Masculine Talk: On the Subconscious Use of Masculine Linguistic Forms among Hebrew-and Arabic-Speaking Women in Israel." *Signs* 32(2): 405–29.
———. 2007b. "Contradictory Location: Assessing the Position of Palestinian Women Citizens of Israel." *Journal of Middle East Women's Studies* 3(3): 45–74.
———. 2007c. *A Business of Your Own*. Jerusalem: National Insurance Institute, Special Projects Fund. (Hebrew)
———. 2009a. *"When I Arrived at the University Something in Me Started to Dance": Making Higher Education Accessible to Older Druze Women*. Research Report Invited by Itach-Ma'aki and the Legal Feminist Clinic, the Faculty of Law, University of Haifa. (Hebrew)
———. 2009b. "Low-Income "Single Moms" in Israel: Redefining the Gender Contract." *Sociological Quarterly* 50(3): 450–73.
———. 2011. *Palestinian-Israeli Women's Employment: The Mystery of Their Absence and the Way to Their Integration into the Formal Labor Force*. Research Report. Haifa: Haifa University Department of Sociology. (Hebrew)
———. 2012. "Holistic, Community-Oriented Empowerment: The Case of Women in Recently Recognized Villages in Galilee." In *Kuluna Hikaya: Action Oriented Research on Al-Tufula Center's Empowerment Approach to Engaging Women in Social Change*, edited by Johayna Hossein. Nazareth: Al-Tufula Center. (Arabic)
———. Forthcoming. "The Gender Contract under Neoliberalism: Palestinian Israeli Women's Labor Force Participation." *Feminist Economics*.
Sa'ar, Amalia, and Sigal Gooldin. 2009. "Intense Engagement: Young Women in Israel Forging Feminist Subjectivities." *Women's Studies International Forum* 32(3): 179–88.
Saban, Ilan. 2011. "Theorizing and Tracing the Legal Dimensions of a Control Framework: Law and the Arab-Palestinian Minority in Israel's First Three Decades (1948–1978)." *Emory International Law Review* 25: 299–378.
Sachs, Dalia, Amalia Sa'ar, and Sarai Aharoni. 2007. "'How can I Feel for Others when I Myself Am Beaten?' The Impact of the Armed Conflict on Women in Israel." *Sex Roles* 57 (7–8): 593–606.
Saler, Michael. 2006. "Modernity and Enchantment: A Historiographic Review." *The American Historical Review* 111 (3): 692–716.
Sa'di, Ahmad H. 2002. "The Peculiarities of Israel's Democracy: Some Theoretical and Practical Implications for Jewish–Arab Relations." *International Journal of Intercultural Relations* 26(2): 119–33.

Sa'di, Ahmad H., and Noah Lewin-Epstein. 2001. "Minority Labour Force Participation in the Post-Fordist Era: The Case of the Arabs in Israeli." *Work, Employment & Society* 15(4): 781–802.

Sambol, Sarit and Orly Benjamin. 2006. "Motherhood and Poverty in Israel: The Place of Motherhood in Poor worker's Lives." *Social Issues in Israel* 1: 11–21.

———. 2007. "Structural Disruptions of Women's Work History: The Narrowing Down of Working Poor's Opportunities Structures." *Israeli Sociology* 9(1): 7–39. (Hebrew)

Schultz, Vicki. 2000. "Life's Work." *Columbia Law Review*: 1881–964.

Schwartz, Eliezer. 2009. *Tariffs of Home-Based Daycare Services Supervised by the Ministry of Industry, Trade and Labor—Description and Analysis.* Jerusalem: Israeli Knesset, Center of Research and Information.

Schwartz, Michal. 2011. "Promoting the Social Rights of Working Women." *Making Globalization Work for Women: The Role of Social Rights and Trade Union Leadership*, edited by Valentine M. Moghadam, Suzanne Franzway, and Mary margaret Fonow, 47–70. Albany: State University of New York Press.

Semyonov, Moshe and Noah Lewin-Epstein. 1987. *Hewers of Wood and Drawers of Water: Noncitizen Arabs in the Israeli Labor Market.* Ithaca, NY: ILR Press.

Sen, Amartya. 1990. "Gender and Cooperative Conflicts." In *Persistent Inequalities: Women and World Development*, edited by Irene Tinker, 123–149. Oxford, New York, Toronto: Oxford University Press, 1990.

———. 1999. *Development as Freedom.* Oxford: Oxford University Press.

Sewell Jr., William H. "A Theory of Structure: Duality, Agency, and Transformation." *American Journal of Sociology* (1992): 1–29.

Shafir, Gershon, and Yoav Peled. 1998. "Citizenship and Stratification in an Ethnic Democracy." *Ethnic and Racial Studies* 21(3): 408–27.

———. 2002. *Being Israeli: The Dynamics of Multiple Citizenship.* Vol. 16. Cambridge: Cambridge University Press.

Shalev, Michael. 1999. "Liberalization and the Transformation of the Political Economy." *The New Israel: Peacemaking and Liberalization*, edited by Gershon Shafir and Yoav Peled, 129–59. Boulder, CO: Westview.

Shalev, Michael and Amit Lazarus. 2013. "The Welfare State as an Employer: An Unacknowledged Avenue of Opportunity for Palestinian Women in Israel." In *Palestinians in the Israeli Labor Market: A Multi-Disciplinary Approach*, edited by Nabil Khattab and Sami Miaari, 153–182: Palgrave Macmillan.

Shalhoub-kevorkian, Nadera. 2004. "Racism, Militarisation and Policing: Police Reactions to Violence Against Palestinian Women in Israel." *Social Identities* 10 (2): 171–193.

Shamir, Ronen. 2005. "Mind the Gap: The Commodification of Corporate Social Responsibility." *Symbolic Interaction* 28(2): 229–53.

———. 2008. "The Age of Responsibilization: On Market-Embedded Morality." *Economy and Society* 37(1): 1–19.

Sharma, Aradhana. 2006. "Crossbreeding Institutions, Breeding Struggle: Women's Empowerment, Neoliberal Governmentality, and State (Re)Formation in India." *Cultural Anthropology*: 60–95.

———. 2008. *Logics of Empowerment: Development, Gender, and Governance in Neoliberal India.* Minneapolis: University of Minnesota Press.

Shiran, Vickie. 2002. "Symmetric Self-Representation: The Contribution of Mizrahi Women to Feminism in Israel." *Impertinence: Mizrahi Feminism*: 12–19.

Shostak-Pascal, Yael. 2011. "Power for the Workers? The Union of Home-Based Early Childhood Caregivers in Israel." Master's thesis, Department of Sociology and Anthropology, University of Haifa. (Hebrew)

Shtewi, Ola. 2014. *Women in the Arab Labor Force.* Haifa: Kayan. (Hebrew)

Simchai, Dalit. 2009. *Flowing Against the Flow: Paradoxes in New Age Vision in Israel.* Haifa: Pardes. (Hebrew)
Singerman, Diane, and Homa Hoodfar. 1996. *Development, Change, and Gender in Cairo: A View from the Household.* Bloomington: Indiana University Press.
Smooha, Sammy. 2002. "The Model of Ethnic Democracy: Israel as a Jewish and Democratic State." *Nations and Nationalism* 8(4): 475–503.
———. 2010. "Arab Jewish Relations in Israel." Washington, DC: United States Institute for Peace. http://www.usip.org/sites/default/files/PW67_Arab-Jewish_Relations_in_Israel.pdf.
Stack, Carol B., and Linda M. Burton. 1993. "Kinscripts." *Journal of Comparative Family Studies* 24: 157–70.
Stadler, Nurit, Edna Lomsky-Feder, and Eyal Ben-Ari. 2008. "Fundamentalism's Encounters with Citizenship: The Haredim in Israel." *Citizenship Studies* 12(3): 215–31.
Steinem, Gloria. 1991. *Revolution from within: A Book of Self-Esteem.* Boston: Little, Brown and Co.
Stephen, Lynn. 2003. "Cultural Citizenship and Labor Rights for Oregon Farmworkers: The Case of Pineros y Campesinos Unidos Del Nordoeste (PCUN)." *Human Organization* 62(1): 27–38.
Stewart, Kenda Ranee. 2012. *In Or Out of Bounds?: The Cultural and Political Implications of Palestinian Women's Soccer in Israel.* PhD Dissertation, University of Iowa.
Strumia, Francesca. 2011. "Remedying the Inequalities of Economic Citizenship in Europe: Cohesion Policy and the Negative Right to Move." *European Law Journal* 17(6): 725–43.
Swirski, Barbara. 2000. "The Citizenship of Jewish and Palestinian Arab Women in Israel." In *Gender and Citizenship in the Middle East,* edited by Suad Josef, 314–44. Syracuse, NY: Syracuse University Press.
Swirski, Shlomo. 1989. *Israel, the Oriental Majority.* London: Zed Books.
———. 1999. *Politics and Education in Israel: Comparisons with the United States.* New York: Falmer.
Swirski, Shlomo, and Etty Konor-Attias. 2012. *Israel: A Social Report 2012.* Tel Aviv: Adva Center. (Hebrew)
Swirski, Shlomo, Etty Konor-Attias, and Ofir Arian. 2013. *Workers, Employers, and the National Income Pie; Report for the Year 2012.* Tel Aviv: Adva Center. (Hebrew)
Swirski, Shlomo, Vered Kraus, Etty Konor-Attias, and Anat Herbst. 2002. *Information about Equality: Single Mothers in Israel.* Tel Aviv: Adva Center. (Hebrew)
Tinker, Irene. 1990. *Persistent Inequalities: Women and World Development.* Oxford: Oxford University Press.
Toledano, Esther, and Tammy Eliav. 2011. *Single-Parent Families 1993–2010.* Jerusalem: National Insurance Institute. (Hebrew)
Torstrick, Rebecca L. 2000. *The Limits of Coexistence: Identity Politics in Israel.* Ann Arbor: University of Michigan Press.
Tzfadia, Erez, and Oren Yiftachel. 2004. "State, Space, and Capital: Immigrants in Israel and Sociospatial Stratification." In *The Power of Property: Israeli Society in the Global Age,* edited by Dani Filk and Uri Ram, 197–222. Jerusalem: Van Leer Jerusalem Institute and Hakibbutz Hameuhad. (Hebrew)
Urciuoli, Bonnie. 2010. "Neoliberal Education." In *Ethnographies of Neoliberalism,* edited by Carol J. Greenhouse, 162–76: Philadelphia: University of Pennsylvania Press.
Walby, Sylvia. 1990. *Theorizing Patriarchy.* Oxford: Blackwell.
———. 1994. "Is Citizenship Gendered?" *Sociology* 28(2): 379–95.
———. 2004. "The European Union and Gender Equality: Emergent Varieties of Gender Regime." *Social Politics: International Studies in Gender, State and Society* 11(1): 4–29.

———. 2005. "Measuring Women's Progress in a Global Era." *International Social Science Journal* 57(184): 371–87.

———. 2012. "Sen and the Measurement of Justice and Capabilities a Problem in Theory and Practice." *Theory, Culture & Society* 29(1): 99–118.

Walby, Sylvia, Jo Armstrong, and Sofia Strid. 2012. "Intersectionality: Multiple Inequalities in Social Theory." *Sociology* 46(2): 224–40.

Wallerstein, Immanuel and Joan Smith. 1991. "Households as an Institution of the World-Economy." In *Gender, Family and Economy: The Triple Overlap*, edited by Rae Lesser Blumberg, 225–243. Newbury Park, London, New Delhi: Sage Publications.

Warren, Tracey, Elizabeth Fox, and Gillian Pascall. 2009. "Innovative Social Policies: Implications for Work–life Balance among Low-waged Women in England." *Gender, Work & Organization* 16 (1): 126–150.

Wessendorf, Susanne. 2008. "Culturalist Discourses on Inclusion and Exclusion: The Swiss Citizenship Debate." *Social Anthropology* 16(2): 187–202.

WGSPWCI, Working Group on the Status of Palestinian Women Citizens of Israel. 2005. *The Status of Palestinian Women Citizens of Israel*. Geneva: Office of the United Nations High Commissioner for Human Rights. http://www2.ohchr.org/english/bodies/cedaw/docs/ngos/WomenCitizens_of_Israel_for_the_session_Israel_CEDAW48.pdf.

Wood, Donna J., Kimberly S. Davenport, Laquita C. Blockson, and Harry J. Van Buren. 2002. "Corporate Involvement in Community Economic Development the Role of US Business Education." *Business & Society* 41(2): 208–41.

Woodyer, Tara, and Hilary Geoghegan. 2012. "(Re) Enchanting Geography? The Nature of Being Critical and the Character of Critique in Human Geography." *Progress in Human Geography*: 195–214.

Yiftachel, Oren. 2006. *Ethnocracy: Land and Identity Politics in Israel/Palestine*. Philadelphia: University of Pennsylvania Press.

Yonah, Yossi, and Ishak Saporta. 2002a. "The Politics of Lands and Housing in Israel: A Wayward Republican Discourse." *Social Identities* 8(1): 91–117.

———. 2002b. "Pre-Vocational Education and the Creation of the Working Class in Israel." In *Mizrahim in Israel: A Critical Observation into Israel's Ethnicity*, edited by Pnina Mutzafi-Haller, Hannan Hever, and Yehouda Shenhav, 68–104. Jerusalem: Van Leer and Hakibutz Hameuhad. (Hebrew)

Yuval-Davis, Nira. 1987. "Woman/Nation/State: The Demographic Race and National Reproduction in Israel." *Radical America* 21(6): 37–59.

———. 1997. "Women, Citizenship and Difference." *Feminist Review*: 4–27.

———. 2006. "Intersectionality and Feminist Politics." *European Journal of Women's Studies* 13(3): 193–209.

———. 2011. *The Politics of Belonging: Intersectional Contestations*. Thousand Oaks, CA: Sage.

Yuval Davis, Nira, and Pnina Werbner, eds. 1999a. *Women, Citizenship and Difference*. London: Zed Books.

———. 1999b. "Introduction: Women and the New Discourse of Citizenship." In *Women, Citizenship and Difference*, edited by Pnina Werbner and Nira Yuval Davis, 1–38. London: Zed Books.

Zehavi, Amos. 2012. "From Enlightened Self-interest to Welfare Coalitions: Overcoming Identity-based Tensions in the Israeli Welfare State." *Social Policy & Administration* 46(5): 562–81.

Zelizer, Viviana A. 2005. *The Purchase of Intimacy*. Princeton, NJ: Princeton University Press.

Zimmerman, Mary K., Jacquelyn S. Litt, and Christine E. Bose. 2006. *Global Dimensions of Gender and Carework*. Palo Alto, CA: Stanford University Press.

Index

Abu-Lughod, Lila, 183
Achoti (Mizrahi feminist group), 110, 123–24, 126
Adva Center, 126
ageism, 19, 78, 85
agricultural work
    Bedouins and, 86, 93
    low wages in, 90–91
    middlemen's role in arranging, 91, 93
    Mizrahi Jews and, 29
    Palestinians and, 30–31, 77, 90–91
    unionization efforts and, 126
    women in, 76–77, 90–91, 124, 126
al-Tufula Center
    Atida project and, 16–17, 21, 77, 120, 128
    author's involvement with, 15–16, 18, 120
    childhood education programs and, 16
    coalition building and, 123
    empowerment workshops and, 120–23
    mission of, 15–16
    Sawa Empowerment Project and, 17–18, 121, 203
ambivalence
    empowerment and, 141, 146, 211
    wage work and, 155–56, 188, 193
Ashkenazi Jews
    economic empowerment initiatives and, 14
    economic liberalization protested by, 66
    feminism among, 123
    immigration to Israel of, 30, 106
    Labor Party and, 55
    Mizrahi Jews contrasted with, 4, 30, 34, 36, 42–43, 66–67, 103, 123
    racism among, 42–43
    socioeconomic status of, 6, 30, 34, 36, 42, 61, 103, 208
    Ultra-Orthodox and, 103
Aswat (Palestinian gay women's group), 124–25
Atida project
    author's involvement in, 16–17, 21
    job training and placement through, 16, 120, 128
    Palestinian women as participants in, 16
    "pink-collar job" aspirations reported in, 86
    vulnerability of low-income women in, 77, 86

Bedouins
    agricultural work and, 86, 93
    economic empowerment initiatives and, 15, 17, 45, 93–94, 141, 145, 203
    housing conditions among, 94–95
    social capital and, 203
    women and, 89, 93–95, 141, 145
Bedouin Village Study, 21, 86, 93, 120, 203
Benjamin, Orly, 76, 90
Berkovitch, Nitza, 19–20, 117, 204–5
Bernstein, Deborah, 90
Bourdieu, Pierre, 184
A Business of One's Own (EEW program), 14
business-organized nonprofit organizations (BONPOs)
    community economic development and, 210, 212

diversity issues and, 53–54
flexibility of, 217
social capital and, 216
social economy and, 48, 50, 53–54

care
    care work, 8, 22–23, 35–36, 78, 89, 152, 156, 161, 165, 168, 170, 201, 217, 221
    childcare, 106, 200, 222
    daycare, 75, 89, 95, 163, 165–70
charisma, 185–87, 221, 223
child care. See under care
citizenship. See also economic citizenship
    affective components of, 196
    alienable versus inalienable aspects of, 206
    basic rights of, 194, 198, 218
    care work marginalized by, 217–18
    cultural implications of, 195–96
    in the European Union, 206–7
    in Israel, 5, 38, 43, 96, 207–8, 222
    Law of Return and, 96
    Marshall's typology of, 198
    as moral construct, 194–95, 206
    neoliberalism and, 5
    "nonproductive" members of society and, 114
    transnational influences on, 195–96
civil rights
    Civil Rights movement (United States, 1960s), 3, 6, 113
    differential distribution of, 194
    economic citizenship and, 199–200
    economic self-sufficiency and, 222
    immigrants and, 38
    Palestinians and, 6, 38, 43
civil society. See also nongovernmental organizations (NGOs)
    apolitical pluralism ideal and, 55
    coalition work and, 63–65
    cross-sectorial collaborations and, 3, 14, 49
    employment opportunities within, 60–62
    empowerment discourse and, 118–19, 151
    legislative policy apparatus and, 159
    liberal notions of, 194
    minority rights and, 127, 212
    networking in, 62–63
    Palestinian community and, 124
    philanthropic organizations and, 61
Class A employees, 79–80, 84
Class B employees, 79–84, 107n2
cleaning women, 76–77, 90, 126, 162
coaching
    affective communication style in, 178
    emotional talk and, 112
    empowerment and, 118–19, 132–34
    neoliberalism and, 136–37
    as private business, 133
    social economy and, 132–34
    views of success in, 149
community economic development (CED)
    asset-building community development (ABCD) and, 202–3, 211
    business school education and, 204
    corporate social responsibility and, 4–5, 49, 204, 207, 210–11
    cross-sectorial collaboration and, 22, 40–41, 201
    democratic culture and, 4–5
    development paradigms and, 40
    diversity as goal in, 211
    economic citizenship and, 201–5, 222
    empowerment emphasis in, 40–41, 203–4, 210
    entrepreneurship and, 45
    feminist approaches and, 40–41, 52, 62
    Israeli political discourse and, 42–43
    neoliberalism and, 4–5, 13, 41–42, 204
    poverty reduction and, 41, 47, 201
    social capital and, 201–4, 211, 222
    social economy and, 42–43, 201
    social solidarity and, 28
Connell, Raewyn, 158–59, 189n2
corporate social responsibility (CSR)
    community economic development and, 4–5, 49, 204, 207, 210–11
    economic citizenship and, 22, 194, 207, 216
    social economy and, 49
cross-sectorial partnerships
    community economic development and, 22, 40–41, 201

networking and, 19
social economy and, 2, 22, 28, 44, 46–51, 56, 59
Cruikshank, Barbara, 114–15, 118, 153
cultural production
    authenticity and, 10
    community economic development and, 40
    empowerment and, 8, 151–52
    Mizrahi Jews and, 42–43
    neoliberalism and, 2
    Palestinians and, 37, 87
    social economy and, 2, 193

daycare. *See under* care
diversity
    business-organized nonprofit organizations (BONPOs) and, 53–54
    community economic development's promotion of, 211
    empowerment and, 22, 141
    Israeli public discourse and, 54
    minority rights reframed as, 4, 209, 219–20
    multiple and contradictory meanings of, 223
    social economy programs and, 53–58, 67, 209–10, 219–20
divorce. *See also* single mothers
    child support and, 105, 154
    domestic violence and, 73
    gender contract breakdown and, 221
    women's economic status and, 73, 75, 77–78, 105–7, 154–56
domestic violence, 72–73, 76, 97, 125–26
domestic work
    compensation for, 200
    daycare as form of, 165–70
    economic value of, 162
    low-income women's responsibility for, 76–79, 91, 95, 105–6, 152, 154, 156–58, 160–62, 168–71, 196
    as source of income, 162–70, 188
Drori, Israel, 92–93

economic citizenship
    civil rights and, 199–200
    community economic development perspective on, 201–5, 222
    corporate social responsibility and, 22, 194, 207, 216
    economic security and, 199–200
    emotional capitalism and, 23
    ethnonationalism and, 5, 22, 39, 209–10
    feminist perspectives on, 197–201, 209, 211–12, 222
    free market perspectives on, 197, 205–7, 222
    gender and, 22–23
    individual economic productivity and, 2–3, 5, 22–23, 28, 193, 197, 200, 207–8, 222
    localization of, 207–15
    multiple and contradictory meanings within, 23, 194, 197, 221–23
    neoliberalism and, 5, 56, 194, 209–16, 219–20, 222
    social economy and, 214–15, 217
    structural inequalities and, 197, 215
Economic Empowerment for Women (EEW)
    author's involvement with, 13–15, 97, 128, 142
    business consulting by, 72, 137
    business hothouse of, 154–55
    A Business of One's Own program and, 14
    diversity as goal at, 129–30
    Haifa Feminist Center and, 125
    ideology of financial supporters of, 27–28
    Isha le Isha Center and, 14
    microentrepreneurship courses and, 50, 97, 128
    workshops run by, 13–14, 97, 128–31, 142–43, 154
economic liberalization. *See also* neoliberalism
    foreign investment and, 32
    immigrant workers and, 32–33, 38
    labor rights weakened by, 32, 81
    moderating the effects of, 193–94
    Organization for Economic Cooperation (OECD) and, 56
    Palestinian economic integration as goal in, 55–56
    polarizing effects of, 7, 33–34
    privatization and, 32, 35, 81–82, 160

protests against, 65–67
social justice and, 42, 219, 223
social welfare services' deterioration and, 3, 33, 35, 42
structural inequalities and, 32–36, 42, 65, 126
emotional capitalism
economic citizenship and, 23
empowerment and, 2, 112, 118, 138, 147, 152, 188–89, 214
enchantment and, 186
narratives of the self in, 112, 118, 132, 138, 221
emotional competence, 10, 112, 152
emotional labor, 9–11
emotional talk. *See also* love-work discourse
empowerment and, 112, 149–50, 176, 181–82, 220
enchantment and, 185–86
intrinsic value of, 9
market-shrewd uses of, 181
paradoxes of low-income women and, 183–85
empowerment
ambivalence and, 141, 146, 211
coaching and, 118–19, 132–34
community economic development and, 40–41, 203–4, 210
as a consumer good, 149
critiques of projects devoted to, 111, 115–17, 220
cultural production and, 8, 151–52
diversity and, 22, 141
emotional capitalism and, 2, 112, 118, 138, 147, 152, 188–89, 214
emotional talk and, 112, 215
enchantment and, 11
feminist perspectives on, 113, 115–17, 119–25, 203
genealogy of concept of, 113–19, 220
immigrants and, 4, 44–45, 47–48, 96–97, 141
leisure culture and, 150, 153
love-work discourse and, 115, 175–78, 183, 187, 189, 214–15, 217, 221
low-income women and, 1–2, 4, 8–9, 11, 13–19, 22–23, 27–28, 40–41, 44–46, 49–53, 57–58, 61–62, 64, 93–94, 97, 110–13, 115–18, 120–23, 126–32, 137–43, 145–46, 150–53, 164, 167, 175–77, 181–82, 187–88, 193, 203, 207, 212–15, 217, 219–20
measurements of, 146–51
Mizrahi Jews and, 4, 14, 44, 124, 213, 216
multiple and contradictory meanings of, 8, 58, 119, 127, 150–52, 220, 223
Palestinians and, 4, 16, 44, 47–48, 54, 56, 61–62, 93, 110–11, 122, 127, 141–42, 167, 209–10, 213–14, 216, 219
self-esteem movement and, 117–18
social economy and, 27–28, 44–46, 51–53, 57–58, 111–12, 143–44, 151, 207, 219
special needs populations and, 47
Ultra-Orthodox Jews and, 4, 15, 44, 47–48, 100, 141, 214
enchantment, 11, 185–86, 214
entitlement
citizenship and, 38
civil forms of, 2–3, 22, 43, 56, 67, 193
emotional capitalism and, 112
individual economic productivity and, 2–3
neoliberalism and, 12–13
wage work providing a sense of, 16
welfare benefits and, 104, 206
women's sense of, 128, 131, 144, 146, 156, 171–72, 213, 220–21

feminism
activism and, 2–3, 6, 13, 20, 22, 27, 59–60, 62–63, 110, 119–31, 134, 136–37, 151, 193
community economic development and, 40–41, 52, 62
economic citizenship and, 197–201, 209, 211–12, 222
empowerment doctrine and, 113, 115–17, 119–25, 144–45
generational differences within, 134
intersectionality and, 5–7, 39, 203, 219–20
microentrepreneurship and, 126
neoliberalism and, 136–37
radical feminism and, 6, 13, 20–21, 28, 50, 59, 111, 120–26, 136, 211

financial citizenship, 204–5
foreign workers. *See* immigrants

Gender and Development (GAD) paradigm, 116, 146
gender contracts
    breakdown of, 105, 107, 221
    care and cash work in, 2–3, 8, 22
    definition of, 158–59
    division of labor and, 157–61, 172, 174, 187, 221
    family-centered *versus* market-centered versions of, 155–56, 160–61, 171, 174, 187–88
    gender bargains and, 158
    gender scripts and, 2, 107, 158, 175
    love-work discourse and, 23, 175
gender regimes, 3, 22, 159–60
General Union of Hebrew Workers in the Land of Israel. *See* Histadrut
GLBTQ. *See* lesbians
Gottfried, Heidi, 158, 161
government organized nongovernmental organizations (GONGOs), 47, 50, 54, 210, 212, 216–17
grassroots grounded projects, 49–51

Haifa Feminist Center Isha L-Isha, 14, 123, 125–26
Harvey, David, 11–12
Herzog, Hanna, 196
Histadrut (General Union of Hebrew Workers in the Land of Israel), 29–33, 35, 80–84, 167
    healthcare and, 35
    labor relations stabilized by, 29
    Mizrahi Jews and, 30
    Palestinians and, 31
    social benefits administered by, 30, 33, 35, 81
Hochschild, Arlie R., 9, 11
Hseiniyye (Bedouin village), 18, 91, 95, 123

Illouz, Eva, 10, 112, 118, 132, 138, 152
immigrants
    civil rights of, 38
    domestic care responsibilities among, 78
    economic empowerment initiatives and, 4, 44–45, 47–48, 96–97, 141

    economic liberalization and increasing numbers of, 32–33, 38
    Israeli labor politics and, 7, 36, 38
    poverty levels among, 37, 96–97, 106
    single mothers among, 97
    support networks among, 106
    textile industry and, 92
    unemployment and, 96, 98
intersectionality, 5–7, 39, 71, 203, 219–20
Isha L-Isha Center. *See* Haifa Feminist Center
Israeli citizenship. *See under* citizenship

Joseph, Suad, 194–95, 216

Kabeer, Naila, 116, 146, 224
Kandiyoti, Deniz, 158, 194
Karim, Lamia, 115–16
Kayan (Arab feminist group), 122–23, 125, 167
Kemp, Adriana, 19–20, 116–17, 127, 204–5
Kessler-Harris, Alice, 198–200, 211, 216–217
Koach La-'ovdim (labor union), 127, 167
Kol Ha'isha organization, 124, 128

labor force participation (LFP) among women, 8, 56, 88–89, 176, 198
lesbians, 6, 120, 123–24
life coaching. *See* coaching
Lindholm, Charles, 10–11, 112, 186–87
love-work discourse. *See also* emotional talk
    economic citizenship and, 23
    economic marginalization of low-income women and, 196–97
    empowerment and, 115, 175–78, 183, 187, 189, 214–15, 217, 221
    gender contracts and, 23, 175

Mahut Center, 15, 18–19, 21, 77–78, 80–86, 125, 128
male breadwinner/female caregiver model, 116, 158, 160–61, 173, 187
Marshall, Thomas H., 198
MATI (*merkaz tipuah yazamut*; state-sponsored centers for fostering entrepreneurship), 46, 50–51, 130, 137, 154

Microentrepreneurship Study, 14, 21, 72, 74–76, 86–87, 97, 104, 137–140
microfinance, 20, 41, 45, 127, 205
Ministry of Industry, Trade, and Labor (MITL). *See also* MATI
　daycare facilities and, 166, 170
　economic empowerment programs and, 46–48, 50
　minimum wage enforcement and, 91
minority rights
　citizenship and, 195
　civil society organizations and, 127, 212
　community economic development and, 46, 50
　Organization of Economic Cooperation and Development and, 56
　reframed as "diversity," 4, 209, 219–20
　social economy and, 151
Mizrahi Jews
　agricultural labor and, 29
　Ashkenazi Jews contrasted with, 4, 30, 34, 36, 42–43, 66–67, 103, 123
　cultural production among, 42–43
　discrimination against, 4, 36, 66, 103
　economic empowerment initiatives and, 4, 14, 44, 124, 213, 216
　economic inequality and, 34, 36
　feminism among, 110, 123–24, 126
　immigration to Israel of, 29–30
　poverty among, 36, 86, 104, 106
　single mothers among, 86, 104
　as social economy project staff, 45
　"social issues" used euphemistically regarding, 42–43
　subordinate status of, 30, 36, 42, 44, 57–58, 66, 86, 103, 106
　textile industry and, 92
　unemployment among, 36, 86
　upward economic mobility among, 31, 36, 42–43, 106
　women, 7, 14, 36, 44–45, 86–87, 90, 92, 103–4, 120, 123–24, 126, 128, 155
Moghadam, Valentine, 199–200
Motzafi-Haller, Pnina, 90

National Insurance Institute (NII), 14–15, 46–47, 77

neoliberalism. *See also* economic liberalization
　citizenship and, 5
　coaching and, 136–37
　community economic development and, 4–5, 13, 41–42, 204
　economic citizenship and, 5, 56, 194, 209–16, 219–20, 222
nongovernmental organizations (NGOs). *See also* civil society
　community economic development and, 40
　economic empowerment initiatives and, 117
　"educational turn" and, 127
　employment opportunities at, 61–62, 133
　government-organized NGOs and, 47, 50, 54, 210, 212, 216–17
nonprofit organizations (NPOs). *See* business-organized nonprofit organizations (BONPOs)

Ong, Ahiwa, 5, 195–96, 209, 216
Organization for Economic Co-operation and Development (OECD), 56, 200
Orthodox Jews. *See* Ultra-Orthodox Jews

Palestinian Israelis
　agricultural work and, 30–31, 77, 90–91
　citizenship status of, 207–8
　civil rights of, 6, 38, 43
　daycare services and, 165, 167–69
　discrimination against and subordinate status of, 4, 6, 30, 33–35, 37, 43, 54–55, 61, 85–90, 94, 96, 106, 122, 203, 207, 209–10, 212
　economic empowerment initiatives and, 4, 16, 44, 47–48, 54, 56, 61–62, 93, 110–11, 122, 127, 141–42, 167, 209–10, 213–14, 216, 219
　economic inequality and, 33–34, 36–37, 87
　gender regimes and gender contracts among, 159–61, 174–76, 188, 221
　grassroots social change organizations and, 50–51
　labor force participation levels among, 88–89

networking among activists and, 63–64
poverty among, 37, 54, 71, 76, 86–87, 96, 98, 174–75
social economy programs and, 47, 54–56
as social economy project staff, 45, 60–62
"social issues" used euphemistically regarding, 43
textile industry and, 92–93, 108n11
unemployment among, 34, 60, 64, 86–87, 89, 96
welfare state's exclusion of, 33–35, 96, 99, 106
women, 6–7, 16, 36, 60–62, 64, 71, 73, 75–79, 85, 87–95, 104, 106, 109–11, 120, 122–23, 127–28, 139, 141–42, 156, 163–65, 168–69, 174–76, 180, 219–21
paradox of subjectivation, 114, 150
patriarchy, 3, 5–6, 158
Peled, Yoav, 208–9
poverty
　community economic development's attempts to address, 41, 47, 201
　divorce and, 106–7
　immigrants and, 37, 96–97, 106
　Israel's levels in comparative context, 33
　Mizrahi Jews and, 36, 86, 104, 106
　Palestinians and, 37, 54, 71, 76, 86–87, 96, 98, 174–75
　reduction initiatives regarding, 3, 27, 39–41, 43, 47, 56, 94, 137, 193, 201, 207, 222
　single mothers and, 104
　social welfare system's attempts to address, 35–36, 193
　Ultra-Orthodox Jews and, 33, 37, 71, 76, 98–103, 108n16
privatization. *See also* economic liberalization
　economic liberalization and, 32, 35, 81–82, 160
　welfare system and, 34–36, 126, 131, 143

Raijman, Rebeca, 32–33
Reber, Dierdra, 112

Reddy, William, 183–85
reproduction, 115, 158–59, 183
Rieff, Philip, 9
Rose, Nikolas, 9

Sawa Empowerment Project, 17–18, 121, 203
self, narratives of, 112, 118, 132, 138, 184, 221
self-governmentality, 113, 115, 137, 187
sexual harassment, 79, 84–85, 89, 107n3, 200
Shafir, Gershon, 208
Sharma, Aradhana, 47, 115–17
single mothers, 86, 97, 103–5
"the social" in Israeli vernacular, 38, 42–44, 53–54, 58, 65–67, 124, 150, 201, 209, 211, 216
social capital, 22, 138, 184, 201–4, 207, 211, 216, 222–223
social economy *(kalkala hevratit)*
　coaching and, 132–34
　community economic development and, 42–43, 201
　cross-class interactions within, 51–53, 210
　cross-sectorial partnerships in, 2, 22, 28, 44, 46–51, 56, 59
　cultural production and, 2, 193
　definition of, 43–44
　diversity promoted in, 53–58, 67, 209–10, 219–20
　economic citizenship and, 214–15, 217
　emotional capitalism and, 221
　empowerment and, 27–28, 44–46, 51–53, 57–58, 111–12, 143–44, 151, 207, 219
　grassroots grounded projects and, 49–51
　Israeli political discourse and, 42
　measurement of success in, 147
　nongovernmental organizations and, 44, 46, 49–51, 57–58
　poverty reduction and, 43, 193
　social justice and, 28, 44, 212
　Zionist foundations and, 47
social justice
　"cottage-cheese" protests (2011) and, 65–66

economic citizenship and, 199
economic liberalization and, 42, 219, 223
empowerment and, 144, 151, 193
feminist perspectives on, 212
social economy and, 28, 44, 212

textile industry, 91–93, 108n11

Ultra-Orthodox Jews
Ashkenazi Jews and, 103
economic empowerment initiatives and, 4, 15, 44, 47–48, 100, 141, 214
employment patterns among, 99–102
Mizrahi Jews and, 103, 155
poverty among, 33, 37, 71, 76, 98–103, 108n16
self-segregation among, 103
welfare benefits and, 98–99
women, 4, 7, 15, 71, 76, 99–103, 141, 168, 180–81, 220
unemployment
community economic development's attempts to address, 41
immigrants and, 96, 98
Mizrahi Jews and, 36, 86
Palestinians and, 34, 60, 64, 86–87, 89, 96
women and, 60, 64, 81–86, 89, 143

Van Leer Research Group Survey, 19–21, 45, 48, 145

vulnerability of low-income women
ageism and, 78, 85
divorce and, 73, 75, 77–78, 87, 104–7, 154–55
domestic care responsibilities and, 76–79, 91, 95, 105–6, 152, 154, 156–58, 160–62, 168–71, 196
domestic violence and, 72–73, 76, 97
sexual harassment and, 79, 84–85, 89, 107, 200
workforce marginalization and, 74–85, 87, 89–93, 98, 105–6, 154, 160, 167–68, 173, 175, 183, 188, 213, 220

Walby, Sylvia, 159, 201
Women in Development (WID) paradigm, 115–16
work
agricultural, 29–31, 76–77, 86, 90–91, 93, 126
care, 8, 22–23, 35–36, 78, 89, 152, 156, 161, 165, 168, 170, 201, 217, 221
domestic, 76–79, 91, 95, 105–6, 152, 154, 156–58, 160–71, 188, 196
paid, 2–3, 8, 16, 22, 155–156, 188, 193
Workers' Advice Center (WAC), 91, 93, 126

Yuval-Davis, Nira, 218

Zionist foundations, 46–47, 49–50, 54, 59

www.ingramcontent.com/pod-product-compliance
Lightning Source LLC
Chambersburg PA
CBHW070917030426
42336CB00014BA/2451